# Fluid Frames

Once the realm of a few stalwart artists, animating with sand, clay, and wet paint is now accessible for all filmmakers with an experimental frame of mind. Created directly under the camera with frame-by-frame stopmotion, this "fluid frame animation" provides a completely unique visual world for animators. While pioneering animators such as Caroline Leaf, Alexander Petrov, and Ishu Patel paved the way, the availability of frame capture programs, compositing software, and digital workflow is opening up new avenues of exploration for artists of all experience levels. This book will walk you through setting up your studio, choosing and working with your materials, and combining the physical under-the-camera production with digital compositing and effects to enhance your animation. It features

- Firsthand advice from experimental animation veterans and rising stars in the field
- Coverage of the digital aspects of experimental animation, including the latest techniques in After Effects CC
- Video tutorials explaining under-the-camera approaches and After Effects enhancements on the book's companion website, www.fluidframes.net.

In addition to the practical advice, you'll find historical and contemporary examples of successful films, step-by-step tutorials for working under the camera and working with the footage digitally, and interviews and tips from artists who are currently pushing the boundaries in these experimental mediums. Stacked with information and images from over 30 artists, this book is an indispensable resource for both the student and professional wishing to get their hands dirty in an increasingly digital world.

**Corrie Francis Parks** animates sand, paint, and other unusual materials. Created with one hand under the camera and the other on the computer keyboard, her films maintain an organic connection to natural materials and traditional production methods while fully integrating digital technology. She teaches and researches animation at the University of Maryland, Baltimore County, and her work has been recognized with fellowships from the MacDowell Colony, Fulbright Foundation, Montana Film Office, and the Mustard Seed Foundation. Her award-winning animated shorts have screened at major festivals on every continent except Antarctica. She looks forward to the day when she can count penguins among her biggest fans.

# Fluid Frames

Experimental Animation with Sand, Clay, Paint, and Pixels

**Corrie Francis Parks**

CRC Press is an imprint of the
Taylor & Francis Group, an Informa business

A FOCAL PRESS BOOK

CRC Press
Taylor & Francis Group
6000 Broken Sound Parkway NW, Suite 300
Boca Raton, FL 33487-2742
© 2016 Taylor & Francis

*CRC Press is an imprint of the Taylor & Francis Group, an informa business*

This book contains information obtained from authentic and highly regarded sources. Reasonable efforts have been made to publish reliable data and information, but the author and publisher cannot assume responsibility for the validity of all materials or the consequences of their use. The authors and publishers have attempted to trace the copyright holders of all material reproduced in this publication and apologize to copyright holders if permission to publish in this form has not been obtained. If any copyright material has not been acknowledged please write and let us know so we may rectify in any future reprint.

Except as permitted under U.S. Copyright Law, no part of this book may be reprinted, reproduced, transmitted, or utilized in any form by any electronic, mechanical, or other means, now known or hereafter invented, including photocopying, microfilming, and recording, or in any information storage or retrieval system, without written permission from the publishers.

For permission to photocopy or use material electronically from this work, please access www.copyright.com (http://www.copyright.com/) or contact the Copyright Clearance Center, Inc. (CCC), 222 Rosewood Drive, Danvers, MA 01923, 978-750-8400. CCC is a not-for-profit organization that provides licenses and registration for a variety of users. For organizations that have been granted a photocopy license by the CCC, a separate system of payment has been arranged.

Trademark Notice: Product or corporate names may be trademarks or registered trademarks, and are used only for identification and explanation without intent to infringe.

*Library of Congress Cataloging in Publication Data*
Parks, Corrie Francis, author.
    Fluid frames : experimental animation with sand, clay, paint, and pixels / by Corrie Francis Parks. — First edition.
        pages cm
    ISBN 978-1-138-19062-7 (hbk) — ISBN 978-1-138-78491-8 (pbk) — ISBN 978-1-315-76810-6 (ebk) 1. Stop-motion animation films. 2. Clay animation films. 3. Computer animation. I. Title.
    TR897.5.P364 2016
    777'.7—dc23                                                2015029168

ISBN: 978-1-138-19062-7 (hbk)
ISBN: 978-1-138-78491-8 (pbk)
ISBN: 978-1-315-76810-6 (ebk)

Typeset in Rockwell and FranklinGothic
by Keystroke, Station Road, Codsall, Wolverhampton

Visit the Taylor & Francis Web site at http://www.taylorandfrancis.com and the CRC Press Web site at http://www.crcpress.com

# Dedication

For David Ehrlich, my mentor, professor, and friend, who pointed me down the fluid frame path and told me to follow my nose.

# Table of Contents

*Acknowledgements* ..... xi

**Introduction: The Experimental Frame of Mind** ..... 1

    Dirty Fingers in the Digital World ..... 1
    Why These Techniques? ..... 4
    Why This Book? ..... 5
    What Is in This Book? ..... 6

## Section I ..... 9

**1. Finding Your Voice** ..... 11

    The Experimental Frame of Mind in the History of Animation ..... 12
    Starting the Journey ..... 17
        Be Alive 19
        Rehearse Before You Perform 19
        Limit Yourself 20
        Ask a Technical Question 20
        Work Abstractly 22
    The Image Stuck in Your Mind ..... 22
    Telling the Story ..... 24
        The Storyboard 24
        Research 26
        Other Structural Methods 27

**2. Lights! Camera! Animation!** ..... 29

    Setting Up Your Studio for Under-the-Camera Animation ..... 29
        Working Surface 30
        The Multiplane 31
    Lights ..... 32
        Top Lights 33
        The Light Box 33

## Contents

| | | |
|---|---|---|
| | The Camera | 35 |
| |     Image Resolution   36 | |
| |     The Lens   37 | |
| |     Setting the Exposure   40 | |
| | Frame Capture | 41 |
| | Additional Advice | 41 |
| |     Lock It Down   41 | |
| |     Staying Healthy Under the Camera   42 | |
| |     Keeping Things in Perspective   42 | |
| **3.** | **A Foundation for Excellence** | **47** |
| | Art that Moves | 48 |
| | Basic Principles of Animated Movement | 48 |
| |     Timing and Spacing   49 | |
| |     Ones . . . Twos . . . Threes . . .   50 | |
| |     Easing   51 | |
| |     Holds and Cycles   52 | |
| |     Staging   52 | |
| |     Squash and Stretch   55 | |
| |     Arcs   55 | |
| |     Anticipation and Follow-Through   57 | |
| |     Overlapping Action   57 | |
| |     Secondary Action   58 | |
| | Fluid Frame Aesthetics | 58 |
| |     In-Camera versus Out-of-Camera   58 | |
| |     Drawn Camera Moves   59 | |
| |     Leaving Trails   59 | |
| |     Animated Transitions   60 | |
| |     The Hand of the Artist   61 | |
| | The Digital Toolbox | 62 |
| |     Thinking in Layers   64 | |
| |     The Staggered Mix   64 | |
| |     Exercise: Staggered Mixes   66 | |
| |     Rotoscoping   70 | |

| | | |
|---|---|---|
| | **Section II** | **73** |
| **4.** | **Animating With Sand and Other Powders** | **75** |
| | Notable Pioneers in Powder Animation | 76 |
| |     Nag and Gisèle Ansorge   76 | |
| |     Kazimierz Urbański   77 | |
| |     Caroline Leaf   78 | |
| |     Ferec Cakó   79 | |
| |     Aleksandra Korejwo   80 | |
| | Exploring the Technique | 81 |
| |     Exercise: Animating a Sandy Morph   82 | |
| | The Sandy Studio | 86 |

Materials 86
Tools 87
In Practice 89
Processing Footage 91
### Planning a Longer Sand Project — 91
### Compositing 101 — 93
Layering in Sand 95
Exercise: Garbage Mattes 98
Blending Modes 100
Exercise: Paint Bucket Effect 101
Color Keying 103
Exercise: Applying a Color Key Effects Stack 103
Exercise: Animated Masks 106
### Adding Color — 110
Exercise: Hand Tinting in Photoshop 110
Exercise: Tints and Filters in After Effects 112
### Combining Sand with Other Animation Techniques — 115
Case Studies from Commercial Projects 115

## 5. The Transforming Painting — 119

### The Life of a Painting — 120
### Notable Pioneers in Painted Animation — 120
Oskar Fischinger 120
Witold Giersz 123
Caroline Leaf 124
Clive Walley 126
Alexander Petrov 128
### Exploring the Technique — 130
Exercise: Motion Painting 130
### Setting Up Your Studio — 132
Your Painting Surface 132
Different Types of Paint 136
Lighting 137
### Things to Have in Your Studio — 138
Exercise: Finger Painting Portrait with Sponge Transition 140
### Digital Approaches to Paint-on-Glass — 144
### Green Screen — 144
Creating the Layers 145
Exercise: Compositing the Roller Coaster of Luv 146
### Moving Beyond the Glass — 150
### Additional Exercises — 153

## 6. Clay Painting and Beyond — 157

### Notable Pioneers in Clay Painting — 158
Ishu Patel 158
Joan Gratz 160
A Survey of Techniques 162

| | |
|---|---|
| Exploring the Technique | 164 |
|     Table and Lighting   164 | |
|     The Clay   165 | |
|     Temperature Regulation   167 | |
|     Tools   167 | |
|     Exercise: Warming Up to the Clay   168 | |
|     Exercise: Clay Compositing   169 | |
| **Moving Beyond the Materials** | 175 |
|     Cut-outs, Drawing, and Further Experimentation   175 | |
| **7. Beyond the Frame** | **179** |
| **Sound Design and Music** | 180 |
|     The Mix   183 | |
| **Digital Output** | 185 |
| **Getting the Film Out** | 186 |
|     The Process Video   187 | |
|     Film Festivals   188 | |
|     Distribution   191 | |
|     Releasing Online   191 | |
|     Alternative Exhibition   192 | |
| **A Final Word** | 193 |
| *Appendix A: Case Studies* | 195 |
|     *Loving Vincent*   195 | |
|     *Truth Has Fallen*   202 | |
|     *Trag/Trace/Spur and Up the Stairs*   209 | |
| *Appendix B: Artists' Profiles* | 215 |
| *Index* | 229 |

# Acknowledgements

It was never my intention to write a book. I have films to make and if the good people at Focal Press had not come knocking on my virtual door asking for a book on sand animation, this particular book would certainly not exist. So the first thanks must go to Lauren Mattos, David Bevans, and Haley Swan, who ushered me through the proposals and manuscript process and ultimately convinced me that people really would read a book on something so arcane as fluid frame animation.

To avoid a long list of appellations, know that every time you come across an artist's name in this book you should send a little thought of thanks to him or her in your mind. Every artist mentioned in these pages has generously and specifically shared their methods, techniques, and films with *you* so that you can make something incredible. Corresponding with these artists has been transformative and inspirational. I am humbled by the graciousness with which they allowed me to probe the inner workings of their creative process. The best expression of thanks will be for you (and me) to take this collective knowledge and push it beyond the pages of this book. Go animate something remarkable.

This book would also be something of a mess if it weren't for the sharp eyes of my technical editor, Josh Harrell, and many fact-checkers and grammar gurus from around the globe. Ed Desroches, Tess Martin, Charles Wilson, Cindy Keefer, Philippe Vaucher, Dan Bailey, Sheila Sofian, Lynn Smith, Martine Chartrand; I will buy you a drink next time we meet. The obliging people at The National Film Board of Canada, Deutsches Filminstitut, ASIFA Switzerland, ASIFA Poland and the Center for Visual Music were beyond helpful in tracking down images, animators, and rights holders. And I would certainly be drowning in rough drafts without my meticulously wonderful research assistant at UMBC, Jacqueline Wojcik, who transcribed hours of interviews, tested tutorials with gusto, and occasionally pointed out the obvious to me when I happened to misplace it.

I also owe a great debt to my parents, a doctor and an accountant, who didn't bat an eye when I told them, at the exuberant age of 13, that I wanted to be an animator. They have been with me all the way. And finally my husband, Thom, who has taken this book-writing thing as just one more zag in lieu of a zig, and I'm sure is very happy to see the sleep-deprived, deadline-obsessed, grump monster he's been living with turn back into his lovely wife. I couldn't have done this without you, my dearest . . . now I'm going to go start my next film.

*Corrie Francis Parks.*

# Introduction
## The Experimental Frame of Mind

**Dirty Fingers in the Digital World**

**Why These Techniques?**

**Why This Book?**

**What Is in This Book?**

## Dirty Fingers in the Digital World

A word I have discovered in writing this book is "haptic." It might be my new favorite word. It means "of or relating to the sense of touch." This describes so well what is happening in animation right now. Artists across all mediums are returning to physical materials as the starting point for their work, boldly employing new technologies to traditionally hand-crafted methods of animating. Not only are viewers fascinated by the artistry of these techniques, but animators also value the haptic experience of working directly with the materials.

This book deals specifically with stopmotion animation techniques created with the haptic materials of sand, clay, and paint. We are about to make a mess, so expect to get dirty! This method of animating is done directly under the camera; every frame is created, shot, and then destroyed in the creation of the next frame. **01**

Working this way requires confidence, intuition, and stamina. Even with the full benefits of digital technology, there is no easy way to harness the physical properties of sand, paint, and clay – the skilled brushwork of a painter, the sculptural eye of a clay animator, the nuanced manipulation of light by a sand animator are still necessary to push through the hours under the camera.

**01** The Crossing – *Marieka Walsh (work in progress).*

## Fluid Frames: The Experimental Frame of Mind

What digital technology has done for under-the-camera animation is to facilitate bolder risk-taking by the creators. Gone are the days when animators would shoot a scene and send a reel of film off to the lab with fingers crossed. My first several films were made on 16mm and I remember nervously threading my footage through the projector, wondering if the days I spent in the camera room had produced anything useable. Now, with real-time feedback from digital cameras, I know immediately if a shot is not working and often have a chance to fix it before it is entirely lost. **02**

Additionally, it seems like anything and everything can be animated. I've seen works animated on laser-burnt toast and a series of popping balloons. An entire beach might be a set for sand animation, or a bunch of scientists can move atoms to create the smallest animated character in the world. **03**

In many films, the novelty of the technique trumps all, intended to surprise and dazzle an audience, gathering as many views as possible regardless of the content. Audiences are fascinated by the artistic process, and a work that involves moving individual grains of sand or shaping wet paint frame-by-frame holds infinitely more wonder than pushing buttons on a computer. (Anyone who has made a CG film knows that just as much time and artistry goes into a well-crafted digital image as any material-based animation. Unfortunately, public perception still sees CG as a shortcut to the time-consuming techniques. To overcome this misperception, many computer-based animators are striving to reveal the physical and artistic components that go into their work as well.) The commercial demand for animation that looks "new and different" signifies that the experimental process has become an essential part of a successful animated film. **04**

Ultimately, the best works are those that use an innovative approach to production, and also relate to the message or emotional tone the film is trying to communicate. Then the audience is moved emotionally, dazzled visually, and the message, whether commercial or artistic, becomes memorable. The

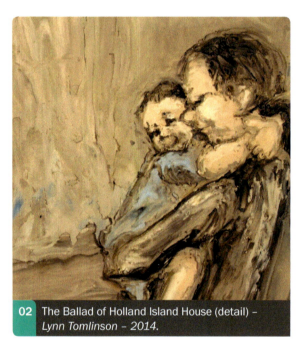

**02** The Ballad of Holland Island House (detail) – *Lynn Tomlinson – 2014.*

**03** Bottle – *Kirsten Lepore – 2010.*

**04** When I Was a Child – *Maryam Kashkoolinia – 2014.*

animations that will be shown generation after generation are those that marry innovative animation techniques with meaningful content.

In order to achieve this harmonious marriage of content and style, animators need to have an *experimental frame of mind*. "Experimental" is a tricky term when applied to animation. Some scholars and artists only apply the term to abstract, non-narrative films. Others use the term more broadly, applying it to animation that uses unusual or innovative production processes, regardless of narrative content. **05**

For the purpose of this book, I prefer Jules Engel's definition:

> Experimental Animation is a personal vision – a concrete record of an artist's discovery of himself.[1]

This removes the emphasis from technique and content and places it on the artist and his or her journey of self-expression. As with every field, those people with bold and often unconventional approaches to animation become catalysts for the slow-moving commercial industry.

Under this broad umbrella, a narrative-based paint-on-glass film, like Patrick Jenkins's *Labyrinth*, **06** and an abstract visual symphony, like Joan Gratz's *Night Weaver*, **07** can both contribute to the conversation that is changing the animation landscape. The overarching creative problem that every artist encounters in each new work is how to express their personal vision. The solution to this problem will come from applying creative thought at every stage of animation production. It may require building a special camera rig, like the one Clive Walley constructed for his abstract films. It may require finding a new material to work with, like the Ansorges did when they started working with sand, or it may require combining techniques, like Lynn Smith did with paper cut-outs and water-soluble crayons. **08 09**

You can bring the experimental frame of mind to your narrative development, sound design, even the way you market and exhibit your finished work. Materials are just one aspect of the solution, and while this book will cover the production methods

**05** Miramare – *Michaela Müller* – 2009.

**06** Labyrinth – *Patrick Jenkins* – 2008.

**07** Night Weaver – *Joan Gratz* – 2015.

unique to sand, paint, and clay, I hope it will also be the starting point for finding new avenues of self-expression through animation.

## Why These Techniques?

Out of the myriad of approaches to experimental animation, why are we focusing on sand, paint, and clay in this book? Their similarities begin with the very nature of the materials. Sand, paint, and clay are materials that have both fluidity and dimension – working with them is like drawing and sculpting simultaneously. Because of their similar physical qualities, a similar working method applies to all three. These materials are animated under the camera, usually on a glass surface. **10** The animator creates one frame by shaping and drawing with the material, records the image with the camera, and then reshapes the materials to make the next frame. Each frame builds upon the one before and at the end of the process there is nothing left except the recorded images. There are no second chances with this type of stopmotion. Everything must be done start to finish, with no way to go back and correct a mistake once the frame has been destroyed. The added difficulty is that the fluidity of these materials make them notoriously difficult to control under the camera.

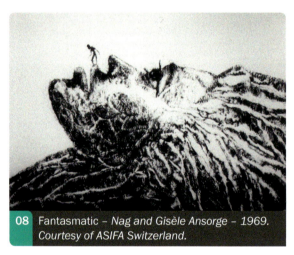

**08** Fantasmatic – *Nag and Gisèle Ansorge* – 1969. Courtesy of ASIFA Switzerland.

**09** Lynn Smith combines paper cut-outs and drawing under the camera in her film Pearl's Diner. (Pearl's Diner – Lynn Smith – 1992.)

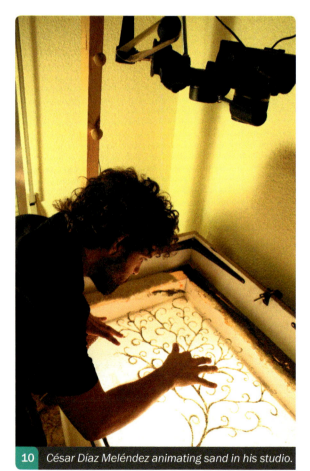

**10** *César Díaz Meléndez animating sand in his studio.*

If the thought of this makes your heart palpitate and palms sweat, you are not alone. Under-the-camera animation is a high-consequence art form and not for the faint of heart! It is a bold choice that comes from an explorative approach to filmmaking. The benefit of working under the camera is the opportunity for a spontaneous adventure. Accidents happen, which can lead to cinematic disasters or great visual discoveries. No matter what type of animation you ultimately choose, you will have many more opportunities to expand your avenues of artistic expression if you approach your art fearlessly! 11

Animators now have a host of new digital tools, which will enhance their practice. Technology has expanded the possibilities of working with these volatile materials. While under-the-camera animation still requires meticulous planning and execution, there is more maneuverability thanks to real-time feedback, digital capture, live-view shooting and post-production magic. What was once the realm of a few fearless pioneers has now become accessible for any animator with a sense of adventure.

## Why This Book?

I know these things because I work in this world of fluid frames. I started my animation career shooting on 16mm film and bootstrapped my way through the transition to digital production. I also began animating as a traditional character animator drawing on paper. As my artistic goals changed, I began to work under the camera, eager for that physical connection with the material. I first discovered paint-on-glass animation, combining it with drawing on paper in my film *Ash Sunday* (2001). 12

Working in the immediacy of the moment was thrilling and stimulating. For my next film, *Tracks* (2003), I tackled sand, but with a particular artistic goal – color. Without digital tools, I had to figure out a way to add color while I was shooting. I discovered theater lighting gels could be cut and taped together into brilliant background scenery that kept the purity of the light coming into the camera. 13 14

For me, the problem-solving is a large part of my attraction to under-the-camera animation. Each film requires a period of research and the opportunity to create something never before seen. That is what keeps me interested – a chance to develop an experimental frame of mind. Both the previous films were shot on 16mm film, which presented a host of challenges.

Once I had fully transitioned to a digital workflow, those challenges were replaced with the new challenge of defining a hybrid hand-crafted aesthetic. Though I work primarily with

**11** *Sheila Sofian animating* Truth Has Fallen *(Truth Has Fallen – Sheila M. Sofian – 2013).*

**12** *My first paint-on-glass film,* Ash Sunday *(Ash Sunday – Corrie Francis Parks – 2001).*

# Fluid Frames: The Experimental Frame of Mind

13   Colored backgrounds for Tracks.

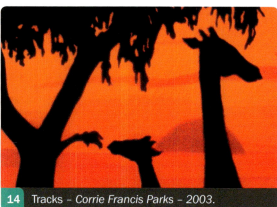

14   Tracks – Corrie Francis Parks – 2003.

15   A Tangled Tale – Corrie Francis Parks – 2013.

16   Animating sandy fish.

sand, the experimental frame of mind has led me to animating paint, cut-outs, objects, drawings and computer-generated effects, as well as a host of other animation techniques. **15**

The opportunity to develop fluid frame animation extends beyond just my own personal process. The artists featured in this book approach their projects with that same experimental frame of mind. My hope is that collecting their discoveries and methods alongside my own will further define and expand the way animation is created. Anything is possible; it is just a matter of how. **16**

## What Is in This Book?

This book will give you the foundation to achieve that "how." Section I will deal with production principles that apply to all these fluid frame techniques. You will find practical steps for developing an idea into a film, setting up your studio for under-the-camera animation, and some general animation techniques that apply to all types of fluid frame animation. Section II will delve into the specifics of sand, paint, and clay, including how to choose and work with your materials and how to transition from the physical process of creating frames to a digital workflow to enhance your animation. Anyone can jump right in and create animation with the introductory exercises – they require minimal equipment and an adventurous attitude. The more advanced compositing exercises do assume a basic familiarity with Adobe After Effects. If you need to brush up on your skills I would recommend finding a good introductory book or online tutorials that will get you comfortable with the After Effects interface and workflow. I also recommend reading through the digital methods for each material, as each chapter builds on the previous. For example, even if you don't plan to animate with sand, many of the basic compositing methods explained in that chapter also apply to paint-on-glass or clay painting.

This book also provides a historical context for inspiration and theoretical considerations for finding your best method of self-expression. These fluid methods of animating are most often relegated to a side note in history books and production manuals. Knowing the history and current state of the art form is not only a source of inspiration, but also a method for learning. Many of the films mentioned in this book are readily available. Go watch them and ask yourself the question: "How did they do that?" **17**

If you are new to filmmaking, this will take you through the entire process of creating a film, from concept to post-production and sending your film out to the world. For veteran animators, you will find mind-expanding creative exercises and a new visual language to apply to your experience. Scattered throughout are interviews and words of wisdom from some of the early practitioners, as well as practical tips from artists who are currently pushing the boundaries in these experimental mediums. I've interviewed over 20 animators working in these techniques; every one has a different approach to their work, and you will too. All I can do is get you started with the right equipment, materials, and some good advice. **18**

There is great pressure in the film industry to be original, but originality always comes as a side effect of pursuing some other goal. Your starting point may be a conceptual idea, a narrative thread or an investigation into material properties, but it should always begin in authentic artistic expression. Caroline Leaf, who teaches animation workshops all over the world, has this observation,

> Original expression comes sort of naturally. I tell [students] to copy me, to look around and if you see anything good that someone else is doing next to you, to copy that too. I think you should copy the technique and then you make it your own. What you want to say will come out and it will be different than what anyone else wants to say.[2]

So view this book as a tool-kit of techniques that will aid you in finding an avenue for your personal voice. Some artists may find they intuitively

**17** Méandres – *Florence Miailhe* – *2013.*

**18** Carmen Torero – *Aleksandra Korejwo* – *1996. Courtesy of TV Studio of Animation Films Ltd. Poznan.*

**19** The Old Man and the Sea – *Alexander Petrov* – *1999. Image courtesy of Pascal Blais Studios. © 2001 Alexander Petrov.*

## Fluid Frames: The Experimental Frame of Mind

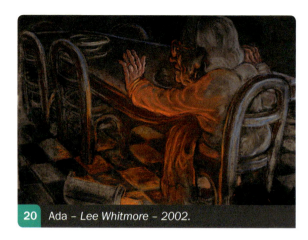

20  Ada – *Lee Whitmore* – 2002.

grasp animating in sand, while others may understand the nature of clay more easily. [19] Still others may find working under the camera far too uncontrollable to suit their artistic goals, and return to other forms of animation with a broader perspective. Wherever you fall after your sojourn into the world of fluid frames, developing an experimental frame of mind will ultimately lead to your most interesting work. [20]

## Notes

1  Engel, Jules. Joy of Movement. Center for Visual Music Online Library. Center for Visual Music, unpublished typescript, n.d. Date accessed: Mar. 16, 2014. http://www.centerforvisualmusic.org/Library.html

2  Leaf, Caroline. Telephone interview. Mar. 26, 2014.

# Section I

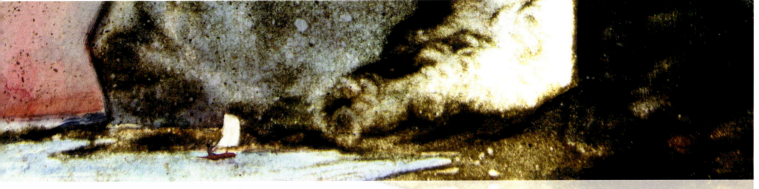

Corrie Francis Parks.

# Chapter 1
# Finding Your Voice

**The Experimental Frame of Mind in the History of Animation**

**Starting the Journey**

    Be Alive
    Rehearse Before You Perform
    Limit Yourself
    Ask a Technical Question
    Work Abstractly

**The Image Stuck in Your Mind**

**Telling the Story**

    The Storyboard
    Research
    Other Structural Methods

Why do you want to make a film? Do you have a compelling story to tell? Have you developed a visual style you want to exhibit? Are you looking for a new way to express yourself artistically? Do you want to sell a product or spread an idea?

    The most groundbreaking and visually engaging films come from animators that have a strong personal vision. The experimental frame of mind has been behind nearly every visual and technological innovation in animation, from the early days of trick films, to the most recent digital renderings. Whether they realize it or not, every animator will be building upon a foundation of experimentation passed down through each new generation. Let's start our own journey with a glance back at how the experimental frame of mind has propelled animators to discover and develop new practical methods of creating. 01 02

## The Experimental Frame of Mind in the History of Animation

The first animators were necessarily experimenters, redefining the new technology of cinema to bring an unconventional visual and narrative experience to their audience. Most mainstream cinematographers in the early 1900s were concerned with recording and documenting live action. However, a few experimental filmmakers, such as Georges Méliès, and James Stuart Blackton, were manipulating the individual frames of filmstrips to create special effects. 03

Building off the traditions of the theater and vaudeville, they popularized the trickfilm genre, bringing figments of the imagination into the pseudo-reality of the cinema. By stopping the camera in the middle of a scene to create magical effects, filmmakers like Méliès and Blackton laid the foundation for further frame-by-frame manipulation. 04

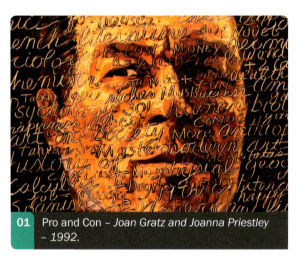

01 Pro and Con – *Joan Gratz and Joanna Priestley – 1992.*

02 Animation from the feature documentary Seed – 2016. Courtesy of Collective Eye Films.

03 In the early days of cinema, Georges Méliès masterfully charmed audiences with camera tricks and fantastical stories. (Georges Méliès – The Mermaid – 1904; A Trip to the Moon – 1901.)

A few years later, Émile Cohl and Winsor McCay built upon the stop-frame idea by making films composed of entirely of drawings. 05

These artists, and others of their era, were able to bring a world of fantasy to the screen because they approached cinema with an experimental frame of mind, thinking not about what it was able to do, but what they needed it to do to realize their personal vision.

As animation developed and became an industry, other experimental thinkers began to take note of its potential. Most notably, a small circle of avant-garde artists in Europe saw animation as an answer to the questions they were wrestling with in painting. With the new tool of cinema, they were able to explore creative problems that had heretofore stumped them. Viking Eggeling was searching for a meaningful system of abstract forms, which resulted in his film *Diagonal Symphony* in 1921. Between 1921 and 1925, Walter Ruttmann was working on a series of animated works he later titled *Opus I–IV*. 06

His experiments reputedly included maneuvering sticks of plasticine under the camera, painting on small glass plates, and manipulating images with mirrors. Hans Richter was working on his abstract Rhythmus series around this time as well. 07

Closely associated with this group was Oskar Fischinger, who pursued his own animated explorations, inventing a wax slicing machine to create

05 *Winsor McCay invested his characters with an endearing emotional range. (Winsor McCay – Gertie the Dinosaur – 1914.)*

04 *James Stuart Blackton created sequences of chalk drawings that transformed on their own. (J. Stuart Blackton – Humorous Phases of Funny Faces – 1906.)*

## Fluid Frames: Finding Your Voice

**06** *Frame sequence from Opus III by Walter Ruttmann – 1921–25. Courtesy of Deutsches Filminstitut, Frankfurt.*

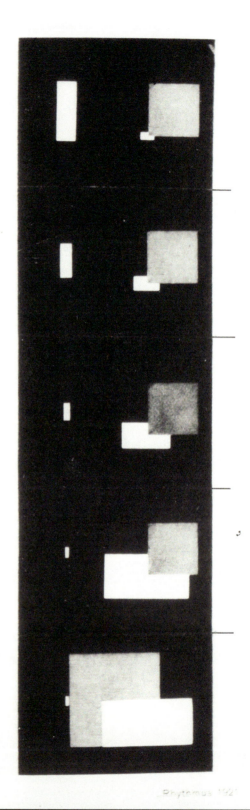

**07** *Sequence from Rhythmus 21 by Hans Richter. Courtesy of Deutsches Filminstitut, Frankfurt.*

abstract animation more efficiently. Fischinger was also making abstract animation commercially viable through advertisement and popular classical music. The Germany of the 1920s fostered an environment in which the experimental frame of mind could flourish, so artists gravitated toward one another, sharing ideas and innovations. One of these animators, Lotte Reiniger, remembers the period as one of great energy and collaboration:

> With each film we could make new discoveries, find new problems, new possibilities, technical and artistic, we were most eager to execute. The whole field was virgin soil and we had all the joys of explorers in an unknown country. It was wonderful.[1]

A project that brought several of these experimentalists together was Reiniger's feature length film, *The Adventures of Prince Achmed* (1926). Reiniger's technique of animating paper jointed paper cut-outs under the camera was revolutionary in itself, but the idea to make a feature length production based on the vision of one animator was unprecedented.

> We did not belong to the [film] industry. We always had been outsiders and we always had done what we wanted to do. Our friends were artists of the same caliber who approached films in their own ways . . . So we were not afraid of the challenge.[2]

To help her, Reiniger gathered a small band of her avant-garde friends and put them in charge of creating animated backgrounds. **08** They built a multiplane camera in an attic in Potsdam and went to work. Bertold Bartosch and Walter Ruttmann animated abstract effects on the lower level using sand, paint, and a wax slicing machine licensed from Oskar Fischinger. Reiniger and other members of the crew animated the cut-outs on the upper levels. The resulting layers of imagery bring together the fairytale world of the Arabian Nights with the time period's cutting-edge abstract animation. **09**

While animation grew into a widespread form of entertainment, experimental animation found its place between the commercial cartoon industry and the world of fine art. Practicing the experimental frame of mind led artists to discover new techniques in animation to serve their specific vision. In 1933, Alexander Alexeieff and Claire Parker developed their unusual pinscreen animation for the film *Night on Bald Mountain*. They wished to capture the "finesses of tone and shading . . . that is known in engraving."[3] The limitations of drawing led them to find a new way to create

**08** *Creating* The Adventures of Prince Achmed. *Lotte Reiniger animates cut-outs as Walter Ruttmann animates sand below while Karl Koch operates the camera above. Courtesy of Christel Strobel, Agentur fuer Primrose Film Productions / Deutsches Filminstitut, Frankfurt.*

"a single picture capable of indefinite modifications."[4] Likewise, Len Lye set out to discover new lab methods with optical printing and experimented with cameraless animation in his scratch-on-film works.[5] Douglass Crockwell investigated progressive painting under the camera in his *Glenn Falls Sequence* (1947).

To further explore ways of creating abstract movement, Crockwell tried squeezing wet paint between sheets of glass and also developed his own wax slicing technique using a meat slicer, describing the resulting animation as "strongly anticipatory and unworldly . . . moving from uncharted point to uncharted point, yet retaining the logic of each minute transition."[6]

According to historian and filmmaker Cecile Starr, experimental filmmaking flourished in North America due to a "growing 16mm market in colleges, museums and film societies" and "the availability of grants and subsidies for experimental filmmaking."[7] Among other grant-making entities, the Museum of Non-Objective Painting (now the Solomon R. Guggenheim Museum) supported several experimental filmmakers through film grants, including Oskar Fischinger, who had, by that time, moved to the United States. Also among the grant recipients was Norman McLaren, whose experimental practice later propelled the National Film Board of Canada (NFB) into a golden era of alternative animation. In 1960, the Annecy Festival was founded to showcase and award animation from around the world.

The same year saw the establishment of the Association Internationale du Film d'Animation / International Animated Film Association (ASIFA) as a way to promote and protect the rights of animators and foster an international camaraderie and exchange of ideas within the medium. Not only was there a way to make films; there were places to show them and meet other animators.

In this vibrant context of creative exploration, the techniques discussed in this book, along with many others, began to appear in multiple contexts. It was as though a collective consciousness of animation was developing. In Poland, Witold Giersz broke

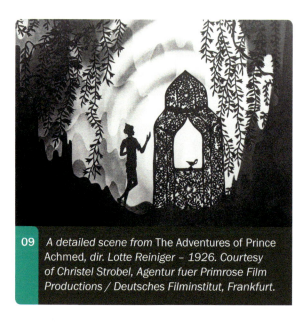

**09** *A detailed scene from* The Adventures of Prince Achmed, *dir. Lotte Reiniger – 1926. Courtesy of Christel Strobel, Agentur fuer Primrose Film Productions / Deutsches Filminstitut, Frankfurt.*

**10** *ASIFA animators from around the world gather at the 1961 Annecy Festival. From left to right: Raymond Maillet, Ivanov-Vano, John Halas, Joy Batchelor, Pierre Barbin, and Paul Grimault. Photo courtesy of The Halas & Batchelor Collection Limited.*

away from the conventional cartoon style of his training and created characters out of splotches of paint in *Little Western* (1960). 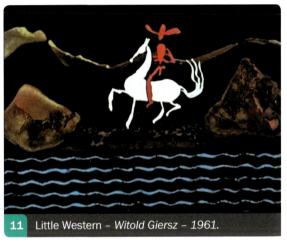 At the same time in Canada, George Dunning was developing a similar style of painted animation in *The Flying Man* (1962). In Switzerland, Nag and Gisèle Ansorge were working on their first film with sand, *Les Corbeaux* (1967),  while across the Atlantic, Caroline Leaf used it to tell the musical tale of *Peter and the Wolf* (1969).

These animators in search of new materials for creative expression placed sand and wet paint under the camera because it served their overarching vision. They followed their inclination and great discoveries ensued.

Today the experimental frame of mind flourishes again. The spread of knowledge and films via the internet creates a collegial atmosphere among the international animation community, where one artist's discoveries can become the foundation for another's experiment. Digital production takes some of the expense and inefficiencies out of the animation process, freeing up the artist to take risks with visual exploration. New avenues of funding, like crowdsourcing and private and commercial patronage, are beginning to make up for the decline of government grants in many countries. If the early pioneers were discovering the New World of animation, we are now about to blast off into the vast expanses of the uncharted universe. We are still explorers on a new frontier. It is an exciting time to be an animator!

## Starting the Journey

Every film, regardless of its subject or technique, will take the viewer on a journey.  Sometimes it is a journey through a story; sometimes the journey revolves around a concept or theme;

**11** Little Western – *Witold Giersz* – *1961*.

**12** The Ravens – *Nag and Gisèle Ansorge* – *1967*. Courtesy of ASIFA Switzerland.

**13** A Tale of Longing – *Xin Li* – *2012*.

**14** When I Was a Child – *Maryam Kashkoolinia* – *2014*.

## Fluid Frames: Finding Your Voice

**15** *When I travel, I will often record the day's events in storyboard form. This page from my sketchbook is from a roadtrip in New Zealand.*

sometimes it is a visual exploration. Most often it is a combination of all these things. The important thing to remember is that every journey starts with a point of inspiration. Caroline Leaf found her starting point in literature. Ishu Patel explored philosophical questions. For Nicolai Troshinsky, it was about eliciting a specific feeling from the audience.

So where do we start searching for the point of inspiration that will carry us through the long hours under the camera? Here are some methods for developing your ideas for an animated project.

## Be Alive

Inspiration starts with our experience of the world. When we connect to what's happening around us, we are able to reroute that connection through our creative activities and make work that will resonate with others. Go to museums, galleries, zoos, beaches, train stations, and parks. Watch people and animals, study art and design, read the newspaper, listen to podcasts, attend lectures. **15**

It's true that animation is a lot of hard work and you may think there is no time for other pursuits, but a well-balanced way of life will add the authenticity of experience to your work and may point you in an unexpected direction.

## Rehearse Before You Perform

Caroline Leaf describes animating under the camera as a performance: "You do it once and that's it. It's sort of nerve wracking, but you do it at a speed where you can control it and feel good about it."[8] We are performers in slow motion under the camera and the key to a good performance are the hours of rehearsal that go into it. An actor would never step onto the stage of a major production and just "wing it." Similarly, we animators must spend time testing our techniques, methods, and ideas before we begin shooting the final frames. **16**

All of these materials move on a flat surface as one mass with malleable qualities. In that way, working with them is a little bit like sculpting. They also can be coerced into fine, linear patterns, so we must wear the hats of painters and drawers as well. Liquid lines, shifting textures, morphing colors, and dimensional paintings are the basis of the fluid frame vocabulary. The physical qualities of our materials should be one of our utmost concerns as we animate. What are the peculiar strengths of sand? What are its challenges? What can we do with paint that is impossible to do in any other medium?

The only way to discover the peculiar qualities of each medium is to spend time playing and experimenting. I use the word "play" deliberately because this rehearsal time should be a fun, low-pressure period where you get to know your materials and equipment. It is a chance to work out any technical problems without deadlines and in the process you may discover some new methods to incorporate into the final performance.

**16** *Experimenting with dripping paint for* A Tangled Tale.

# Fluid Frames: Finding Your Voice

> **Animated Anecdote**
> 
> *Once, when I was playing around with some sand footage in Photoshop, I accidentally hit the key that inverts the image. Suddenly my sand had turned into snow! I liked the way it looked so much I made the short film* Snow *to explore the idea further.* **17**

**17** Sand magically turned to snow by accidentally hitting the wrong button.

## Limit Yourself

Sometimes creativity can be jumpstarted by imposing rules or limitations on the creative process. Nicolai Troshinsky wanted to explore the feeling of being lost in *Astigmatismo* (2013). To create an authentic exploration of that theme, he asked four different collaborators – a character designer, a background artist, a sound designer, and a group of musicians – to create different pieces of the film in their style. He gave the artists no guidance, so they would have to start at the point of feeling lost and work toward clarity. Then, when Troshinsky received each artist's work, he had to puzzle them together into a coherent film. This made the feeling of being lost as his own starting point as well. Troshinsky had to work creatively around the pre-established structure the other artists had provided, and these limitations connected directly with the theme he was exploring. **18**

Troshinsky chose to work this way because the creative process was as important as the film itself:

> We spent almost three years making this very short film, and since I could not guarantee that it would turn out good, I hoped that the process itself would be interesting. In the end if the film was a train wreck, it didn't matter because I had a great time making it.[9]

This is a great working philosophy for an animator! Because we spend so much time with each frame, we must find ways to make the work feel like play. Of course, Troshinsky's film did turn out to be excellent because when an animator enjoys the work that enjoyment seeps into every frame and is evident in the final film.

## Ask a Technical Question

One way to focus your exploration of a medium is to work toward a technical goal. After many years of animating clay painting completely in-camera, Joan Gratz wanted to learn how to use Photoshop and After Effects. The film *Puffer Girl* (2009) developed along with Gratz's knowledge of these programs, and her discoveries along the way would cause her to continuously revisit and add to the animation:

> It ended up taking a couple years to [make the film] just because every time I learned something new, I could do something new on the film. There were so many different kinds of animation in that film, so for me it was constantly interesting.[10]

In this surreal journey through an underwater dream world, Gratz used live action footage filmed in aquariums, processed with Photoshop filters, and composited with her clay painting animation. **19 20**

18  Background designs by Cecilia Ramieri and character designs by Gina Thorstensen were the visual inspiration for Nicolai Troshinsky's Astigmatismo – 2013.

19  Joan Gratz filmed jellyfish in an aquarium as the base of this scene in Puffer Girl.

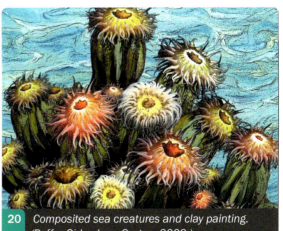

20  Composited sea creatures and clay painting. (Puffer Girl – Joan Gratz – 2009.)

**Animated Anecdote**

Joan Gratz discovered an unusual animating material for her film Puffer Girl. "There's a very big Japanese market up in Portland so I went and bought this 55-dollar octopus. Because he had already been steamed, he had a nice appearance but he was not flexible at all. So I shot him partly as a 3-dimensional object and then I scanned him and animated him in Photoshop . . . One good tip I learned is to always clean your scanner well after you've scanned your octopus, because otherwise you can really regret it!" **21**

**21** Puffer Girl – Joan Gratz – 2009.

**22** Textural experimentation in The Orange Umbrella – 2009.

## Work Abstractly

My paint-on-glass short *The Orange Umbrella* (2009) started as a textural experiment. I was interested in seeing how painted texture evolved, so I chose a limited color palette and very simple movements, dabbing paint with a sponge in one section and making long strokes with a wide brush in another. The simple design allowed me to work very quickly and not get too attached to each frame. I could look at my work and then do another experiment right away, keeping up the momentum. After several hours of disjointed experiments, I created a longer series of transformations between textures reminiscent of a rapidly changing landscape. I later decided to add the cut-out character against the abstract background as an anchor point for the viewer. The transformations provided the visual motivation for developing a simple narrative structure around the character. **22**

## The Image Stuck in Your Mind

It's impossible to tell an animator exactly how to start a film. Studios have their own protocols for visual and story development, but when it comes to an individual artist, anything goes. I will tell you how my films have come about and perhaps that will help you think more specifically about how to develop your initial ideas into a full production.

My films usually start with a strong image that I can't get out of my head. Figure 23 shows the first sketches that eventually developed into *A Tangled Tale* (2013). **23**

The metaphor of two entangled fish germinated from an emotional moment in my personal life that I felt needed to be expressed artistically. I sketched and developed the premise of the story and then set it aside because I was working on other things. It was not until two years later, when I returned to sand animation, that I revisited the story and found a film waiting to be made.

When I am fanning that first spark of inspiration, I do a lot of drawing. I let one image build off another, not thinking too hard about where they are heading. During my development phase on

*A Tangled Tale*, I pulled my charcoal sticks out of the back of my art box and started smearing and smudging images of fish. **24** Getting messy helped loosen my mind and the intense black of the charcoal approximated the look of sand, letting me use my drawing skills to work through my ideas quickly.

I like to sketch on paper, but I have a colleague who "sketches" with a camera – taking photographs as a form of visual research. He gathers many, many images and then begins to whittle them down as his ideas formulate. Maybe you prefer to draw on the computer. Just remember that a sketch is something fast and inconsequential. If

**23** *Rough storyboard for* A Tangled Tale *– 2013.*

it doesn't work out, move on quickly to the next one to keep the ideas flowing. This is both the most exciting and the most terrifying part of the film. The options are endless and can be paralyzing, which is why it is important to just plow ahead and not worry about whether what you make will eventually be useful. 25

## Telling the Story

As my pile of concept art grows, certain images start to rise naturally to the surface, becoming the visual turning points of the film. At this stage I may start writing a more detailed script, or stick to developing things visually, depending on the film. This is a trick I learned from a writer that flexes the storytelling muscles:

24 Working out story ideas on index cards.

- Write each major plot point of a story on an index card.
- Shuffle the index cards and lay them out in a random order.
- Now on blank index cards, write connecting details that reconnect the original plot points in the new order.

Sometimes shaking things up (literally) can lead to new narrative discoveries and a stronger film over all. The danger is getting too attached to your first idea and becoming convinced it is the only way to make the film.

## The Storyboard

As I write things down, I use thumbnail drawings to work out the narrative connections between these key moments. Thumbnails are a small series of drawings that block out a scene or a sequence. They are great way to get your visual ideas down quickly as they pop into your head. 26 Eventually,

25 Concept sketch and finished frame by Ishu Patel for United Airlines commercial. Courtesy of Ishu Patel.

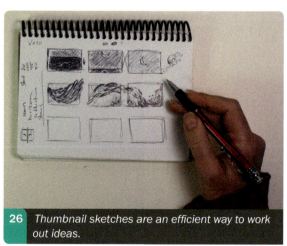

26 Thumbnail sketches are an efficient way to work out ideas.

you can develop these thumbnail sequences into a detailed storyboard, which then will be your guide for the animation.

A film is broken down into scenes (everything in one location), scenes are broken into shots (action from a single camera angle), and shots are broken into moments (emotional highlights or shifts in the action within a shot). The rule of thumb is to create a storyboard panel for every emotional or action shift of your film. This becomes the backbone of how the action will progress from moment to moment, shot to shot, scene to scene. Storyboards are very helpful for both narrative and non-narrative films. **27**

Some animators will take their storyboards a step further and create an animatic by editing their panels in sequence to match a rough soundtrack. This is a way to fine-tune the timing and see if your editing is working before you commit to the hours under the camera.

For independent animators, there is an infinite number of ways you can storyboard and script a film. How you approach these will depend on what information you need to record for yourself and what information you need to communicate for others. If you are applying for grants, starting a crowdfunding campaign or working with a team of other artists, you will need to communicate the ideas behind your film in a clear, enticing manner so that anyone can understand them (and hopefully support your project!). In these situations, an animatic is about as close as you can get to watching the film before you have made any animation.

On the other hand, if you are working alone, then you are the only one who needs to know where the film is going and you may not even need a storyboard. In *The Street* (1976), Caroline Leaf used the soundtrack and a few sketches as a guide to take her from scene to scene with spontaneous transformations.[11] César Díaz Meléndez also does not use a storyboard, saying he is too eager to get started on a scene to draw out all the details:

> Sometimes, if the scene is very clear in my head, I can just start. If not, I draw a rough sketch and then I start. But it's always right before I start to shoot. I don't spend one month doing a storyboard. I can't do that![12] **28**

Meléndez's expertise working with sand and his foundational knowledge of the principles of animation allow him to forge ahead without the security of a tightly planned scene.

> "When I am thinking of an idea for a new film, the most important thing to me is to know how the film ends. Without an ending (where one usually places the message of the film) there is not really an idea. So, all my storyboards must come to an ending before I go into production."
>
> – Gil Alkabetz

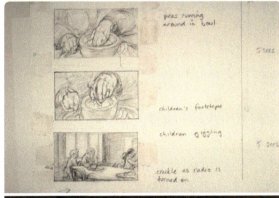

**27** *Storyboard and final drawing from Lee Whitmore's Ada.*

## Research

Even the artists who don't work with storyboards spend a lot of time developing their story or idea. Some films require meticulous research, both visual and factual. Before she made *Pearl's Diner* (1992), Lynn Smith visited dozens of diners, sketching and eavesdropping on the patrons' conversations. Lee Whitmore dug into her own memories with factual research for *The Safe House* (2006):

> I felt the period of the story had to be evoked exactly and accurately. As good as my memory is I couldn't rely completely on it this time. So I researched everything from period telephones and firemen's helmets to what ASIO and police cars were like.[13] 29

Martine Chartrand discovered an unexpectedly rich backstory when she began researching the history of a favorite folk song, *MacPherson* (2012). Investigating the song's composer, Félix Leclerc, she learned about their intimate family connection with the man that inspired the song: "I visited the Leclerc family home, where Macpherson used to listen to Félix's sister play the piano . . . It was the beginning of a great adventure."[14] 30 Instead of

28 *César Díaz Meléndez working on Zepo.*

30 *Frank Randolph Macpherson in the Leclerc living room, as imagined by Martine Chartrand. Macpherson ©2012 National Film Board of Canada, All rights reserved.*

29 *Lee Whitmore used historic TV footage and newspaper clippings as well as her own childhood memories to recreate scenes surrounding the Petrov Affair in The Safe House. (The Safe House – Lee Whitmore – 2006.)*

31 *Night Weaver – Joan Gratz – 2015.*

focusing her film only on the folk tale outlined in the song, Chartrand was able to weave in the life story of Frank Randolph Macpherson.

Visual research may involve learning a new artistic process, or gaining life experiences. For *A Tangled Tale*, I learned to fly fish. Even though a fisherman never appears in the film, the time I spent on the river with my fly rod helped me think like a fish. I knew my research had paid off when I showed the film to a fishing guide and he told me he felt the same thrill watching my sandy animated fish take the fly as he does on a real river when a fish strikes his fly.

## Other Structural Methods

This conceptual development is just as important for films that do not rely on a traditional narrative. Whether you plan to work with abstract or non-objective imagery, or use representational imagery in a non-narrative structure, your film will require significant deliberation and planning. It must also take the viewer on a journey so the audience does not end up confused, or even worse, bored! Bärbel Neubauer, who makes abstract films by painting and scratching on filmstrips, explains that determining the mental method of creating is particularly important to the abstract filmmaker because it can provide a framework for the physical process:

> There are as many possibilities for creating abstract films as there are for all other kinds of filmmaking. The artist can work in a meditative way, in a structural way, in an intellectual way and/or in an interpretational way . . . Many abstract filmmakers want to enjoy the process of making the film, experiencing and experimenting with the medium.[15] **31**

If you plan to work abstractly, consider the following methods as possible starting points for guiding your process:

- Animate to a musical or mathematically determined rhythmic structure.
- Create visual poetry using a literary structure, like a visual limerick or a haiku.
- Institute sets of visual rules for color, shape, or movement patterns that repeat and change over the course of the film.
- Work through stream of consciousness by animating straight ahead, letting images develop intuitively.
- Use a computer to generate randomness and link it with your visual imagery.

Neubauer also points out, it is often the mistakes that lead to new discoveries and ideas, which is true with all experimental processes. As you acquire the experimental frame of mind, you will find it extends not only to all forms of animation, but can be applied to the situations we encounter outside the studio as well. Whether you are working with a narrative structure or non-narrative structure, making a strong film is a balancing act between self-expression and connecting with an audience. You are a creative, resourceful animator with something to share with the world. Let's get to work!

## Notes

1. Starr, Cecile, and Robert Russett. Experimental Animation: Origins of a New Art. New York, NY: Da Capo, 1988, p. 77.
2. Ibid.
3. Parker, Claire, and Alexander Alexeieff. "New Abstract Process." Cinema Quarterly 3.1 (1934): 34. MOMA Library. Date accessed: Mar. 15, 2015. https://archive.org/details/cinemaquarterly103gdro
4. Ibid., p. 34.
5. Starr and Russett, pp. 66–69.
6. Crockwell, Douglass. "A Background to Free Animation." Film Culture 32 (Spring 1964): 30–31.
7. Starr and Russett, p. 100.
8. Leaf, Caroline. Telephone interview. Mar. 26, 2014.
9. Troshinsky, Nicolai. Telephone interview. Feb. 20, 2014.
10. Gratz, Joan. Telephone interview. October 14, 2014.
11. Leaf, Caroline. "An Interview with Caroline Leaf in English." Interview by Midhat "Ajan" Ajanovic. 2002. Date accessed: Feb. 20, 2014. http://www.ajan.se/index.php?option=com_content&task=view&id=46&Itemid=43
12. Meléndez, César Díaz. Telephone interview. May 21, 2014.
13. Whitmore, Lee. Hand-drawn Histories: The Films of Lee Whitmore. 2011. DVD Booklet.
14. "Martine Chartrand: Visual Artist-Filmmaker." MacPherson Press Kit. National Film Board of Canada, n.d. Date accessed: Mar. 28, 2015. http://martinechartrand.net/medias/MacPherson_PressKit.pdf
15. Neubauer, Bärbel. "Thoughts on Abstract Animation." Animation Journal 7.2 (1999): 58–62.

*Thomas Parks.*

# Chapter 2
# Lights! Camera! Animation!

**Setting Up Your Studio for Under-the-Camera Animation**
  Working Surface
  The Multiplane

**Lights**
  Top Light
  The Light Box

**The Camera**
  Image Resolution
  The Lens
  Setting the Exposure

**Frame Capture**

**Additional Advice**
  Lock it Down
  Staying Healthy Under the Camera
  Keeping Things in Perspective

## Setting Up Your Studio for Under-the-Camera Animation

Shooting animation under the camera means you will be spending a lot of time in your camera room. With that in mind, having a functional, comfortable workspace will help you create better animation. Naturally, not everyone has access to the ideal studio space. When I started animating, my first camera room was 4x5-foot closet in my bedroom and I still managed to maintain a very active artistic and commercial practice. `01`

Since then, I have moved my studio several times, and I had to transform each new space into a place where my creative brain could focus and expand.

Here's a list of questions to ask yourself when setting up your workspace:

- Do you like to work standing up or sitting on a stool or chair?
- Do you need inspiring images covering the walls or does blank space keep you focused?
- Do you like to listen to music or podcasts while you work or is silence your friend?
- Does it help you to be surrounded by others while you are working? Does sharing a studio with another artist appeal to you?

A studio is an evolving space, and it will grow as you grow as an artist. If you find yourself stuck creatively, maybe it's time to rearrange the furniture, buy a new piece of equipment to play with, or visit other animators and see how they construct their space. Your studio should be both sacred and adjustable and, most importantly, a place you want to spend your time. **02**

Practically, there are certain things you'll need to animate under the camera with the materials covered later in this book. These are:

- Working surface – table, light box, or multiplane setup
- Lights – top light, backlight, or both
- Camera – digital still camera, film, video camera, or webcam
- Frame capture software – not necessary but very convenient.

## Working Surface

Just about every animator I talked to for this book has a customized animation table that suits their working methods. Each one brought the experimental frame of mind to the construction of their studio and figured out what special functions their vision required. The size and style of your working surface will vary based on your individual production needs, but at the very least you will want a table at a comfortable height with the capability of being lit from above or below. **03**

The techniques in this book are often animated on glass or Plexiglas. Plexiglas is lightweight and inexpensive and has a very slight texture that some

**01** A closet is the perfect place for a camera room.

**02** Lynn Tomlinson's living room studio. Courtesy of Lynn Tomlinson.

paint-on-glass animators find helps paint stick to the surface. Glass is sturdier, resisting scratches from scraping palette knives or rubbing sand. For sand animators, glass also minimizes the static electricity that can build up on the surface and make the sand spontaneously jump out of place. For this reason most sand animators animate on glass. Other surfaces work as well. Patrick Jenkins paints on linoleum tiles because he likes how the texture interacts with the paint. Joan Gratz paints with clay on a masonite board. Some artists, like Alexander Petrov and Martine Chartrand, paint on clear, acetate cels taped to the glass so they can easily slide reference images underneath.

A sturdy piece of glass makes a great base for your working surface and you can always place a Plexiglas sheet or acetate cel on top. You can have glass cut to any size at a glass shop. For larger working surfaces, choose a fairly thick sheet of glass, at least ¼ to ½ of an inch. If you can afford it, get tempered glass, which is much stronger than standard window glass and doesn't scratch as easily. I have a tendency to lean on my table a bit while working and it would be tragic and dangerous if I fell through it! Pay a little extra to have the edges sealed (i.e. smoothed down) so you don't cut yourself while handling it, or you can tape the edges with strong masking tape. If you are working with top light, look for non-reflective glass (frequently used in picture framing). It is expensive, but you won't have to deal with tricky reflections from the lights and camera.

## The Multiplane

If you are planning to work in layers, you may want to construct a multiplane, which is multiple layers of glass stacked under the camera. With a multiplane, you can separate parts of your animation onto the different layers so they don't intermingle. This is convenient if you have two colors you don't want to mix together, or if you have a background image that you want to keep separate from the foreground action.

A multiplane is a customizable thing. It can be as simple as propping up a layer of glass above your table, or as complex as Clive Walley's highly engineered 4D camera rig. Nicolai Troshinsky's multiplane stretched from floor to ceiling because he needed to manipulate the depth of field in *Astigmatismo*. Through trial and error, Troshinsky determined the distance necessary between each level to achieve the precise focus shifts between distant and close-up parts of the scene.[1] **04 05**

**03** The sand animation studio where I made *A Tangled Tale*.

**04** The layered multiplane used in *Astigmatismo*. Courtesy of Nicolai Troshinsky.

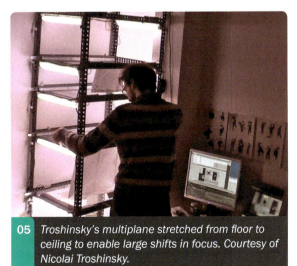
**05** Troshinsky's multiplane stretched from floor to ceiling to enable large shifts in focus. Courtesy of Nicolai Troshinsky.

Bernard Lajoie, technical director on Alexander Petrov's *The Old Man and the Sea* (1999), built a custom animation stand that would accommodate an IMAX camera. The stand had four glass plates that slid in and out like drawers. Petrov would make changes to the necessary level and slide the drawers into place, at which point an electric sensor would indicate they were back in exact alignment. Everything had to be perfectly precise because the slightest misalignment would be magnified enormously on the IMAX screen.[2]

If you wish to build a multiplane, start with something simple, like Tess Martin's homemade layering system. **06** Leave enough space between the layers so you can reach your hand in and make changes to the lower levels, if necessary. See what you can achieve with just two layers, and how your material looks when it is stacked. Once you have worked like this for a little while, you will learn what special modifications you might want. You may decide you need sliding mounts to pull out your layers, or a special lighting system to eliminate shadows. Your studio is your customizable workspace, so let it evolve with your production needs.

## Lights

Top lighting is when light illuminates the top of the artwork. Backlighting is when the light comes from behind the artwork, creating a silhouette or backlit image. **07 08**

Back in the days of film, lighting had to be very carefully calibrated with the correct film stock so the color and exposure would be accurate to life. Digital cameras give us much more flexibility with lighting because we can adjust the settings within the camera based on what lighting we have

**06** *A simple multiplane. Courtesy of Tess Martin.*

**07** *The Safe House by Lee Whitmore is top lit gouache – 2006.*

**08** *The Umbrella by Xin Li is backlit oil paint – 2011.*

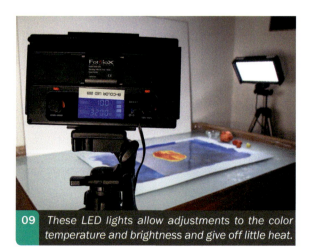

**09** *These LED lights allow adjustments to the color temperature and brightness and give off little heat.*

available. LED lights are a less expensive and more energy efficient option to large studio lights. **09 10**

A dimmer switch will allow you to precisely control the amount of light that goes into the camera. Check the specifications before installing one, as certain types of lights have special requirements. Some lights need time to warm up before they reach their full brightness, so turn them on while you are getting your supplies ready. You may not notice the difference with the naked eye, but the sensitive camera will!

## Top Lights

With top lighting, reflections off the glass can sometimes be a problem, which is why I recommend non-reflective glass. A polarizing filter on the camera lens will also help in eliminating glare, or you can add a touch of backlight. I have found that the combination of backlight and top light works very well for paint-on-glass and clay painting.

You will also need some sort of diffusion method to soften the light hitting the image and reduce harsh shadows. You can buy diffusion paper to go over the lights, use a professional softbox or try bouncing light off a piece of white foam core above the artwork. The farther back your lights are from the artwork, the more diffuse the lights will be. Of course more diffuse light also means less light on the artwork, so you will have to compensate for this with your exposure settings. **11**

The standard light placement is at a 45° angle on either side of the image surface. Of course, this is just a starting point and you will want to make your own adjustments according to the effects you want to achieve. While I was shooting tests for *Ash Sunday*, I tried all sorts of lighting combinations to eliminate the shadow the paint cast onto the paper below the glass. Nothing worked, so I accentuated the shadow by using thicker glass and eliminating all diffusion. Then I wrote the shadow into the story as an additional character. **12**

## The Light Box

If you wish to have your work lit from underneath, the simplest solution is to buy a light box from an art supply or photography store. Look for one that

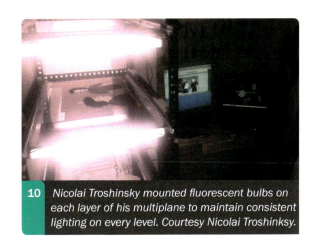

**10** *Nicolai Troshinsky mounted fluorescent bulbs on each layer of his multiplane to maintain consistent lighting on every level. Courtesy Nicolai Troshinksy.*

**11** *Bounced light makes for an even illumination over the artwork.*

**12** *Ash Sunday – Corrie Francis Parks – 2001.*

can provide a consistent diffusion across the surface, as sometimes the bulb will illuminate one section of the box very brightly and leave the rest in a dull, underexposed state. **13**

At some point, you may find it more economical to build your own light box so you can have a larger working surface. There are a number of ways to do this, but the basic idea is to build an encasement for customizable lighting. Inside the box you can use linkable under-cabinet lights or strips of LEDs arranged to provide even illumination.

If you are working with backlit techniques, you will need some way to diffuse the light as it comes through the glass so it spreads evenly and softly. Milk glass (also known as opal glass) is a white, opaque glass that provides near-perfect diffusion. However, it is expensive and hard to find. Other options include adhering white window privacy film to the glass or taping a few layers of translucent architecture paper on the underside of your glass. Bouncing and reflecting the light from underneath also helps create an even illumination. **14**

Your studio needs will depend on your production and the way you like to work. Creativity doesn't end with the artwork; it is your tool for anything that gets in the way of your production. Don't be intimidated by construction projects; you can enlist help. Michaela Müller asked her father to help her build a camera and light box that could rotate as one unit so she could incorporate slowly dripping paint in her animation. **15**

Robbe Vervaeke's grandfather helped him construct a metal-framed easel for his large-format paint-on-glass. Lynn Smith's custom 16mm camera stand, which she used to shoot several of her films, was designed and built by George Perkins in 1972, a master tinkerer who worked for the Physics Department at Harvard helping graduate students construct unique models in order to

**13** Working on a manufactured light box.

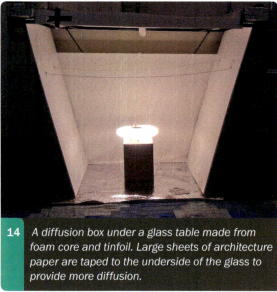

**14** A diffusion box under a glass table made from foam core and tinfoil. Large sheets of architecture paper are taped to the underside of the glass to provide more diffusion.

> "You need to be constantly managing your work area. If you don't, then you won't make animation. It can be cluttered and it can be dirty, but you need to be able to move stuff and change stuff, to move your lights and your camera, expand your work area. And if it doesn't work, do something else."
>
> – Robbe Vervaeke

test their ideas. Later, Smith had the stand modified to accommodate a digital camera. We are not in this alone. Let your limitations be the reason to involve someone else in your production, for both you and your collaborators will find the experience full of unexpected rewards.

## The Camera

The most common way to shoot animation is using a Digital Single Reflex Lens (DSLR) camera. It's also possible to shoot animation with a webcam, digital video camera, or even a phone. Don't let finances keep you from animating! Just start with what you have. **17**

However, if you shoot with a DSLR, you will be able to fine-tune the image before the shoot and afterwards during post-production. In this section, we will go through some of the basics of choosing and adjusting a DSLR for under-the-camera animation.

A DSLR is made up of a camera body and a lens. A power adapter is a nice accessory to have for your camera so your battery won't die in the

**15** *Michaela Müller's tilting camera. Photo by Corrie Francis Parks.*

**Animated Anecdote**

*After hacking together my first sand table from a WalMart computer desk, I needed to build a camera stand. I headed to the local hardware store with a sketch of what I wanted and no idea where to start. The lady at the front counter sent me upstairs to consult with Max (aka MacGyver). He took one look at my sketch and got this twinkle of glee in his eye and off we went on a whirlwind around the hardware store collecting items and consulting with several other employees along the way. I could tell they were attacking the problem with as much creative gusto as I brought to my films. I ended up constructing the camera stand out of some discarded 2x4-foot scraps, steel plumbing parts (I now know what a flange is for), and a few nuts and bolts. On my last of several trips to the store, I brought a thank-you note and a big plate of cookies for all the employees that took on such an unusual creative problem with such enthusiasm.* **16**

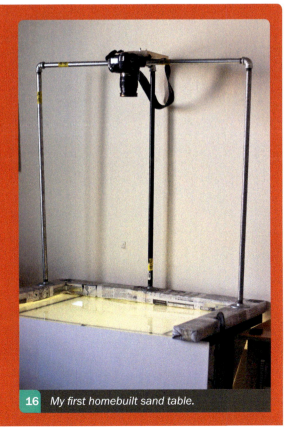

**16** *My first homebuilt sand table.*

17  A phone camera stand in use at an animation workshop for teachers led by Diane Kuthy and Lynn Tomlinson at Towson University. Photo by Hannah Simms.

18  A Canon DSLR set up for shooting animation.

middle of a shot. You will need a cable to connect the camera to the computer as well. Check with the camera's manufacturer to find out what kind you will need. The brand of your camera doesn't matter, but there are some features to look for when choosing a camera body. **18**

## Image Resolution

All cameras have a maximum resolution for the images they capture. Usually an image captured by a DSLR will be at a much greater resolution than one from a high definition video camera, which might shoot in full HD (1920x1080 pixels) or even 4K (3084x2160). High resolution images give you options for digital manipulations. For example, if the final format of my film is full HD and my camera shoots an image that is 5184x2986, I will be able to zoom into the image 2.5 times and not lose any image quality. However, if my film is 4K resolution, I will be able to zoom in much less before the pixels become visible. If you are using a webcam or digital video camera, pay particular attention to the image resolution. Many modern cameras are able to shoot in high definition (1920x1080) but also have lower resolution settings. Always capture at the highest resolution possible because it is much easier to scale down an image than to scale it up. Of course, there is a tradeoff: The bigger the image resolution, the larger the file size. You will need more storage space and processing power on your computer to work with the footage. **19**

Most DSLRs have the option to shoot in RAW format. A RAW image file has not been processed and has the most information available in each pixel for digital development. Different camera brands have their own internal processing methods for making JPEG files in the camera, but a RAW file allows you to determine the development

> **#ProTip** ALWAYS back up your footage and project files on an external storage drive that you keep in a safe place away from the computer! In the event your computer breaks down, or is stolen or damaged, you at least won't have lost the hours you spent under the camera.

settings for the sequences. Shooting in RAW format results in bigger file sizes, but you have the option to take the images into programs like Adobe Lightroom or Photoshop and adjust nearly every setting, even after you have shot a scene. If you get your exposure perfect when you shoot, it is not necessary to shoot in RAW, so that can save you a lot of file space over the course of a film. However, if you like to manipulate the exposure, white balance, saturation, or sharpness of your images, RAW files are the better choice. Because I do a lot of post-processing to my sand footage, I almost always shoot in RAW and batch process each sequence in Lightroom.

## The Lens

The lens you choose will affect how your final image looks more than the body of the camera. All the light, color, and dimensionality of the world around us must pass through a series of glass layers before it is recorded on the camera sensor. The higher quality the glass and engineering with that process, the more true to life those digital images will be. [20] When you are spending your creative energy animating worldly

**19** *The image on the left was shot at 5184x3186, the image on the right at 720x400 and was scaled up 750% to match the size of the first image. You can see the noticeable difference in sharpness.*

**20** *Different lenses provide different optical properties.*

materials under the camera, each frame is a work of art, so if you are going to spend some money somewhere, spend it on your camera lens. Here are some things to consider when choosing a lens.

**Focal Length:** Fixed or prime lenses come in many different focal lengths (e.g. 28mm, 50mm, 80mm). The focal length is the distance from the lens to the sensor in the camera. A smaller number (i.e. 28mm, wide angle) means the lens has a wider field of view; more of what is in front of the camera will fit within the frame. A longer focal length (i.e. 200mm, telephoto) means a narrow field of view, and you will see only a small portion of what is in front of the camera represented on the frame. **21**

Many DSLR cameras are sold with some sort of zoom lens. Zoom lenses have a range of focal lengths (e.g. 18–200mm) so you can choose to have a wider or narrow field of view. The flexibility of being able to set your own focal length is useful, but in exchange for this flexibility you will sacrifice sharpness and clarity in your image. Additionally, when the camera is mounted with the lens pointing down at the table or floor, gravity will want to pull the lens out to its fullest zoom. For professional projects, it is better to have a fixed lens and be able to adjust the height of the camera above your working surface.

**Depth of Field:** The difference in focus between the nearest and furthest object in the field of view is called the depth of field and can be manipulated through the aperture settings on the lens. This f-stop setting is the ratio between the width of the lens and its focal length. Changing the f-stop (e.g f/1.8, f/4, f/22) changes the width of the opening and thus affects how much of our scene will be in focus. For example, if your f-stop is set to f/22 and you focus on an object very close to the camera, the objects in the background will also be in focus. If the f-stop is set at f/1.8, then only one part of the foreground image will be in focus and the background will be very blurry. **22**

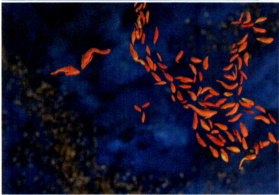
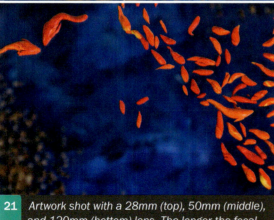

**21** Artwork shot with a 28mm (top), 50mm (middle), and 120mm (bottom) lens. The longer the focal length of the lens, the smaller the field of view.

**#ProTip** *Some lenses have an image stabilizing feature. Be sure to turn this off when you shoot animation because the stabilizer will cause slight changes in the alignment, resulting in jittery footage.*

This is particularly important to keep in mind when working with multiplane set-ups, because you may want to have only one layer in focus and the others out of focus. In this case you would use a wide aperture like f/1.8 to give you a shallow depth of field. Or you may want every layer in focus, in which case you would need a very narrow aperture like f/22. Nicolai Troshinsky used this to his advantage in *Astigmatismo*. This short about a boy who loses his glasses masterfully plays with depth of field. Troshinsky shot the film on a five-layer multiplane setup with carefully planned shifts of focus to leave the audience feeling disoriented like his character. He used a Canon EF 85mm f/1.2 lens, which gave him an extremely wide depth of field. **23**

Every lens has a sweet spot where the image is at its most sharp and clear. Usually, this is somewhere in the middle of its aperture range. Photographers will conduct a series of focus tests through an aperture range to find the sweet spot on

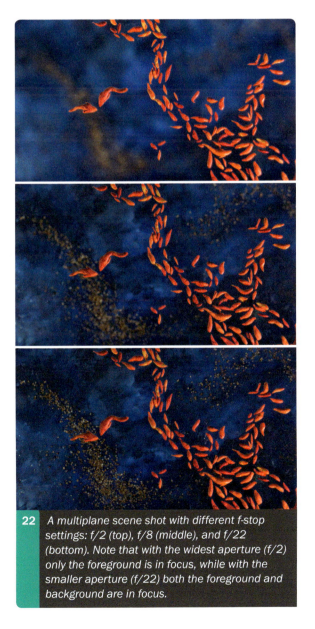

**22** *A multiplane scene shot with different f-stop settings: f/2 (top), f/8 (middle), and f/22 (bottom). Note that with the widest aperture (f/2) only the foreground is in focus, while with the smaller aperture (f/22) both the foreground and background are in focus.*

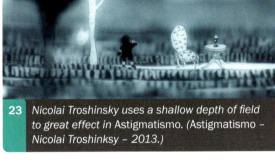

**23** *Nicolai Troshinsky uses a shallow depth of field to great effect in* Astigmatismo. *(Astigmatismo – Nicolai Troshinksy – 2013.)*

a lens. Unless you have a specific reason for working on the widest or narrowest settings, keep your aperture set as close to the sweet spot as possible.

### Setting the Exposure

Another benefit of a DSLR over webcams and point-and-shoot cameras is you have very precise control over how you expose the image, which is a balancing act between aperture, shutter speed, and ISO. These three settings are all related to how much light passes through the lens to the camera sensor and determine how light or dark the image is.

***Aperture:*** We discussed the fine details of aperture when we picked out our lens. Here is where your aesthetic tastes come into play, so we will set this first. Determine what you want in focus, then set the aperture to achieve the desired depth of field. If you are shooting on just one level and don't need to worry about depth of field, set the aperture in that sweet spot for your lens to get the sharpest image and to avoid any vignette.

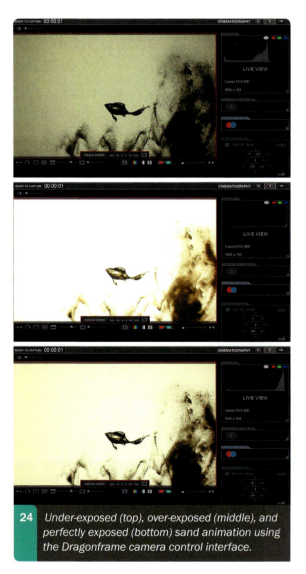

**24** Under-exposed (top), over-exposed (middle), and perfectly exposed (bottom) sand animation using the Dragonframe camera control interface.

***Shutter Speed:*** Shutter speed is how fast the camera opens and closes to allow the light to hit the sensor and create an image. You can make the shutter speed slower and allow more light onto the sensor, or faster and allow less light in. Always use a remote or a keystroke to activate the shutter on your camera. Pressing the shutter button with your finger will create a slight movement in the camera and cause jitter in your final animation. If your camera is mounted securely on a tripod or camera stand, you should be able to have a fairly slow shutter speed without risking a blurred image. However, if the shutter speed is very slow, you might notice some digital artifacts called "noise" in the final image.

***ISO:*** ISO used to refer to the film speed, i.e. how much light was required to expose a piece of film. Now there is a digital equivalent. If you need a faster shutter speed and don't want to change your aperture settings, you can increase the ISO. The tradeoff is that a high ISO can create noise in an image, which may not fit your aesthetic. The ISO is something you would change only if you can't make the shutter speed and aperture setting work together. Keep your ISO around 100–200 if possible.

Take some test shots, changing the shutter speed, aperture, and ISO until you find an exposure that accurately represents your artistic goals. You will need to test your exposure for every scene, particularly for backlit work. A scene with a lot of white will need to be exposed differently than a scene with a lot of dark colors. **24**

## Frame Capture

Once you have your working surface, lights, and camera arranged, the only thing left is a way to get the frames you record into the computer. Your digital camera can capture a sequence of images and you could download them after you finish shooting. However, there are several software programs on the market that will let you view a live feed from your camera while you are animating, which will make your life infinitely easier! There are many out there, some free or inexpensive and some professional grade with professional prices. These are some of the essential and convenient functions you will want to have in frame capture software:

- Live View: You can see what the camera is seeing on the computer.
- Onion-skinning: You can see previously recorded images superimposed on the live image. Very handy to keep your movements between frames uniform and forms accurate. **25**
- Video Playback: While animating, you can play back what you have recorded and see how things are going.
- Frame Export: Once you are done animating, you can export your work in a useable format for future editing, like an uncompressed video file or frame sequence.

Other great features to look for:

- Camera Controls: ability to adjust camera settings, exposure, and focus
- Motion/Control/Lighting Controls: control studio lights and motion rigs for complex shots
- Rotoscoping or Reference footage: you can load an image or movie and see it over the live feed as a reference for your animation.

Most programs will let you download a trial version before you pay so always try before you buy! Check that you like the user interface and that your camera is compatible.

## Additional Advice

The benefit of this book is it is a collective repository of what many animators have learned through experience. Most of them have figured it out as they go along. Here's a host of things that I would have loved to know when I started working under the camera.

### Lock It Down

Weight and lock down everything that could get moved while you shoot. There's nothing more frustrating than accidentally bumping the table in the middle of a scene and throwing the alignment with

**25** *Using a guide layer and onion skin in Dragonframe software.*

the camera off. Even worse is having a wobbly camera stand that makes the shot jitter. Tape the legs of your tripod to the table or floor and weight the center column with sand bags or bolt your camera mount to the wall. I also use tape and sticky tack to attach my light box to the table and brace the table against a wall to minimize any movement.

Leaving a "hot set" means leaving in the middle of a scene because you need to sleep, eat, or just go outside and breathe some fresh air. When taking a break, protect your work by placing a large sheet of foam core or an extra plate of glass over your working area to protect it from curious fingers or bits of dust. When you get back, let your lights warm up for a while before you start to shoot and always double check the exposure and framing in case something has shifted while you were away.

### Staying Healthy Under the Camera

Because of the long hours, animating under the camera can take a toll on your health and wellbeing. Here are a few things to keep you feeling good throughout the process.

- Make your work table at a comfortable height so you don't have to bend over much. I stand on an anti-fatigue mat while animating, which keeps me from getting leg cramps and backaches.
- Set a timer to go off every 30 minutes. When it goes off, stand up, walk around the room, wave your arms, look out the window at something far away, do a toe-touch and some arm circles, then get back to it.
- If you are using backlighting and are staring into the light for long hours, get some lightly tinted glasses to protect your eyes.
- Use a dust mask if you are working with very fine grain sand, pastels, or other dusty materials.
- Make sure you have proper ventilation, especially if you are working with oils and turpentine.

### Keeping Things in Perspective

Inevitably in the middle of a shot there comes a moment when we wonder what we have gotten ourselves into. Destroying and reconstructing each frame seems like an endless process and we wonder why we decided to have so many things moving! Ultimately, we ask ourselves, "How long will this take?"

You are not alone! Here's an anecdotal comparison of the pace at which the stalwart animators in this book work:

- On *Soup of the Day*, Lynn Smith could spend all day on one image when the image contained many characters or was part of a complex drawn camera move (or both!) When working on *Pearl's Diner* with paper cut-outs and water-based Crapas crayons, she averaged five to six images in a day. 27

***Animated Anecdote***
*While working on* Truth Has Fallen, *Sheila Sofian stepped away from her paint-on-glass for a moment. When she came back, she found her cat, Diva, had wandered across her painting, leaving paw prints in the wet paint. She now uses a wire covering to protect her work from curious cats!* 26

26 Sheila Sofian's cat protector. Courtesy of Sheila M. Sofian.

- On the more complex shots in *MacPherson*, Martine Chartrand would be able to finish four to eight painted images a day. Sometimes creating the backgrounds would take her an entire day.
- Joan Gratz's pace for her clay painting varies from less that 1 to 12 images per day.
- When animating a single fish swimming in *A Tangled Tale*, I could sometimes complete 100 images in a day. But on a more complex image, like the moving portrait of Darwin and his owl for the documentary *Seed*, I barely managed 20 images in one day.
- On the opposite end of the spectrum, Robbe Vervaeke will complete 60–120 images of painted animation a day, depending on how complex and detailed the scene is.
- Shira Avni's personal record is 200 images in one day! "But," she says, "I was doing something very simple." Usually she averages between 5 and 20 images per day.

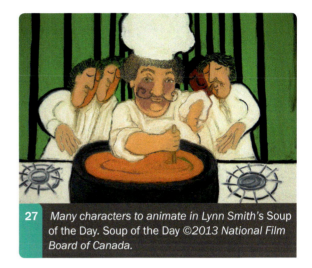

**27** *Many characters to animate in Lynn Smith's* Soup of the Day. *Soup of the Day ©2013 National Film Board of Canada.*

Because this moment of fatigue will inevitably come, we must prepare mentally as well as physically. A good part of our mental preparation comes from that rehearsal time mentioned in the previous chapter. Playing develops fluency in our chosen technique so when we do sit down to create our final work we can better achieve "a state of flow." This is a state of mind frequently referred to by athletes, artists, or other professionals, when they are fully immersed and focused on their area of expertise.

Sometimes it's enough to just know what to expect and have a plan, like Shira Avni's preparations for a long shoot: "I prepare myself with music that will inspire me for long hours, food, cut off the internet access, and plan an open schedule that allows for a long day (and often overnight) of work."[3] **28**

Michaela Müller prepares for each scene by spending time visualizing. Using her storyboard as a guide, she mentally watches each shot in her mind:

> With *Miramare* . . . every day, when I went to bed, when I woke up in the morning, I stayed with my eyes closed and tried to watch the film. I tried to learn the film by heart and then watch it and feel it. That's how I then improvised it . . . It's like meditation – I get distracted all the time, it's very hard![4]

**28** *Shira Avni working with backlit clay under the camera. ©2006 National Film Board of Canada. Photo credit: Caroline Hayeur.*

Added confidence can also come from constructing references. **29** Lee Whitmore created three-dimensional models of the dining room in *Ada* (2002). Since the room was so important to the film, she needed to draw it from every possible angle. When it came time to do *The Safe House* (2006), she took the same approach, making a model of the street where the story takes place. Alexander Petrov filmed and sketched his father-in-law as a model for *The Old Man and the Sea*: "Using living people whom I know well and love, these people with their personalities, help me to make the personalities of my painted characters believable. This is the case for practically all of my films."[5] Using familiar faces as the basis for his characters gave Petrov an added motivation and emotional investment in the hours under the camera. **30**

Pacing yourself is also important. Martine Chartrand received some very good advice from Petrov in her early days of animating: "He said to me, 'Now you have to work with the hardest of your scenes first and make it very complicated. Then you will understand the difficulty of animating and push yourself not to be comfortable with the easy scenes.'"[6] While working on the most complex scenes at the beginning of your production may feel like jumping into the deep end, taking the plunge will increase your learning curve and make the entire film better. If you know a particular shot is going to be a massive undertaking, do it early in the production when you have energy and enthusiasm and time to address the challenges.

Chartrand also observes:

persevering is not the problem . . . it's overcoming the feelings of isolation . . . I created my films *Black Soul* and *MacPherson* under a 35mm camera, without any computer. Animating under a 35mm camera, 10 hours per day for years, demands great concentration, and circumstances dictate that I work alone . . . I am not connected to the virtual world of communication . . .[7]

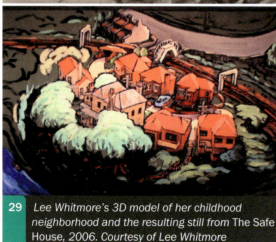

**29** *Lee Whitmore's 3D model of her childhood neighborhood and the resulting still from* The Safe House, *2006. Courtesy of Lee Whitmore*

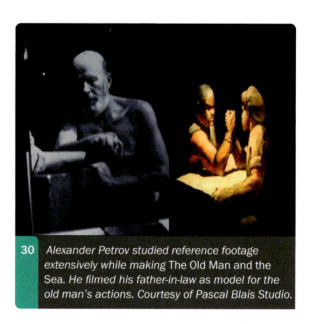

**30** *Alexander Petrov studied reference footage extensively while making* The Old Man and the Sea. *He filmed his father-in-law as model for the old man's actions. Courtesy of Pascal Blais Studio.*

The demands of the outside world may be a distraction you need to avoid, or it may help you with your production. Lynn Tomlinson says that sharing her work over social media helped motivate her to complete *The Ballad of Holland Island House* (2014):

> My research, my working relationships and network of artists that give me feedback and encouragement are digital and online. That's how I motivate myself. I would say to myself, "Okay, if I can do one second, I'll let myself post a still and people will give me likes and then I will feel encouraged to continue."[8]

The key to maintaining your energy and motivation through an entire production is having a balanced life. Be sure to spend time away from your work with friends and family, or rent a studio space in an area with other artists so you will occasionally have a built-in opportunity for social interaction. Maintaining a good mental attitude is just as important as staying physically healthy!

We want to step into the spotlight of the camera with as much preparation as possible, so we can animate with confidence. Every animator will have a different comfort level with the uncontrollable aspects of these materials. Some we can eliminate through our preparations, and some we must simply embrace as part of the under-the-camera method. There may seem to be mountains of preparations and mounds of uncertainty ahead. Immersed in your production, if you find yourself in need of encouragement, remember the words of Martine Chartrand,

31 Black Soul by Martine Chartrand ©2000 National Film Board of Canada.

> More than anything, you feel very spoiled taking so long to work on your film . . . you want to finish your film as quickly as possible, and in the best possible way, and still manage to maintain the fire of inspiration. All that is very hard and it makes you want to leave the ring. But you can't. You have to hang on, to make people dream.[9] 31

## Notes

1 Troshinsky, Nicolai. Telephone interview. Feb. 20, 2014.
2 Cotte, Olivier. Secrets of Oscar-winning Animation: Behind the Scenes of 13 Classic Short Animations. Amsterdam: Elsevier/Focal, 2006, p. 208.
3 Avni, Shira, Telephone interview. Oct. 24, 2014.
4 Müller, Michaela. Personal interview. Mar. 20, 2015.
5 Alexander Petrov: The Making of "Mermaid" and "The Old Man and the Sea." Dir. Alexander Petrov. Panorama Animation Film Studio, c. 2000. Dailymotion.com. Subtitles in English by Niffiwan.
6 Chartrand, Martine. Email interview. Jan. 11, 2015.
7 "MacPherson: A Film by Martine Chartrand." MacPherson Press Kit. National Film Board of Canada, n.d. Date accessed: Mar. 28, 2015. http://martinechartrand.net/medias/MacPherson_PressKit.pdf

8 Tomlinson, Lynn. Personal interview. Oct. 13, 2014.
9 "Martine Chartrand: Visual Artist-Filmmaker." MacPherson Press Kit. National Film Board of Canada, n.d. Date accessed: Mar. 28, 2015. http://martinechartrand.net/medias/MacPherson_PressKit.pdf

*Corrie Francis Parks.*

# Chapter 3
# A Foundation for Excellence

**Art that Moves**

**Basic Principles of Animated Movement**

    Timing and Spacing
    Ones . . . Twos . . . Threes . . .
    Easing
    Holds and Cycles
    Staging
    Squash and Stretch
    Arcs
    Anticipation and Follow-Through
    Overlapping Action
    Secondary Action

**Fluid Frame Aesthetics**

    In-Camera versus Out-of-Camera
    Drawn Camera Moves
    Leaving Trails
    Animated Transitions
    The Hand of the Artist

**The Digital Toolbox**

    Thinking in Layers
    The Staggered Mix
    Exercise: Staggered Mixes
    Rotoscoping

## Art that Moves

Animators are artists of motion, and the things that make great art also make great animation. **01** Words like composition, form, pattern, texture, and color should be at the forefront of our minds as we design each frame. The best equipment and most up-to-date software in the world cannot make you a good animator. It is the time spent observing, researching, and practicing that results in authentic, believable animation.

Eventually, when we do sit down for the final performance, we are better able to achieve what psychologists call "a state of flow." This is a state of mind frequently referred to by athletes, artists, or other professionals, when they are fully immersed and focused on their area of expertise. Working under the camera provides an ideal environment for getting into this state of mind, but it requires confidence in your materials and trust in your intuition. **02**

In this chapter, we'll learn some of the fundamentals that apply to all forms of animation and some of the specific practices common to animating in fluid frame techniques. Study these things and put them in your bag of tricks so you will have them handy when it comes time to perform under the camera.

## Basic Principles of Animated Movement

Becoming confident animators means we frequently have to refresh our foundational skills. We are bringing our characters and stories, even the very materials we work with, into a vibrant, animated existence. To do this, we must be aware not only of how to create aesthetically pleasing images, but also of how our audience will experience those images. Any animated work is a conversation between the artist, the material, and the viewer. Clear communication is essential for a good conversation.

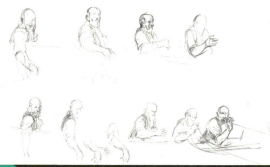

**01** Mona Lisa Descending a Staircase – *Joan Gratz – 1992.*

**02** *Through hundreds of sketches and studies, Alexander Petrov developed an intuitive familiarity with his main character in* The Old Man and the Sea *so animating him under the camera would be a natural outflow of his internal vision for a scene. Courtesy of Pascal Blais Studio.*

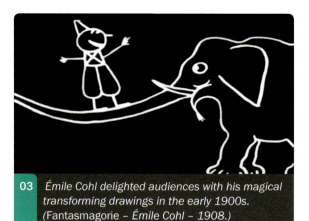

**03** Émile Cohl delighted audiences with his magical transforming drawings in the early 1900s. (Fantasmagorie – Émile Cohl – 1908.)

In the early days of animation, animators were challenged by the technical limitations of film projection and the sheer number of drawings that needed to be created. It was a magical feat just to show an audience a drawing that moved. 03 As new methods of creating and shooting animation were developed, like the mechanical animation camera, and cel animation, production became more efficient, freeing up time for the animator to focus on the emotive qualities of his animation. The traditional "Disney-style" character animation evolved over several decades as artists at major studios experimented not only with their drawings but also with the words to describe them. Eventually a language developed with words like "squash and stretch," "anticipation," and "line of action" becoming part of every animator's vocabulary. 04

The visual language they developed has trickled down into nearly every animation we see today, varying in its interpretation according to the individual or studio styles. When it comes to fluid frame animation, a solid understanding of things like anticipation, squash and stretch, and lines of action will allow you to better harness the unique properties of your materials and achieve an effective visual impact on your audience. I've adapted these foundational principles of animation for fluid frame animators. This overview is brief, but I fully support further exploration. These principles are all based on real phenomena we observe in the world around us. However, in animation, they are exaggerated and pushed to the extreme, creating dynamic, interesting movement that goes beyond reality.

04 *A great film comes from understanding the expressive potential of motion. (Storyboard from The Well – Philippe Vaucher – 2013.)*

## Timing and Spacing

Frames are the common denominator across all animation mediums and the building blocks of seconds. We create every minute of animation "frame-by-frame." 05 Frame rates vary by format – film runs at 24 frames per second (fps), NTSC video at 29.97fps, PAL video at 25fps, etc. Digital video allows you to set your own frame rates, but it is usually best to conform to a known standard so that your work can be seen in a variety of venues.

Also, a project will typically have a constant frame rate defined by the director. Everyone working on the production will use that same frame rate. That way, when they bring their work together, everything will time consistently. Variations aside, the important thing is to know how many frames are in one second, because this is the basis of our timing. In this book, we will be using 24 frames per second (fps) as our constant project rate.

0 : 01 : 57 : 22
one minute,
fifty-seven seconds,
twenty-two frames

05

When we talk about timing in animation, we are really talking about where each part of the action falls in the frame count. For example, if I want to animate a fly zipping across the screen and I know it should take one second to cross, then I know I will need 24 frames. If the fly is followed by a bumbling bee that takes two seconds to cross the screen, I will need an additional 48 frames for the bee. 06

## Ones... Twos... Threes...

As you can see, the frames are already adding up! However, we can often get away with filming each image for two frames, which cuts our work in half. In this situation, we would only have to draw the zippy fly 12 times, but we would still end up with 24 frames because each frame would be doubled. **07**

This is called *animating on twos* or double-framing. On some occasions, we can even get away with animating on threes. But beware! What you save in time, you lose in fluidity and your animation might look choppy. On the flipside, animating on ones will give you ultra-smooth animation, which might be just the thing for very complex movements. Most animators will mix it up quite a bit, shooting some parts of the action on twos and switching to ones or threes when the motion calls for it. Regardless, your choice to animate on ones, twos, or threes should be deliberate and made before you start animating.

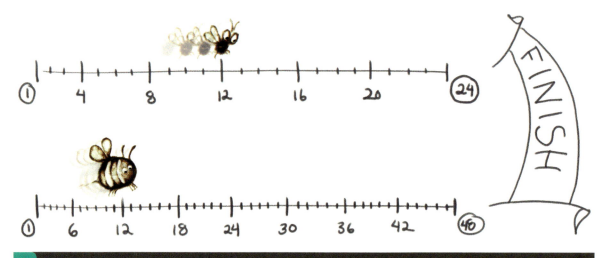

**06** 24 drawings shot on ones equals one second of animation.

**07** *12 drawings shot on twos equals 24 frames (one second of animation).*

Once you know how many drawings an action will take (timing), the way that action unfolds lies in the spacing between those drawings. Notice that the space between the drawings of the zippy fly is much greater than the space between the bumbling bee, because he covers the ground much faster. Large changes between drawings result in faster action and small changes result in slower action. Consistent spacing between drawings will result in a smooth, consistent speed, but the lyrical quality of animation comes when we start deliberately varying the spacing to achieve variation in the movement.

## Easing

Think of a train pulling out of a station. The whistle blows and it starts to inch along the tracks, gradually picking up momentum until it reaches its cruising speed. As it approaches the next station, it slows and finally comes to a stop. **08**

With every movement, there is always some sort of revving up or winding down. Therefore, the space between drawings in this sequence gradually increases as the train pulls out of a station – it will *ease out* of the station. Likewise the space between the drawings gets shorter and shorter as it approaches its new station – *easing in*. Our bumbling bee landing on a flower will ease into the landing, slowing down and dropping lightly. Then when he takes off, he will rev up to speed as he flies off. **09** Applying easing softens the movements of our characters and makes them seem more natural.

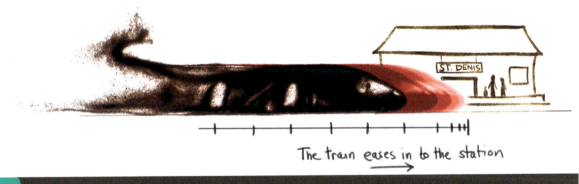

**08** The train eases in to the station.

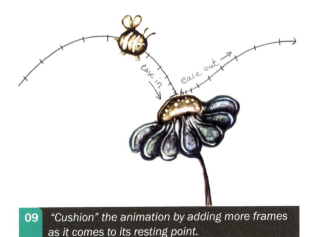

**09** "Cushion" the animation by adding more frames as it comes to its resting point.

**#ProTip** Some animators will refer to easing "in or out of an action" rather than "in or out of a pose." The result is the same; just the terminology is reversed. You might also hear the terms "cushioning" or "slow in and slow out." They all refer to the same thing.

## Holds and Cycles

Another timing technique is creating holds and cycles. A **hold** is when a character or image holds still in one position. One way to make a hold is to just take multiple frames of the same drawing until you have enough frames for however long the hold is. The drawback of this method is that the texture of the paint or sand, which up until this point has been shimmering and moving with vitality, suddenly stops dead, leaving the image lifeless. A better solution is to create an ***evolving hold***. In an evolving hold, the shape of the image does not change but the texture retains subtle movement. To get this effect, I will gently touch the material with my fingers or a brush in each frame. Even though it appears that nothing has moved, if I do this in every frame, the interior of my image will shimmer with life. Another option is to run your brush or finger along the outline of the image to create a dynamic edge. This little bit of movement keeps the audience engaged and expectant during the hold. It also gives the image a sense of life, even while it is holding still.

If you are working digitally, you might also find the opportunity to use a ***cycle***. A cycle is a movement that ends where it begins and can be looped an infinite number of times. **10**

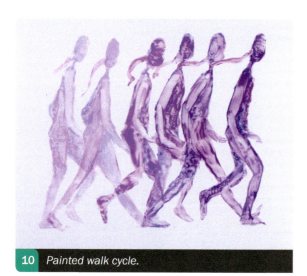

**10** Painted walk cycle.

A common application is a walk cycle. An animator might animate 12 frames of a character taking two steps then cycle those images as she moves the background behind the character. You can also create a cycle with subtle movement in the texture to use as a hold. This is difficult to do in fluid frame animation because the texture of the materials will change significantly between the first and last frame, creating a visible jump every time it cycles back. A style that incorporates large, bold changes in the texture between frames will mask this problem because the changes are already so significant between frames. Or you must take the opposite approach and be particularly precise about matching the texture from the first to last frame. In a few situations it works well, and in many a cycle looks glaringly obvious. It is worth testing out to see if you can make a cycle work with your animation style, but you may find that getting it right is more trouble than just animating the frames themselves.

## Staging

***Staging*** is how you present a shot to your viewers. Like a theater director or choreographer, we must always be aware of what the audience can see and how they will interpret it. Everything happening on screen works together and brings the viewer the experience we want them to have. Good staging is a combination of three different decisions:

> *"I think an image, wherever you present it, should have a legendary quality . . . You need to be able to keep looking at it, even if it passes by in a film for a second. That's the way images get stuck in your head and you carry them along with you wherever you go. You should be able to take a film along with you as if it's baggage . . . It's a fantasy of mine that if you ever were to encounter a shrimp on the ground on a street somewhere, you would immediately think back to* Norman.*"*
>
> *– Robbe Vervaeke*

### Where You Place Your Subject and Characters

Different camera angles and shots have different effects on a viewer. A close-up shot is intimate and direct. The emphasis is on emotion. A long shot allows us to take in the character's surroundings and understand the context of the scene. **11** **12**

A Dutch angle will heighten the tension in a scene, while a flat camera angle will provide a stage for comedy. Which shot you choose directly affects how your viewer will experience the film, so stage appropriately!

Additionally, what's going on in the background can affect how the viewer understands the action. A cluttered, busy background will fight for the audience's attention and your character may get lost. Find ways to pull your character out of the background through lighting, composition, or focus. **13**

### How You Pose Your Subject and Characters

So much can be conveyed within the attitude of a pose. Staging is your opportunity to say something before you even consider words or action. The right amount of exaggeration is the key to a strong pose. We are used to seeing things happen in the real world, but when it comes to animation, we expect more. Take your drawing and "push the pose" further by exaggerating the attitude. **14**

When staging a shot, consider what you can see in a split second. A good way to do this is to look at the silhouette of the pose. **15** If you can

**11** *An extreme close-up opens an intimate window into a character's psyche. (Norman – Robbe Vervaeke – 2012.)*

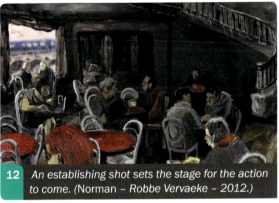

**12** *An establishing shot sets the stage for the action to come. (Norman – Robbe Vervaeke – 2012.)*

**13** *Maryam Kashkoolinia's film* Tunnel *(2012) effectively creates the claustrophobic atmosphere of being underground.*

**14**

Fluid Frames: A Foundation for Excellence

15  A good way to test the strength of your pose is to look at the silhouette. Which of these characters has a stronger pose?

16  In this image sequence, the character in the background mimics the action of the character in the foreground as the focus shifts between the two. (Astigmatismo – Nicolai Troshinsky – 2013.)

generally tell what is going on without all the little details, you know the viewer will not have any trouble.

### *How You Time the Action*

Animation is a visually dense medium and our brains can get overwhelmed taking it all in. In order to have clear staging, be deliberate about what actions are happening on screen. Sometimes, the best option is to have only one thing happening at a time. Or two actions can relate and complement each other if they are carefully planned and staged.

In this scene from *Astigmatismo*, the actions of the boy in the foreground are mirrored by the girl in the background, but only one character is in focus at any given time. The slightly offset movements create one unified action that relates the two characters together, even though they are far apart. **16** More complex combinations of actions can work beautifully in tandem if they are well planned. Think of yourself as a choreographer, moving the supporting cast of actions around the star ballerina of the main action. **17**

## Squash and Stretch

Everything has some malleability. The forces that affect an object change its shape, causing it to *squash and stretch*. Our faces and bodies squash and stretch as we move. **18**

Squash and stretch is another way of exaggerating the reality we see around us for the sake of believable animation. A naturalistic approach may use very subtle squash and stretch while a very cartoony, comical approach will greatly exaggerate the effect.

Observe, however, that as things squash and stretch their way around this world, their volume remains constant. Think of a water balloon with a life of its own. No matter how it twists, turns, bounces, and flops, the amount of water inside stays the same, it just gets squashed and stretched into different positions. **19**

This can be applied quite literally in some cases because we are actually dealing with a physical amount of material. A great exercise to practice this principle is to place a pile of sand or clay on the glass and animate it through a series of squashes and stretches, seeing how exaggerated you can get without adding or subtracting any material.

## Arcs

Thanks to gravity, almost everything in the physical world moves in arcs. Consequently, our animation will feel more natural when we base it on arcs of motion.

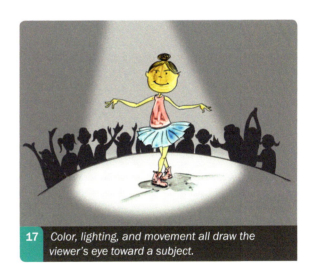

**17** *Color, lighting, and movement all draw the viewer's eye toward a subject.*

**18**

# Fluid Frames: A Foundation for Excellence

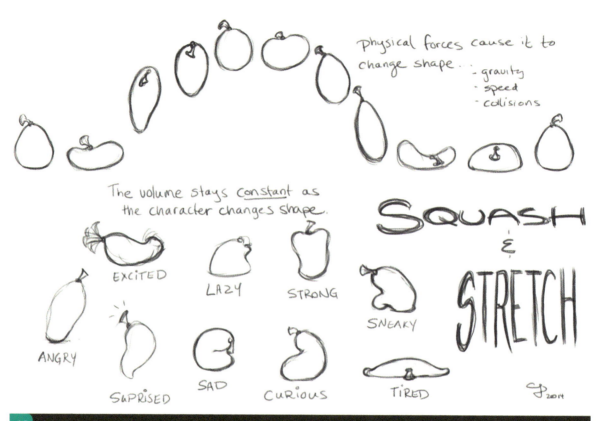

**19** *A water balloon's volume stays constant, even as it squashes and stretches.*

**20** *Arcs create pleasing, naturalistic movement. Vezo – Courtesy of Nomadic Pictures.*

**21** *A strong line of action makes a pose easy to understand.*

You will notice in particular with materials like sand, paint, and clay that straight lines are difficult to control and move, but curved designs bring out the natural fluidity of the material. The animation will seem to flow from your fingertips and into the arcs of the material. **20**

A pose or a movement will also have a line of action, which is its strongest directional arc. All the other details of the pose should be built around this strong line and support it. **21**

## Anticipation and Follow-Through

Every action can be broken down into three parts – preparing for the action, doing the action, and recovering from the action.

*Anticipation* is the act that comes before the action. Time for a break. Put the book down, stand up, and jump as high as you can into the air . . .

Notice that before you went up, you went down, bending your knees, swinging your arms back, activating your muscles. You were anticipating the jump and preparing for it. Without anticipation, an action would feel abrupt and robotic. Anticipation can be subtle, like a slight nod of the head before standing up, or it can be exaggerated like an elaborate wind-up for a pitch. As a character is "getting ready" in those few frames, the audience is also getting ready to absorb whatever comes next.

While we are up getting some exercise, jump up into the air one more time. This time notice how you land. If you really did jump as high as you can, you landed, absorbing the shock with bent knees and using your arms to regain balance. Probably your head bobbed forward and down a bit too. *Follow through* is the continuation of an action beyond its end. When a soccer player kicks a ball, her foot never just stops at the ball, it continues around her body after the ball is long gone. **22**

**22** The anticipation and follow-through of an action can sometimes communicate more than the action itself.

## Overlapping Action

Closely related to follow-through, **overlapping action** is motion that is connected to the main action but a little bit behind, i.e. "overlapping." Loose parts, like clothing, hair, or tails, echo the main action with slight variations depending on what they are made of. A heavy dinosaur tail will have a more subdued arc than a fluffy squirrel tail, but both follow the line of action of the primary animation. **23**

**23** Overlapping action follows the arc of the main action, only a little bit behind.

These trailing bits and pieces also have momentum of their own, so they will carry on moving even when the primary action has stopped. Here are some things that will have overlapping action.

- clothing
- hair
- tails
- loose flesh
- things being carried, like bags or backpacks
- liquids
- long stringy things like seaweed, fishing line, snakes, and worms.

### Secondary Action

*Secondary action* is additional motion that is unconnected to but supports and reinforces the primary action. This is the whipped cream on the animation cake! Secondary actions are subtle and do not distract from the main action (that would be poor staging).

For example, I can take a bow (primary action), but as I bow I may flutter my fingers and wrist to add a little sparkle to my attitude (secondary action). **24** If, instead of this little flutter, I waved my arms wildly like a windmill, that would detract from the bow and the scene would become confusing.

Practice working these fundamentals into all your animation projects, no matter the medium you use. Eventually, they will become intuitive. When you are working under the camera, where consequences are higher, you'll find they are second nature and your animation will have a life of its own.

## Fluid Frame Aesthetics

### In-Camera versus Out-of-Camera

With all the digital tools at their fingertips, animators are faced with a choice: we can animate all effects, camera movements, layering, and other complex aspects of animation while shooting so it is entirely *in-camera*; or, we can add some of those complexities after the shoot through specific digital processes, thus continuing the animation work *out-of-camera*. The benefit of working entirely in-camera is that when you are done shooting, the film is essentially done. However, the process of shooting will likely be longer and more complex. Working out-of-camera will allow you to separate that complexity into its parts, shooting one layer at a time and then bringing them all together afterwards. You will also be able to add effects like camera movement, color adjustments, and three-dimensional environments, which would be difficult or even impossible to do in-camera. The drawback is that getting a seamless composite with these materials is quite difficult and requires meticulous attention and skill during the

**24** Secondary action will add a little extra bit of flair that makes your animation stand out.

post-production phase. Working out-of-camera may save time during the shoot, but inevitably that time is put back into the post-production work so don't think of it as an easier path. Beautiful films have been made both ways, so it is really a matter of skill and preference.

## Drawn Camera Moves

The camera, whether physical or replicated in the computer, has a certain rigidity based on the laws of physics. An animator has the freedom to redefine those rules by drawing the camera moves, and no techniques embrace this method so well as animating under the camera. A *drawn camera move* manipulates the structural environment through redrawing the perspective every frame. The complex twisting of space you see in films by Caroline Leaf and Lynn Smith may seem intimidating at first, but there is actually a lot of flexibility in animating these moves. 25

Lynn Smith has an intuitive sense of the intricate camera moves she draws in her films, but tells beginners not to worry about getting it perfect:

> I can visualize the pivot points and I allow the pivot points to change. As the camera comes around, the space extrudes. This is when I like to change the pivot point. It may sound complicated, but it's ultimately very forgiving. There's so much going on that if you make some odd mistake in the corner, the brain is still processing everything else going on and is not able to process the mistake. So just jump into the deep end of the pool and try animating a drawn camera move.[1]

## Leaving Trails

Imagine you are animating a character with wet paint walking across the screen. You create one frame with a painted background and take your frame. Then to make the next frame, you have to move the paint forward and fill in the gap behind it. Because of the disturbance in the paint behind the character, the effect is a trail of motion behind the main motion. 26

Leaving trails is a technique that lets the audience have a glimpse of the animation process. This can add a fascinating extra dimension to a film, one

25  *A drawn camera move in Lynn Smith's* Soup of the Day. *This sequence shows every third painting of the animation as the camera moves through the restaurant.* Soup of the Day ©2013 National Film Board of Canada.

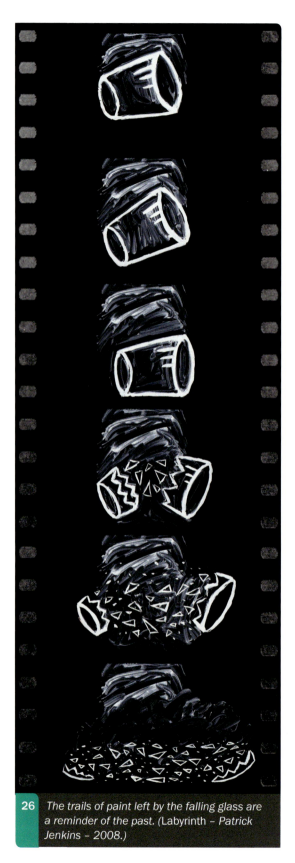

26  *The trails of paint left by the falling glass are a reminder of the past. (Labyrinth – Patrick Jenkins – 2008.)*

in which the process becomes part of the overall experience. However, there is also the risk that the composition will become too cluttered with all the trailing animation.

Should you wish to avoid this disturbance, you have an extra challenge. Some possible ways include designing the image so that the space behind the character is easy to fill. For example, having a figure come out of black shadows instead of a textured background eliminates the problem because it is easy to fill the solid color behind the moving character. Another possibility is to animate on a multiplane, or to digitally composite the foreground over the background. **27**

Or there is the option to meticulously repaint or reform the background each frame. In general, the audience is focused on the character and won't notice the small imperfections in your cover-up job.

## Animated Transitions

Cinematic editing is a language of its own, and most of us are fairly fluent in understanding a story told through cuts, fades, and dissolves. We understand that a cut can either change our perspective within a scene or change the time and location completely. A dissolve might indicate the passage of time, a fade to black might leave us with our own assumptions about what is happening between scenes. In animation, we have the added tool of making an animated transition between scenes, which broadens the range of emotional and narrative effects we can have on our audience. **28**

27  *Meléndez carefully composed his shots so he could animate on a multiplane without leaving trails. (Zepo – César Díaz Meléndez – 2014.)*

Veteran effects animator John Benson once challenged me to never cut into a new scene, but always use an animated transition. I was working on *Conversing with Aotearoa* (2006), an animated documentary with a lot of transitions, and many times I was tempted to take the easy road and cut or dissolve between shots. However, I took his advice seriously and found creative ways to move from one scene to the next. Many audience members have told me afterwards that the transitions made them pay greater attention to each scene, because they never knew where it was going to end up. Animated transitions keep the audience on their toes and visually engaged. They take elements of one scene draw them into the scene ahead with natural flow.

An animated transition can be as simple as a textural abstract wipe across the screen, or as elaborate as a carefully planned perspective morph from one scene to the next. **29** Because our work under the camera is constantly evolving, we have even more potential for interesting morphs between scenes than most forms of animation.

## The Hand of the Artist

With these fluid frame techniques, the artist is more intimately connected to the audience because the very fact that these inert materials are moving indicates the hand of the artist is at work. In some situations, acknowledging this outright can draw the

> **Animated Anecdote** Caroline Leaf's films in particular make exclusive use of the animated transition. She developed the shifting perspective and morphing shapes that define her style purely through necessity: "I can't remember ever learning how to edit. I was scared to end a shot because I didn't understand what it would connect to. So to make a morph into the next shot was the safest way to keep going." Leaf's aesthetic has now become a recognizable influence in many paint, clay, and sand animation films.

**28** *One of Joan Gratz's exquisite morphs. (Mona Lisa Descending a Staircase – Joan Gratz – 1992.)*

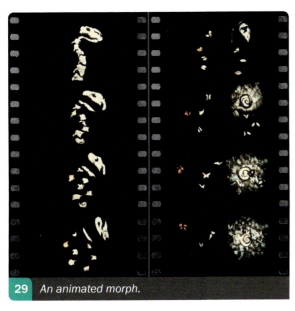

**29** *An animated morph.*

**30** *A nod to the material in Meléndez's commissioned project for Earth University. Courtesy of César Díaz Meléndez.*

audience into the artistic process and incite a sense of wonder that remains throughout the film. Starting a film with a shot of the artist creating a scene or having the artist's hand come in and interact with the material at different moments initiates the audience into our secret world. **30**

Ending with the hand of the artist clearing away the screen or writing the credits, as Caroline Leaf does at the end of *The Owl Who Married a Goose* (1974), can have the same overall effect, only it is postponed until the audience has fully experienced the story.

If you decide to reveal yourself in this way, be fully aware of the effect it will have and that it has been done many times in many ways before you. Done at the wrong time and in the wrong context, the hand will seem like a gimmick or a kitsch way of grabbing attention. But done well, it will draw your audience into a new understanding of the film.

## The Digital Toolbox

Working digitally brings plenty of advantages to fluid frame animation. For one, you don't need a highly engineered movable camera stand to make pans and zooms. Most digital cameras shoot at a high enough resolution that you can zoom in to at least 200% in post-production without losing quality, some even much more than that. How far you can go will depend on the maximum resolution of your camera. That is why shooting in the highest quality with the sharpest lens is important – it gives you the most flexibility for moving within your image.

In *A Tangled Tale*, I created high-resolution sand paintings for the background and choreographed the animation around those environments, while the camera tracked along with the movement. **31**

A word of caution when using digital editing programs to pan around your animation sequences: The computer interpolates movement very smoothly. When combined with handmade animation, this smooth motion can sometimes seem out of place, especially if we are animating on twos or threes. For example, if your character is walking in place and you wish to pan the background behind her, you will notice the background moves back every frame while her feet remain in the same place for two frames, making it look like the ground is slipping under her. This "slippage" can be disconcerting to watch, or just appear amateur. The best solution would be to animate the walk cycle on ones so every background frame is matched with a frame of the cycle. You have more flexibility with fast movements like running or things that roll, swim, or fly because they aren't in direct contact with the ground. In such situations, you can get away with animating movement on twos while the background is being moved by the computer on ones.

A few tips for animating camera movements in post:

- I always make a *Master Null* in After Effects, to which I parent any layers that aren't already

**31** *This large composited scene allowed me to zoom and pan in After Effects.*

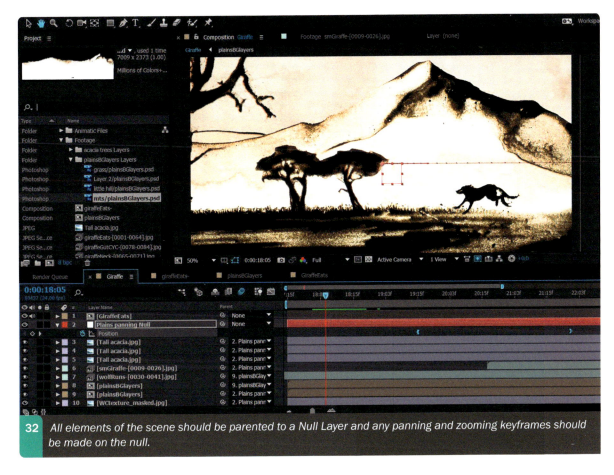

**32** *All elements of the scene should be parented to a Null Layer and any panning and zooming keyframes should be made on the null.*

attached to another layer. I then keyframe my pans and zooms on the Null Layer using the position, scale, and rotation values. That way if I need to make some smaller adjustments to different layers, or add some extra texture layers later, I won't need to fiddle with the overall choreography of the scene. **32**

- Use the *Ease Out* and *Ease In* features to smooth the movement. In After Effects, you can get even more sophisticated in adjusting the motion and speed graphs for each keyframe. **33**
- Adding a little rotation to your camera moves can also break that mathematical feel that comes from computer-generated movement.
- When all else fails, Motion Blur can save the day. But use it sparingly and deliberately! **34**
- Think about the X, Y, and Z axes. A great possibility in the digital world is to take your animation beyond the flat plane of the glass and add the third dimension.

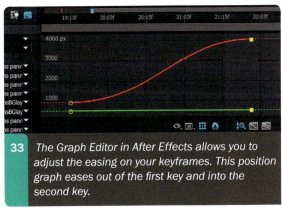

**33** *The Graph Editor in After Effects allows you to adjust the easing on your keyframes. This position graph eases out of the first key and into the second key.*

# Fluid Frames: A Foundation for Excellence

**34** Motion Blur can add an extra bit of fluidity to a pan, if used sparingly.

**35** I used dozens of nested layers for this animated Christmas card.

## Thinking in Layers

Another great digital enhancement is layering. Where we used to be limited by the physical layers on a multiplane camera, now we can have hundreds of layers. In After Effects, you can nest compositions of layers within other compositions, as I did in these shots from *Heart of the World*. **35**

Each glowing parachute woman is a separate cycling layer, which is part of a small group and the small groups are nested into the larger groups which then move en masse over the six layers of background animation!

If you plan to do any digital compositing, think about how your composition might be broken down into layers. In 2D animation, animators will separate different characters and even parts of characters like arms or mouths on individual layers to save time animating. Different mediums have different limitations, but in general you can shoot in layers and composite afterwards in any of the techniques covered in this book.

Think about the scene you want to create: What elements will be moving? Will there be anything that does not move? Are there some parts of the scene (like background elements, or complicated characters) which will be much easier if you animate them separately? Will certain characters touch or overlap? Will you transition to the next scene with a cut or a morph? These questions will help you decide if you should work in layers and how to approach your scene design if you do. There are some specific considerations to take into account with each of these techniques, so we will cover detailed compositing techniques for each technique in the chapters to come.

## The Staggered Mix

The *staggered mix* is a camera technique which creates a sequence of cross-fades between drawings to soften the movement. The result is similar to leaving trails, but has the softness of a dissolve, giving the impression that one frame is morphing into the next. The formula for the staggered mix was used and refined by Norman McLaren at the National Film Board of Canada and his formula was passed down to animators such as Frederick Back and Ishu Patel.[2] It is most effective for slow, dreamy movement, and growing or evolving subjects like plants, water, and clouds.

A Foundation for Excellence  Chapter 3

In a traditional staggered mix shot on film, each frame contains three exposures: the main image (exposed at 50%) and the image before and image after (both at 25%). Thus the main image has a ghost image preceding it and following it and the frame is 100% exposed. **36**

It's now possible to digitally recreate the staggered mix without having to do multiple exposures and complex camera passes. We can also get much more sophisticated with our dissolves and mixes, playing with the length of exposures and density of the dissolves. **37**

The variations are endless. You can have a mix that staggers only behind and leaves trails of the action, or a mix that staggers only ahead and leads the action forward. You could extend the mix to show a dozen frames before and after.

Though it may seem like this is an easy way to do fewer drawings, Patel notes that the staggered mix "works best if the drawings are not too far apart,"[3] so don't think of it as a way to smooth out jerky animation. Ideally, you will have the same number of drawings as if you were just animating the scene normally. Rather, consider it an effect to add to your animation at the appropriate times. In *Afterlife* (1978), Patel starts the film with regular, frame-by-frame animation. Then when the character leaves his body and enters the nether world between life and death, he uses the staggered mix to create an otherworldly experience for the viewer. At the end of the film, he returns to a normal shooting method to complete the circle.

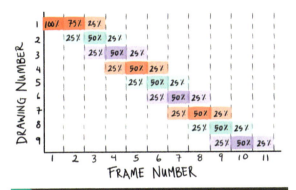

**36** When shooting on film, a staggered mix is done by taking multiple exposures of each frame at different exposure percentages. This makes the images overlap and blend together.

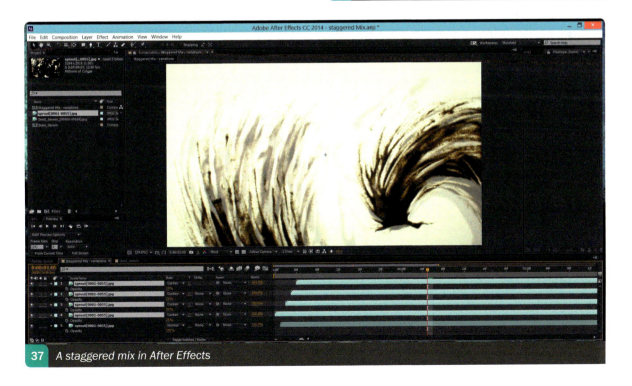

**37** A staggered mix in After Effects

# Fluid Frames: A Foundation for Excellence

**38** The dreamy blending of frames creates a very specific atmosphere. Use it deliberately and sparingly. (Spring – Xin Li – in progress.)

After Effects has several time manipulation effects which can replicate a staggered mix fairly well. **38** The CC Wide Time effect in After Effects is the most straightforward approach to a staggered mix, but you can also experiment with Echo, Time Warp and frame blending for some very unusual results. While you can control some of the settings with these effects, you may want more precision in the footage at some point, in which case you will want to do a staggered mix using layer opacity. Here is a comparative exercise that will show you how the CC Wide Time effect compares with a layered mix. For this exercise you can download the Darwin Staggered Mix sample footage from fluidframes.net.

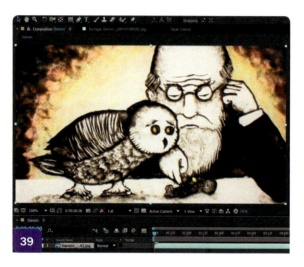

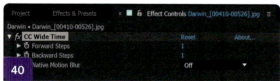

## Exercise

### Staggered Mixes

1. Make a new composition (Ctrl N) at 1920x1080, 24fps. Import the Darwin image sequence, set the frame rate for the sequence to 12fps, and drag it into your composition. **39**

2. In the Effects and Presets panel, search for CC Wide Time. Grab the CC Wide Time effect and apply it to the layer. **40**

3. Open the Effects Settings. This is where we will set how many frames are visible in the mix. You will see Forward Steps and Backward Steps: Forward Steps are the number of upcoming frames that are revealed, and Backward Steps are the number of trailing frames that are revealed. Since this footage is playing at 12fps inside a 24fps composition, each frame has been duplicated by After Effects. We must keep this in mind when we set our Forward Steps and Backward Steps. Set Forward Steps to 1, Backward Steps to 0, and scrub through the footage. You will notice that only every other frame has a ghost image, causing a stutter when we play back the footage. To fix this our numbers must be in multiples of 2. Set Forward Steps to 2 and scrub through the footage. Now

you will see that each frame has a ghost image of the following frame. Set Backward Steps to 6 and you will see trailing frames. **41**

4. As you can see, there are a lot of frames blending together, which looks great during the slower movements of the plant growing, but gets muddled during the larger movements at the beginning. I want this effect to only happen during the growing plant and final morph into the night scene. To do this, set some keyframes for the Forward and Backward Steps. Move the time indicator to when the plant begins to grow (0:00:03:22) and click on the stopwatch symbol next to Forward and Backward steps to set a key for these properties. **42**

5. Now move the time indicator back four frames (0:00:03:18). Set the Forward and Backward Steps to 0. A keyframe will be created automatically. Play back the footage and see the effect of the mix on the growth of the plant and the following transition. Make some more keyframes for the Forward and Backward steps to further adjust the mix to your liking. **43**

6. CC Wide Time is a quick, straightforward way to create a staggered mix that does the job in most situations. Occasionally I will take another approach, using duplicate layers and opacity settings, if I want more specific control over the blending modes, for example, or if I want very specific control over the opacity of individual frames.

7. Now, as a comparison, we will make a staggered mix using layer opacity. Make a new composition (Ctrl N) within the same project. Drag the Darwin image sequence into the composition.

8. Duplicate the layer three times (Ctrl D). Open the Opacity (T) setting for each layer. Set the top three layers to 25%. **44**

9. Drag the top sequence forward two frames. This layer is your Leading Image. Drag the bottom layer forward two frames. This is your Main Image. Drag the second layer four frames forward and the third layer six frames forward. These two are the two Trailing Images. (Note that we are again working in multiples of two because the sequence is at 12fps in a 24fps composition.) 45

10. If you move the time indicator to the first frame of the Leading Image layer, you should see the Main Image, a ghosted image of the upcoming frame and two ghosted images of the trailing frame. We will now add keyframes to the Opacity levels so the mix will start at the same time as our CC Wide Time version.

11. Move the time indicator to when the plant begins to grow (0:00:04:02) and set an Opacity keyframe for the top three layers. Then move the time indicator back four frames (0:00:03:22) and set the Opacity to 0. 46

12. Notice that by staggering the layers, you lose the last few frames of your sequence because of the overlap. You can either Time Remap the footage to hold on the last frame, or you can animate a few extra frames at the end of the sequence to cover the gap. The number of extra frames you need will be the same as the number of layers you plan to mix on the main layer, so in this basic mix, I added three extra frames at the end and can cut out the last bit of the composition. 47

A Foundation for Excellence  Chapter 3

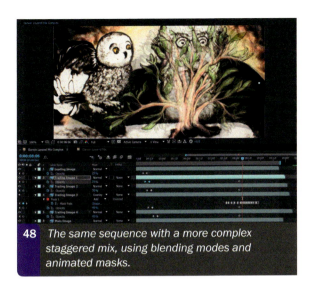

48  The same sequence with a more complex staggered mix, using blending modes and animated masks.

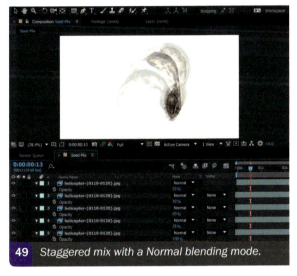

49  Staggered mix with a Normal blending mode.

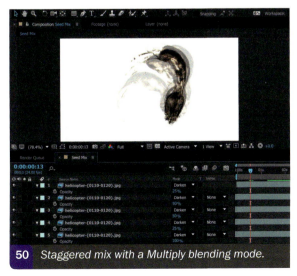

50  Staggered mix with a Multiply blending mode.

13. Right now this mix looks very similar to the CC Wide Time effect, but the benefit of working with layers is that you have precise control over the opacity settings, blending modes, and staggering of each layer. Can you imagine how you might take this technique further for some more extravagant mixes? 48

14. Try changing the blending modes to Add or Multiply and see how that affects the look of the mix. The effect will differ if you have a white background, black background, or fully colored images. How you mix for sand will be different than how you mix for clay and paint. In general, keeping the main layer on the bottom at 100% opacity will ensure you always have a strong base for any variations on the staggered mix you try above. 49 50

## Rotoscoping

Technology now makes it much easier to use reference footage when shooting stopmotion. Many frame capture programs will let you load a video sequence and overlay it frame-by-frame as you shoot. This way you can match live action footage, or draw a rough sequence of animation ahead of time to guide your work under the camera.

In his current production *Fighting Pablo*, Robbe Vervaeke collaborates with an assistant animator who creates hand-drawn sequences that are then projected on his painting surface.

> It's a concession to speed because I don't want to spend eight years making a single film and end up impoverished and hungry. So we're looking for another way to make the animation go smoother and more fluid . . . The danger is the fact that the animation might not feel like painted animation anymore so we're going to have to devise a way to make sure that his animation prioritizes the feel of the film.[4] 51

Lynn Tomlinson edited a video compilation of inspirational paintings, drawings, and videos into a mash-up version of *The Ballad of Holland Island House*. She then used the mash-up as a visual reference, loading it as a guide layer in her frame capture program and following the motion in the video as she animated. 52

This takes much of the risk out of the process of working straight ahead. Be wary though, of relying too much on predetermined footage. Meticulously tracing your guide layer turns animating into mechanical work. One of the joys of animating under the camera is the possibility of spontaneity and play. Building confidence in your method and artistic ability through experiments and tests will ultimately give you more freedom to use reference footage as it is intended – a starting point for creative expression.

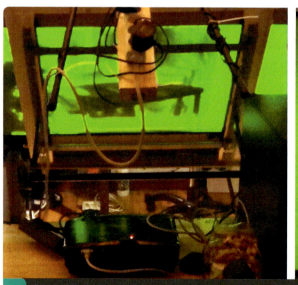

**51** Robbe Vervaeke projects reference animation on the back of his glass-painting surface. Courtesy of Robbe Vervaeke.

Animating under the camera is a specialized technique, but it is rooted in the traditions of art and motion. Even as you take on this experimental frame of mind, continue solidifying your base of knowledge – artistic design, filmmaking techniques, and classic animation methods – so you will have a firm platform to spring into the world of experimentation.

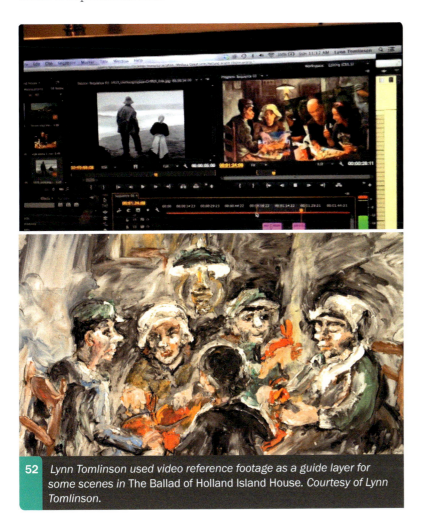

52  Lynn Tomlinson used video reference footage as a guide layer for some scenes in The Ballad of Holland Island House. *Courtesy of Lynn Tomlinson.*

## Notes

1  Smith, Lynn. Telephone interview. Jan. 25, 2015.
2  Patel, Ishu. Telephone interview. Oct. 3, 2014.
3  Ibid.
4  Vervaeke, Robbe. Telephone interview. Feb. 4, 2015.

# Section II

*Thomas Parks.*

# Chapter 4
# Animating With Sand and Other Powders

**Notable Pioneers in Powder Animation**
    Nag and Gisèle Ansorge
    Kazimierz Urbański
    Caroline Leaf
    Ferec Cakó
    Aleksandra Korejwo

**Exploring the Technique**
    Exercise: Animating a Sandy Morph

**The Sandy Studio**
    Materials
    Tools
    In Practice
    Processing Footage

**Planning a Longer Sand Project**

**Compositing 101**
    Layering in Sand
    Exercise: Garbage Mattes
    Blending Modes
    Exercise: Paint Bucket Effect
    Color Keying
    Exercise: Applying a Color Key Effects Stack
    Exercise: Animated Masks

**Adding Color**
    Exercise: Hand Tinting in Photoshop
    Exercise: Tints and Filters in After Effects

**Combining Sand with Other Animation Techniques**
    Case Studies from Commercial Projects

# Fluid Frames: Animated Sand and Other Powders

Any child at the beach will quickly realize the vast expanses of sand are an open canvas for creative exploration. But who would think that those tiny grains could be a medium for harnessing pure light into nuanced chiaroscuro under the camera? **01**

Sand animation encompasses delicate textures alongside bold, contrasting shapes and each artist that encounters the material interprets its uses in a new way. Powder animation, as it is sometimes called, is not limited to sand either. Salt is used in a similar way, as well as other granular substances.

If you have encountered sand animation before, it was probably in a film by Caroline Leaf or through a school assignment. **02** The fact that you are reading this book tells me that your interest was piqued, not spent, by this strange form of animation. Sand animation is my particular specialty, so as we begin to tap the potential of this little-known medium, I would like to personally welcome you into the world of sandy animation!

**01** The Crossing – *Marieka Walsh.*

**02** The Owl Who Married a Goose ©1974 National Film Board of Canada, All rights reserved.

## Notable Pioneers in Powder Animation

Sand animation came into its own in a time when animators were eagerly trying new materials and techniques. Swiss animator and historian Rolf Bächler observes,

> Like with many other inventions in the history of film, there were several people in different places experimenting independently with similar materials at roughly around the same time. In the pre-digital world images could not be spread as easily and instantly as they are now, and a new animation technique had to travel physically as a film print if it was to be discovered elsewhere.[1]

Thus, the first influential films made exclusively with sand and other powdered substances came to light in several different areas of the globe.

### Nag and Gisèle Ansorge

In Switzerland in the 1960s, Ernest "Nag" and Gisèle Ansorge were making live action commercial films to support their more experimental endeavors. **03**

In one of these commercial films, they used sand to depict circulating blood.

> As a pharmacist, Gisèle was familiar with loose material of all kinds, and tested every substance within reach, ending with quartz sand of a certain grain size . . . They would sift the sand for the right calibration, soak it in black china ink and then grind the dyed grains in a mortar.[2]

After three years of experimenting and refining the technique, the Ansorges presented their first short, *Les Corbeaux* (*The Ravens*) in 1967 at the prestigious Annecy International Animation Festival. 04

The enthusiastic response, and their fascination with the material, led to a lifetime of work in sand resulting in ten short films and many commissions.

The Ansorges's films are sometimes narrative and sometimes surreal journeys. Gisèle primarily manipulated the sand while Nag operated the camera and took care of the editing. One thing that marks their work is the use of imaginative transformations from scene to scene. Gisèle's masterful command of the material combined with an unabashed approach to unconventional narrative led to films that explored the inner psyche of their relationship and philosophy. 05 The Ansorges also made a sustainable career out of sand animation by making films for children and advertisements. 06

## Kazimierz Urbański

In Poland in the 1960s, Kazimierz Urbański was also experimenting with new techniques. He chose to use salt on a black board, becoming the yin to the Ansorges's yang. His students followed in his footsteps with many works, including Piotr Muszalski's *Toccata and Fugue in D Minor* (1994),

04 | The Ravens –1967. Courtesy of ASIFA Switzerland.

05 | Smile 3 – 1975. Courtesy of ASIFA Switzerland.

03 | Nag and Gisèle Ansorge ©Aline Kundig / www.alinekundig.com.

06 | The Little Boy Who Stole the Moon – 1988. Courtesy of ASIFA Switzerland.

and *The Awakening* (2000) by Waldemar Mordarski. The most well known and prolific of Urbański's students is Aleksandra Korejwo. More on her in a bit. **07**

## Caroline Leaf

Also in the 1960s, a young Harvard architectural student was invited to take the university's first animation class. Feeling that drawing wasn't her strong suit, she went to the beach and came back with a bucket of sand to move under the camera. The resulting film, *Sand* or *Peter and the Wolf* (1969), was Caroline Leaf's first film and the beginning of a groundbreaking animation career. **08**

Her mentor and professor, Derek Lamb, was executive producer at the National Film Board of Canada's English Animation Studio, and he soon invited Leaf to Montreal to continue her work. While at the NFB, Leaf made several short films in sand, paint-on-glass, and scratching on celluloid.

Leaf's early sand films emphasize the shape and form of the sand, and her characters have minimal details. In *The Owl Who Married a Goose* (1974), positive and negative space intermingle as passing characters melt into each other and reform on the other side, preserving a clean and elegant design throughout the animation. Leaf manages to convey a sense of depth and space in the white void of the background by growing and shrinking the characters as though they were walking toward or away from the camera. In the distance, the characters are black silhouettes but as they approach the camera we see more details in their feathers and refined shapes in the eye, approximating atmospheric distance. **09**

Remarkably, the landscape surrounding the characters is in our imaginations without any actual imagery on Leaf's part. Leaf also transforms the positive space in the film so by the end, what was white has become black and what was black is now white, reflecting both a seasonal

**07** *Toccata and Fugue in D Minor – 1994 – Piotr Muszalski. Courtesy of TV Studio of Animation Films Ltd. Poznan.*

**08** *Caroline Leaf's first film – Sand or Peter and the Wolf (1969) – made at Harvard.*

**09** *Positive and negative shapes define the composition and movement in Leaf's landmark film* The Owl Who Married a Goose. *©1974 National Film Board of Canada, All rights reserved.*

change and a reversal in the Owl's fate as a lover.

Leaf's next and final sand film, *The Metamorphosis of Mr. Samsa* (1977), employs more tonal variance and texture, as well as far more sophisticated perspective shifts and camera angles. Based loosely on Kafka's tale of a man who turns into an insect, Leaf's seamless transitions take us back and forth between the dark world of Gregor's personal misery and the expectations of the friends and family outside his little room. **10**

Looking at Leaf's entire body of work, the progression of her personal style is clearly evident in the increasing visual complexity displayed in each film.

## Ferenc Cakó

Ferenc Cakó from Hungary began working with sand in the 1980s. After many years of working with puppets and clay, Cakó was searching for a way to tap into his roots as a graphic artist and create drawing-based films. "I experimented with paints and powders and eventually with sand, which allowed me to move fast."[3] Cakó is less concerned with studied motion and more interested in how the transformative quality of the sand can enhance his overarching themes. His first film, *Ab Ova* (1987), won the Palme d'Or at Cannes in 1987. In this film and many others, Cakó uses both sand and clay, mixing the three-dimensional world of stopmotion with the two-dimensional world of sand. "The biggest advantage for me with this type of animation, as opposed to the hand drawn animation, was the constant room for improvisation."[4] **11**

*Ab Ova* opens with images of birth and growth. As the music takes a violent turn, the slow gentle morphs of the opening are replaced by abrupt cutting and sand being thrown across the delicate drawings, which disintegrate into abstraction. The maternal instinct of the beginning is replaced by the instinct of Cain and Abel. Cakó presents symbolic interpretations of human conflict, which make symbolic use of a cycle of destruction and formation, bringing us to a final, climactic revelation of three-dimensional humanity, emerging from the pattern of conflict.

The physical qualities of the sand are just as important as the thematic imagery. **12**

**10** Leaf expands into tonal variations and pattern with sand in The Metamorphosis of Mr. Samsa. ©1977 National Film Board of Canada, All rights reserved.

**11** Ab Ova – Ferenc Cakó – 1987.

**12** Fészek (Nest) – Ferenc Cakó – 1992.

## Fluid Frames: Animated Sand and Other Powders

13  Ferenc Cakó and the live sand animation performance. Photo credit: Szabolcs Bánlaki.

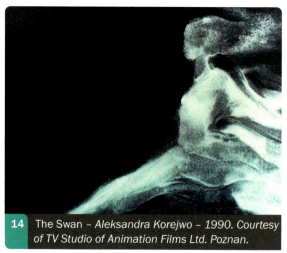

14  The Swan – Aleksandra Korejwo – 1990. Courtesy of TV Studio of Animation Films Ltd. Poznan.

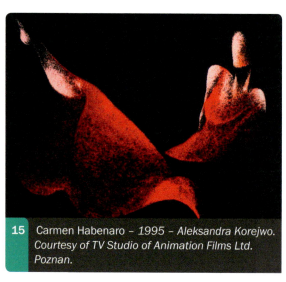

15  Carmen Habenaro – 1995 – Aleksandra Korejwo. Courtesy of TV Studio of Animation Films Ltd. Poznan.

We frequently see the artist's hand at work and it is clear Cakó is just as fascinated by the process of creating as he is by the ideas he is communicating. It makes sense, then, that he was the first to make live sand animation performances. In such a performance, the artist tells a story, usually with musical accompaniment, by drawing in the sand while the audience watches a projection of the artist's hands at work. Though not created frame-by-frame, this performance art is often referred to as sand animation. The magic in these performances lies in watching the artist transform one drawing into another with a few strokes of the fingers. Live performance and stopmotion sand animation are complementary art forms. **13**

Cakó prepares for both the live sand performance and the stopmotion films in a similar manner, creating concept drawings and a script ahead of time to guide the imagery.

> Since I have to work tightly together with the music, I don't practice drawing, because I can do that, but I do learn the order of the pictures, so that they correspond to the rhythm . . . As the musician practices the piece, here the drawing should be rehearsed to be "in tune with" the music.[5]

### Aleksandra Korejwo

Another artist that belongs in this group of pioneers is Polish animator Aleksandra Korejwo. Her delicate, lyrical films are made by carefully moving colored salt on a velvet background. Korejwo's animation was inspired by her childhood fascination with Walt Disney films and a lifelong love of music and dance.[6] **14**

In fact, her first inclination was to make films that were colored music for the eyes. Watching her films, the viewer will get the impression that Korejwo is somehow aware of every single grain of salt on the screen, moving them with delicate attention and precision. Her style is immediately recognizable for its shimmering color palette and lyrical movement patterns based on dance and opera. Developing this unique style has contributed to Korejwo's success at film festivals and in the commercial market. She has made numerous advertisements in salt, working for companies that valued the specific artistic quality of her personal style. 15

Looking back, we may call these animators pioneers of powder animation, but at the time they were simply working with an interesting material that best suited their temperament and the stories they wanted to tell. What attracted these artists to sand was not the novelty of working with a strange material, but the actual properties of that material. You can draw with the sand, but in that drawing process you push, mold, spread, and confine it. The combination of dimensional and linear properties can be frustrating for some artists and liberating for others. The only way to test your affinity is to dig into the sandbox and give it a try!

## Exploring the Technique

There are many things I could tell you about sand animation. We could talk about texture and light, color and layering, pre- and post-production. Eventually, we will get to a lot of these things, but at the beginning, the best way to learn is to dig your hands in and start animating. Let's not worry about perfection or plan a major opus. Let me simply introduce you to the sand.

To start, we will need just the most basic setup: a light table, a camera, and a frame capture program, all of which we learned about in Chapter 3. You will also need a glass box that you can put on the light table to contain the sand. Otherwise it will spread out and get all over your studio. You can make a box quite easily with a sheet of glass, some foam core, and masking tape 16 Make sure the walls of the box are fairly high and all the seams are taped securely so no sand can escape.

And, of course, you will need some sand. Any sand will do – something you picked up on your last trip to the beach perhaps, or maybe from the hardware store or your nearest craft store. I find a quart is usually enough to start with. If you like working on a large surface, you may need more. I run my beach sand through a kitchen sieve to filter out any larger grains or odd bits of seaweed and shell. 18

> **#ProTip** *Sand likes to get in every nook and cranny in the studio. I wrap my keyboard camera buttons and anything I might get dirty while animating in plastic wrap before I start.*

16 A young animator plays in a home-made sandbox. Photo credit: Kevin Fosse.

> **#ProTip** *Even though I can see the edge of my frame in the frame capture program, I use a dry-erase marker to put little marks in the corner. That way, when I'm looking at the glass, I know what will be on screen and what will be off.* 17

## Fluid Frames: Animated Sand and Other Powders

If you are concerned about the sanitation of your local beach, you can wash the sand by putting it in a big bucket with a bit of dish soap and swishing it around. After the sand settles, pour out as much water as you can then rinse several times. Spread the wet sand on an old bed sheet in the sun to dry (which may take a day or two depending on how much sand you have).

**18** The beach near her parent's home where Caroline Leaf got her sand. Courtesy of Caroline Leaf.

*"For me the trick is to lose the fear . . . in the beginning, I thought, 'Oh, if I breathe maybe the sand will be ruined.' I did just little tiny things. I was afraid to move the sand. Don't be afraid with the sand! You can move it. Push it around."* **19**

– César Díaz Meléndez

**19** César Díaz Meléndez's home-made multiplane light table.

*When I do workshops, I introduce the technique with the idea of doing morphs. It's not because you can't do a morph with some other media like pencil and paper, but . . . the plasticity of the sand and morphing seem to go together so they reinforce each other.*

– Caroline Leaf

### Exercise

### Animating a Sandy Morph

(For this exercise, set the playback frame rate in your capture program to 12 frames per second.)

1. Put a small pile of sand in the middle of your table. **20**

2. Use your entire hand to spread out the sand. Push it around a bit and note how it spills over the glass. See how much you can pile up before it starts to tumble down. See how thinly you can spread it and what sort of patterns you can make with your fingers. **21**

**20**

Animated Sand and Other Powders  Chapter 4              83

21

22

23

24

3. Feel the warmth of the lights coming through the sand and warming your hands. Spend five to ten minutes just playing and letting your mind relax. This is you and the sand saying "Hello!" **22**

4. As you and the sand get to know each other, you may start to see recognizable shapes emerge, just as you might see shapes in the clouds on a warm spring day. Use your fingers to help one of those shapes emerge and become more defined. Add a few details but don't get too caught up in making it perfect. If you are feeling a bit hesitant about your abilities, just stick to a silhouette.

5. Once satisfied, take a frame. Now we will create an evolving hold. Use your finger or a paintbrush to lightly trace the edges without changing the original shape. If your image has any areas where a bit of light is showing through, pat those gently with your fingertips or hand, then take a second frame. Do this several more times, tracing the outline and lightly patting the textured parts before taking a frame. Don't worry if you aren't perfectly consistent. This puts just a little bit of movement in the sand and keeps it alive even while holding still. A more subtle approach is to tap the glass next to the drawing a few times – the vibration will shift grains just enough to provide a little shimmer. Repeat this process until you have 12 frames (a one-second evolving hold). **23**

6. Over the next 12–24 frames, we are going to morph the image you have before you on the sand table into the new image. In your mind, break down the morph into incremental changes. You can plan this out by sketching out some thumbnails to guide you, or you can improvise and let the sand lead you to a new image as you move it. **24** Think about some of the basic animation principles we discussed in Chapter 3 that might apply, like easing or anticipation and follow-through. When I'm moving a large patch of sand, I work from the outside in, pushing the edge of the sand first to a new position so I can retain the basic shape and size of my drawing in the next frame, then I realign the interior details

# Fluid Frames: Animated Sand and Other Powders

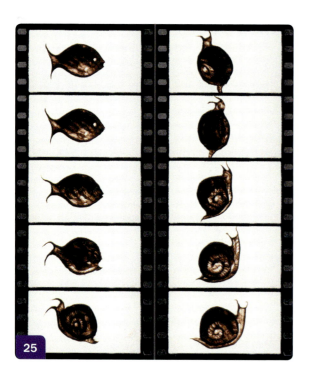

25

with the outer edge. Finally, I'll smooth the edge with my fingers or a paintbrush.

7. Once the morph is complete, create another evolving hold for 12 frames by tracing the outline or tapping the glass by your new drawing. 25

8. You should now have three to four seconds of animation! Play it back and see what it looks like. We will continue working with this image in a few minutes so leave it on the table as you read the next section.

26 *Marieka Walsh's detailed rendering of a scene for* The Crossing.

You may have noticed with this first part of the exercise that there are several approaches to moving the sand. You can push it into piles and use your entire hand to move it on the glass or you can take a more delicate approach and use the tips of your fingers and fine brushes to create detailed lines and shading. We start off with simple drawings and silhouettes because we can move along quickly from frame to frame, making things move without getting caught up in the details. However, as you work more with the sand, you will start to develop a style that is suited to your temperament and aesthetic preferences. For example, Marieka Walsh's films are full of shading and

27 *A simple stylistic approach in Maryam Kashkoolinia's* When I was a Child *reflects the subject of the film.*

28 *Sand can become a linear drawing tool, as César Díaz Meléndez shows us in* No Corras Tanto – 2009.

Animated Sand and Other Powders  Chapter 4

moving texture. 26 Maryam Kashkoolinia uses simple character design and solid shapes, while César Díaz Meléndez's work has a linear quality that he manipulates quickly and intuitively. 27 28

These animators harness different qualities of the sand to create their own unique aesthetic. They use the same tools and the same basic setup but the results are very different. Trust your intuition as you continue to experiment with sand and discover what feels enjoyable and natural to you. That will eventually become your own unique style.

> **Animated Anecdote**
>
> "I remember one of the biggest and most important 'Aha!' moments was after I had made a number of films. I had always moved things back and forth across the screen. I was doing The Owl Who Married a Goose and suddenly I saw that the white was infinite space. It was depth and that was a huge revelation to me . . . After that I started moving things back and forth in depth as well as across."
>
> – Caroline Leaf

> "You've just got to go with the light. It's all about using the light to make things look good . . . you can do things that look really good with the sand because you have all this lightplay going on."
>
> – Anna Humphries

> "What I love about sand animation . . . is the darkness. I like the idea that you are pulling something out of darkness. You're peeling through that sand and finding texture and tone. I always start with a lot of sand on the lightbox and am teasing those images out."
>
> – Marieka Walsh

29

Let's continue with the animation we started, this time paying attention to the white space around the sand.

9. Picking up where we left off, let's bring our drawing "closer" to the audience by making it incrementally bigger. 29

10. I will use the current frame as a starting point, pushing the sand outward along the edge to make the shape expand. Once I have the outline for the new frame, I fill in holes left in the sand.
    Slowly my drawing is filling the screen. I add more sand with each frame to fill more of the space. Continue animating until sand is filling almost all of the frame. 30

11. Positive and negative space can become interchangeable. Continue to grow your drawing until it fills the entire frame, but now with each frame begin to pull away the sand from inside

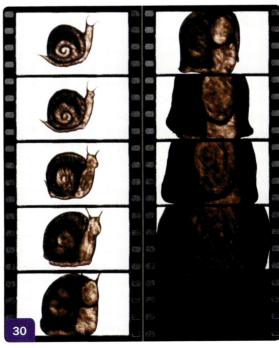

30

the frame to reveal another drawing. Here we have an entirely different artistic look, with the white as the positive space and the sand as the negative space. **31**

12. Move your new drawing around. Remember to draw the next frame before obliterating the last one. As a finale, transform it into a negative space version of the very first drawing.

31

**32** *Samples of sands and salts I've collected from friends around the world. The variations in texture and color offer a broad palette.*

**33** *Dazzling gems created in colored sand by Anna Humphries for the music video* It Might Be Real *– 2012.*

## The Sandy Studio

### Materials

Different types of sand have different qualities and part of the fun is learning what hidden imagery is in each type. Large grains of sand reflect light beautifully, like little glass stones, but they do not stick to each other well and are difficult to form into shapes. Very fine sand can create ethereal shapes and be spread smoothly over glass. You can get brightly colored sand at craft stores and it can either be top lit or backlit. **32 33**

Sand is not the only thing you can animate. Any sort of powder or granules can be fluidly manipulated on a flat surface. For his films *Cumulus* and *The Well*, Philippe Vaucher used salt colored with food dye:

> I have a small bowl, fill it with salt, and drop fifteen drops of undiluted dye in and mix it up

> *"The sand that I like the best is some sand that a friend got for me from a river inlet just off a beach. It's really fine and it feels like velvet. It's beautiful to work with."*
>
> – Marieka Walsh

Animated Sand and Other Powders  Chapter 4     87

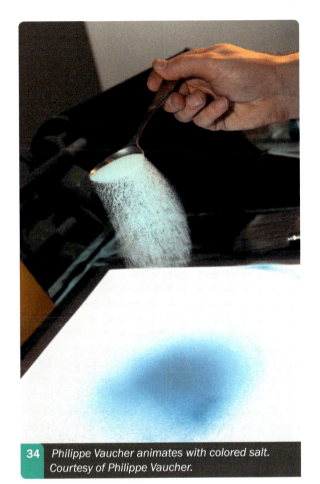

34  Philippe Vaucher animates with colored salt. Courtesy of Philippe Vaucher.

35  *The Well* – Philippe Vaucher – 2013.

36  Students animating with sugar at South Dakota State University.

with a spoon. After about 10 to 15 minutes of constant mixing, it's done . . . I tried different salts. Kosher salt is too thick, it looks pixilated - you see the blocks. So, a nice, fine salt works best."[7] 34 35

Sugar has a different quality than salt; baking soda is very fine and adheres to itself in unusual ways; you could use ground coffee, tea leaves, garden soil . . . what else can you think of? Perhaps a combination of various sands and salts will suit your work. 36 Finding the right material for your project can be an experiment in its own right. Start with what is readily available and turn its limitations into assets.

## Tools

In sand animation, your hands are your closest and most effective tools. Don't be afraid to get them dirty! See how many different types of marks you can make with the anatomy of your hands: fingertips, the fleshy part below the thumb, nails, palms, knuckles, the length of your pinky finger.

Paint brushes will give you a beautiful smooth line and are useful for pushing sand around in places that are too small for fingers. Different brushes will have different levels of stiffness and springiness. Philippe Vaucher uses rubber-nibbed brushes and foam brushes, available at arts stores or online. I most often use a soft flathead watercolor brush. Sometimes static will build up on the brush and the sand will stick

## Fluid Frames: Animated Sand and Other Powders

to it, depending on the type of fibers and the mineral content of the sand, so you will need to try out some different brushes to find out what works best for you.

Sharp, pointy objects like a kebab skewer or a blending stump are great for adding small details and drawing delicate lines. **37**

**37** *My favorite sand tools.*

You will also want tools for applying, spreading, and collecting sand. Plastering tools are useful for creating even gradients. Tibetan monks have a variety of tools they use to make intricate sand mandalas, one of which is a metal cone for drawing very precise lines with a thin stream of sand. You can make your own by rolling a piece of paper into a tight cone and using your finger to control the amount of sand out of the end. Feathers are great for clearing away sand or adding unusual textures. **38 39 40 41**

Textures are also fun to play with. You can press stamps, buttons, or other everyday objects into the sand to create patterns. **42**

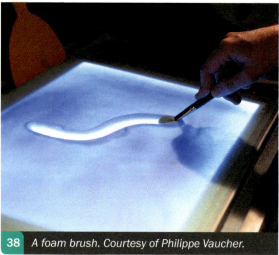

**38** *A foam brush. Courtesy of Philippe Vaucher.*

**40** *Scoop and brush. Courtesy of Philippe Vaucher.*

**39** *Plaster scraper. Courtesy of Philippe Vaucher.*

**41** *Tibetan Chak Pur tool for sand mandalas. Courtesy of Lynn Smith.*

Animated Sand and Other Powders  Chapter 4

Get in touch with your inner three-year-old and go play in the sandbox!

## In Practice

Here are some other project ideas for exploring sand:

- Make a series of abstract transitions from a fully black screen to a fully white screen. Think of abstract ways to bring the sand on and off the screen using form and texture. **43**
- Start with a negative space image and think of a way to transition to a positive space image. **44** **45**

**42** Lynn Smith pressed small objects into the sand to create textures for the film Siena – 1999. Courtesy of Lynn Smith.

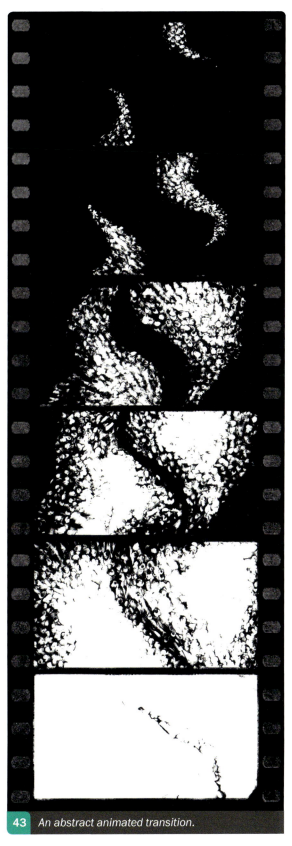

**43** An abstract animated transition.

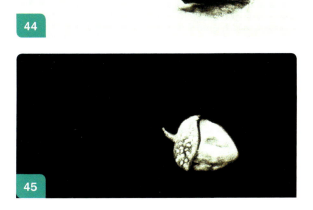

**44**

**45**

## Fluid Frames: Animated Sand and Other Powders

- Find different tools to make textures in the sand. **46**
- Things like a comb, a dry sponge, or bubble wrap can make interesting sand textures. Try animating the textures by redoing them each frame and observing the different rhythms that come from each type of texture.
- Create a ball with shading, then animate an imaginary light source moving around the ball by changing the density of the sand. **47**

**46** *A garden made from kitchen utensils: 1 – meat tenderizer, 2 – sifter, 3 – lemon juicer, 4 – clothespin, 5 – crumpled aluminium foil.*

**47** *I used a roll of masking tape as a stencil to get this perfectly round ball.*

**48** *Processing footage in Adobe Lightroom.*

## Processing Footage

My personal workflow includes processing footage after it is shot. This is an optional step and can be skipped if you are completely satisfied with your exposure and composition during the shoot. However, one of the great benefits of shooting digitally is the option to make adjustments outside the camera.

Once I have shot a scene, I export it as a RAW frame sequence. Then I process the frames in Adobe Lightroom before I do anything further with them. I might crop out the edges of my sand table, adjust the white balance, and adjust the contrast and sharpness to bring out the best in the sand. I also export them as a PNG, JPG, or TIFF sequence to their own folder with a descriptive name. This keeps everything organized so when I have dozens of layers in After Effects, I know what I'm working with. **48**

If you don't have Lightroom, you can create an automated batch process in Photoshop that will develop an entire folder of frames or use a similar function in Adobe Bridge. Since you will have hundreds of frames, it's best to find a photo editing program that can automate your adjustments.

> **#ProTip** *Create healthy working habits for yourself from the beginning. Wear a dust mask or bandana if you find yourself getting sensitive to the particles that inevitably get stirred up while animating. When you take breaks, turn on the overhead lights or go outside so your eyes can recover from the intensity of the lightbox.*

## Planning a Longer Sand Project

The best ideas come from the work. I love to experiment with materials because I often make unexpected discoveries when I don't have a specific goal in mind. After taking some time to get to know the sand, your brain will be sprouting with things you want to try, images you want to create, perhaps even the beginning of a story or a character that has risen out of the sandbox. At some point, you will want to plan a longer project in sand.

Let's look at two first films, by César Díaz Meléndez and Marieka Walsh. Both artists were new to sand animation and did not do extensive experimenting beforehand. They both had become excited about sand as a material for animation and had an idea they wanted to execute. The resulting films could not be more different.

After working 12 years in TV series animation, Meléndez began animating in sand in his spare time just for fun, and the ideas were multiplying. His first sand film, *No Corras Tanto* (2009), is a music video for his band, El Combolinga. **49**

> That was my excuse to try all the experiments I had in my head for the sand. What will happen if I blow on the sand? What will happen if I put some objects in there or if I use different colors? It was the perfect excuse to make every shot an experiment.[8]

The imagery moves between abstract moments and refined linear drawing but is always a playful and varied investigation of the properties of moving sand.

**49** No Corras Tanto – *César Díaz Meléndez – 2009.*

## Fluid Frames: Animated Sand and Other Powders

The improvisational aspect of the film was both a benefit and a detriment to Meléndez's workflow: "It was crazy because I didn't have any screenplay or storyboard. Each day I spent more time thinking of what to do than actually making animation."[9] Meléndez's eye for movement, developed over his years as a commercial animator, comes through in the segments of perfect lip sync and masterful human movement. Just when we are getting too caught up in the imagery, a shift from backlight to top light reminds us that we are watching moving sand. Also serving this purpose are the frequent appearances of the hand of the artist. Meléndez wants to bring the audience with him on his journey of experimentation and is careful not to let us fall behind. Watching his later films, it is clear that some of the discoveries made in *No Corras Tanto* became part of Meléndez's signature style. **50**

Marieka Walsh's first film, *The Hunter* (2011), was also sparked from her very first experiments. **51**

> I saw *The Owl Who Married a Goose* and . . . was really drawn to the tonal ranges you can get with sand, how fluid it was and what Caroline Leaf did with it. That afternoon I started building a box and got some sand and spent the entire weekend drawing things in sand and experimenting . . . Those first few images are what sparked the story of *The Hunter*.[10] **52**

**50** No Corras Tanto – *César Díaz Meléndez – 2009.*

**51** The Hunter – *Marieka Walsh – 2011.*

**52** Marieka Walsh animating The Hunter. *Photo credit: Toula Anastas.*

Walsh took those images and built a story around them, learning by doing. In contrast to Meléndez's very loose stream of consciousness, Walsh had a highly structured story that was driving the imagery. Her imagery maximizes those tonal qualities of the sand which made her fall in love with the medium. To move us through the plot, she uses classic editing techniques, close-ups, and long shots, which also help minimize the need for movement in her highly detailed drawings and create an appropriate atmosphere for the dramatic storyline. **53**

Walsh shot on 35mm film, so was unable to use any reference footage or even see her animation until the film had been developed. The first shot took her five days instead of her estimated half a day,[11] and she quickly realized that making the film she wanted to make would require an act of perseverance and determination.

> The big problem I had with *The Hunter* was everything just moved way too fast. Even though I felt like I was moving things in the smallest increments, they just weren't small enough. Now, sometimes I say to myself, if I can't see that they've moved, that's a good thing.[12]

Toward the end of the film, Walsh had the negative scanned and was able to work with a compositor to incorporate walk cycles and layering in some of the shots.

Both animators will readily tell you that their first films were incredible learning experiences and solidified their love for sand. Their subsequent work evolved in sophistication both in the storytelling and technique, but they would never have gotten there if they had not simply jumped in and started animating. The advanced techniques we will cover in the next chapter may help you grow as an artist and give you ideas, but if they start to feel overwhelming, simply close the book for a while and get animating. Experience is the best teacher and an experimental frame of mind will always lead you in the right direction.

**53** The Hunter – *Marieka Walsh* – 2011.

## Compositing 101

In Chapter 3, we touched on the pros and cons of animating everything in-camera versus adding effects and movement in post. When it comes to sand, post-production should be a deliberate aesthetic choice based on how you want your final work to look. There are some very specific situations where compositing will save you a lot of time, but more often, trying to replicate an in-camera look through shortcuts and tricks will cost you more effort than working entirely in-camera – and will likely not look as authentic!

When running tests for her film *The Crossing*, Marieka Walsh tried several different ways to create the expansive ocean scenes with constant movement: "Ideally when I'm experimenting, I'm saying, 'Let's find the way that looks the best and will save me time.' But it usually works out to be, 'Well, this looks the best, but it's not going to save me any time!'"[13] Sometimes it takes Walsh up to 30 minutes to create one frame of animation, but the payoff for her perseverance is a screen full of undulating sand, something that no special plug-in or filter could ever replicate.

The touch of the artist's hand in a physical material is something that can't be faked. 54

Philippe Vaucher uses extensive compositing in *The Well* (2013) and he also notes that it does not save any time:

> You think it's going to be such a timesaver, and it is while you're at the camera, but I spent almost as much time compositing as animating. It's tedious. I think I spent eight months animating and six months compositing on *The Well*. However, I would not have been able to get the degree of complexity in my shots [without compositing].[14] 55

54 *The Crossing – Marieka Walsh.*

As Vaucher notes, digital post-production can transform your raw animation into something astounding. In *A Tangled Tale*, I used After Effects mesh warps to create the underwater background movement and I hand tinted every frame of sand to add vibrant color to my characters. 56

These processes didn't save me any time, but they were more suited to my working preferences (i.e. I would rather hand tint each frame in Photoshop than deal with colored sand under the

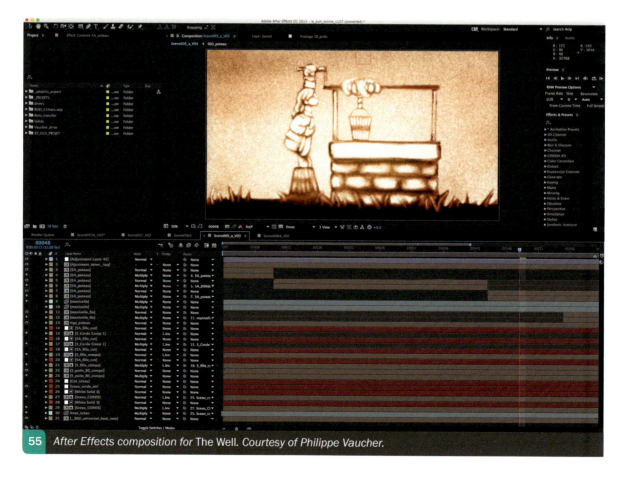

55 *After Effects composition for* The Well. *Courtesy of Philippe Vaucher.*

camera). My goal was to retain the organic feel of the imagery and blur the line between digital and in-camera animation. When you realize it will take just as much work to bring the digital and physical into seamless harmony as it will if you chose to do everything in-camera, then you are able to make a deliberate choice as to how and where to spend your time. 57

## Layering in Sand

The most obvious way to animate sand is on one level entirely in-camera. The background and foreground elements are all composed of one unit of sand and so movement in one area affects movement in another. But sometimes we want to separate out elements of a shot and work with them individually, which means we must work in layers. Layering can be done in-camera with a multiplane, or it can be done digitally by shooting sequences separately and compositing them together.

Working in-camera usually means creating the backgrounds for each shot on the lower level of the multiplane and animating the foreground on the upper level. One effect of the multiplane is when the light comes through the background layer, it reflects off the edges of the sand on the top layer, leaving a visible halo around the drawing. The intensity of this halo depends on the distance between the foreground and background plane, and how much light is filtering through the foreground. Walsh observes, "It's quite hard to overcome the 'halo' effect and often I find an in-camera multiplane shot in sand can actually look like a badly composited image!"[15] Being aware of this effect, you may decide to incorporate it into the design of your animation, as Anna Humphries did in her music video *It Might Be Real* (2012). 58

The other approach to layering is to film each layer of your animation separately and then composite them together in the computer. The halo effect is still a problem with this approach. In fact, it is more evident without some finely calibrated settings in the compositing software. Deciding what approach to use for your sand animation will be a combination of your digital skill-set (whether you know or are willing to learn compositing software), your studio (whether you can build a multiplane), and how you prefer to animate (whether you can keep track of all the movements in an entire scene or do you prefer to focus on animating one thing at a time).

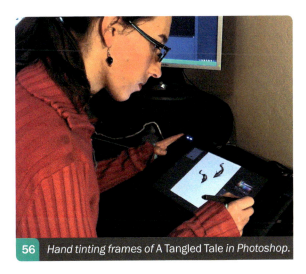
56　*Hand tinting frames of* A Tangled Tale *in Photoshop.*

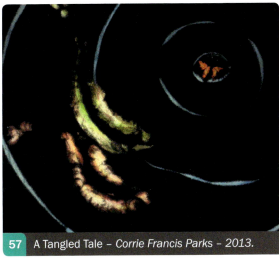
57　*A Tangled Tale –* Corrie Francis Parks *– 2013.*

58　*The "halo effect" on a multiplane. (*It Might Be Real *– Anna Humphries – 2012.)*

Fluid Frames: Animated Sand and Other Powders

Here's a practical example. This character is walking through a landscape into the distance. **59** We have three layering options for creating this scene:

- *Animate the entire scene in-camera on one layer.* This eliminates any need for post-production. However, you will face the challenge of redrawing the background as the girl moves through it toward the tree. There will inevitably be a bit of inconsistency and a trail of movement behind the girl. This could be an aesthetic decision.
- *Create the background on a lower level of a multiplane and the silhouette of the girl on the upper level.* This could work very well. We could even move elements in the background as long as we have space to reach in-between the layers, or we can slide the lower layer out.
- *Animate the background and foreground together in two separate takes and then composite the two layers together.* This also will work well and there are multiple compositing methods which will replicate shooting on a multiplane. **60**

**59**

**60** *Separating layers for compositing.*

> **Animated Anecdote**
>
> Marieka Walsh used a time-saving trick for animating a detailed face of a character in *The Crossing*. *In this shot below where the sea captain falls into the water,* she glued sand in the shape of the captain's face to a small piece of clear acetate. Then she only had to move the acetate like a cut-out and animate the body around it. Sprinkling a little sand on the top and around the edges of the acetate gives the little bit of movement, while the difficult features stay consistent. **61**
>
>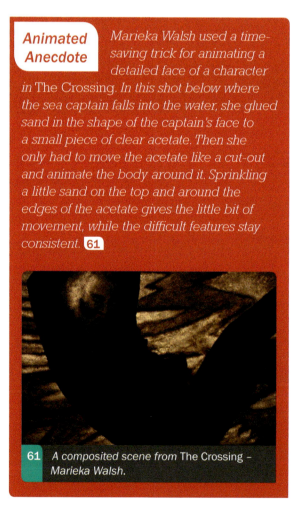
>
> **61** *A composited scene from* The Crossing *– Marieka Walsh.*

Animated Sand and Other Powders  Chapter 4

In this situation, choosing what method to use really comes down to personal preference and your digital skill-set.

Now let's throw an extra challenge into the mix. Our foreground character isn't a silhouette any more. She has some subtle shading that we want to preserve as she moves over the background. **63**

Looking again at our three approaches to layering:

- *Single layer in-camera.* Animating all on one layer will be essentially the same as if the girl were a silhouette. No changes there.
- *Two layers on a multiplane.* In Figure 64 we see the problem. We can see the background through the girl and that's ruining the solidity of our character. **64**

Fixing this on the multiplane can be tricky. If we reach under or slide out the lower level to clear away the sand behind the girl, we risk moving something we don't want to move, plus we have to rebuild the background as she moves into the distance. We might as well animate everything on one layer if we are going to do that. Alternatively, we could recompose the background so the area where the girl is going to move does not have any sand in it and avoid the problem all together. **65**

63

> **#ProTip** In *Tracks* I worked on one layer and did everything in-camera. I made trees out of cut black paper and placed them under the glass tray in each scene. Because the animals were all strong silhouettes, the paper cut-outs looked like they were also sand but I didn't have to worry about accidentally messing them up while animating. **62**
>
>
>
> 62  *Tracks* was shot entirely in-camera on one layer.

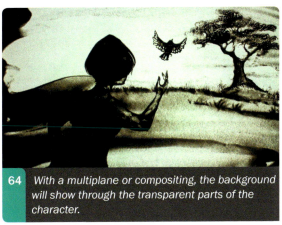

64  With a multiplane or compositing, the background will show through the transparent parts of the character.

65  Recomposing the background so the character doesn't cross over any sand will avoid the problem.

# Fluid Frames: Animated Sand and Other Powders

- *Digitally compositing.* Shooting the two layers separately will not pose any problems while animating, but compositing becomes more complicated in this sort of scene. If you simply key out the white, the lighter areas inside the girl's body will become transparent, turning her into a ghost. We will have to use more advanced keying and masking to keep the solidity of our character.

Speaking of keying and masking, let's go over some basic techniques so when it does come time to decide whether to work in-camera or composite, you will understand what you are getting into. The following are some After Effects tutorials for bringing multiple layers of sand animation together. I recommend having a basic familiarity with the After Effects interface before diving into these exercises. You can find the source files for all the compositing tutorials online at this book's website.

## Exercise

### Garbage Mattes

A Garbage Matte cuts out all the visual "garbage" that might be lurking around the edge of your frame from uneven lighting or renegade sand creeping into frame. We tried to get rid of most of that when we exposed and processed our footage, but sometimes it just can't be helped. When I have footage that needs a bit of love, I start by creating a Garbage Matte around the animation to clean it up. In Figure 66 I have an animated sequence of an egg that has quite a bit of mess around the edges. 66

66 This image is in need of a garbage matte!

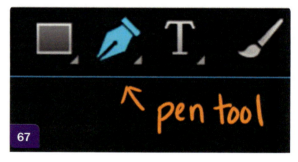

67

1. Create a new composition and import the sand footage at 12fps. Scrub through the footage so you get a sense of where the animation is going. Your mask needs to be big enough to encompass any movement in your footage but tight enough to cut out the garbage.

2. Select the sand layer by clicking on it. Then select the Pen Tool (G) and draw a mask, point by point, around the sand image. 67

   A click-hold and drag with the pen tool will make Bezier handles appear, which is useful if you want a curved mask. Since the sand drops down to the bottom of the frame in this sequence, I've scrubbed to the end of the sequence so I can make sure I get all the animation within the mask. 68

68

Animated Sand and Other Powders **Chapter 4**

3. Close the mask by connecting the last dot with the first. Now all the garbage around the edge of the frame disappears. (I changed the background color of my composition to red so I could see the edge of the mask.) **69**

4. Next we'll feather (soften) the edges of the mask to make sure it blends in to the background. Click on the little arrow to the right of the layer to open the layer properties and then open the Mask Properties (M). In the Mask Properties, you'll see the Feather (F) property. Adjust the value until you have a nice soft edge. The pixels will depend on the resolution of your composition. I've set mine to 50 pixels. **70 71**

5. Finally, we will put a fresh white background underneath the egg layer so we have a clean slate for any other compositing. Go to Layer > New > Solid (Ctrl Y) and create a white solid. **72** Place the solid in the composition under your footage. **73**

6. This is looking great. Scrub once more through the footage to make sure the feathering didn't encroach on any of the animation. Now we have a clean slate for more advanced compositing techniques.

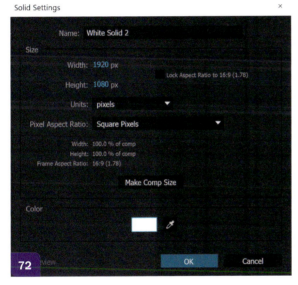

There are several ways to approach digital compositing for sand animation. The method you choose will depend greatly on what your footage looks like and what you want to achieve. Understanding your compositing options before you shoot the animation will also save you time and trouble during post-production.

## Blending Modes

Solid black silhouettes are the easiest footage to composite because you can use After Effects blending modes. With blending modes there is no need for color keying or masks. You can find the blending mode options in the Timeline panel right next to the layer name. **74**

Blending modes control how each layer interacts with layers beneath it. In the Multiply mode, After Effects multiplies color channel values with the underlying layers using a rather complex mathematical formula that accentuates the darker values and eliminates the lighter values. The practical result (if you can't get your head around that) is that any white pixels in your sand footage will become transparent while black pixels will darken the underlying footage. If you have a black silhouette on a white background, setting the blending mode to Multiply will result in the black silhouette remaining while the surrounding white disappears and allows the background to show through. **75**

There are blending modes for other situations as well. If you are working with negative space images, use the Screen blending mode, which will preserve the bright whites and eliminate the blacks from the footage. **76**

**75** *A Multiply blending mode applied.*

Animated Sand and Other Powders  Chapter 4

The Multiply and Screen blending modes work best with high-contrast footage and strong silhouette shapes. Other blending modes might have very specific applications, which you can explore in your experiments. Unfortunately, they won't work for most situations. For example, if your layers have any tonal variations, such as the shading in the body of the girl in Figure 77, the blending will begin to look forced as one layer moves over another. In this case you will have to consider other compositing options. **77**

76  *The angels in the foreground were animated on a separate layer and then combined using the Screen blending mode.*

77

## Exercise

### Paint Bucket Effect

If you have a strong edge to your image, the Paint Bucket will be the first compositing effect to try out. This allows you to create a mask outside the image. For this example, we'll use some footage from my film *A Tangled Tale*. **78** **79**

1. Create a composition and place the frame sequence of the fish swimming over the background plate. Set the sand layer blending mode to Multiply. **80**

78

79

80

## Fluid Frames: Animated Sand and Other Powders

2. Duplicate (Ctrl D) the frame sequence and set the top layer's blending mode to Normal.

3. Open Effects and Presets (Window > Effects and Presets). Search for the Paint Bucket effect and apply it to the top layer. **81** The area surrounding the fish will turn to the default Fill Color, a bright red.

4. At the center of the image, there is a circle with a crosshair. This is the Fill Point. **82** You can grab this circle and move it to a part of the screen that will not have any sand in it throughout the sequence. If necessary, you can set keyframes for the position of the Fill Point.

5. In the effects panel, set Stroke > Spread, check the box for Invert Fill and set Blending Mode > Stencil Alpha. Everything that was bright red now becomes transparent and we can see the background plate behind the fish. **83**

6. To refine the choke on the matte, you can adjust the Tolerance and Spread Radius settings.

7. Remember how we put a second layer of the fish footage with a Multiply blending mode underneath the layer with the Paint Bucket effect? Find that layer and turn it off and on, noticing the difference in the edge of the drawing. Paint Bucket allows us to choke back the matte to get rid of the halo at the expense of the fine grainy texture. This extra layer multiplied underneath brings back that texture along the edge.

8. As a final check, scrub through the footage to make sure nothing has gone awry. All the settings can be keyframed, including the position of the Fill Point. Occasionally I have needed to use more than one Fill Point to cover all the areas that need to be keyed out.

## Color Keying

If you find you have to animate the Fill Point too often, or use multiple Fill Points, it's time to look for another solution. When there is too much movement in the footage to realistically use the Paint Bucket, another useful compositing technique is color keying. Color keying means the computer evaluates a specified color in an image and replaces it with transparency so that an object can be lifted off of one background and placed on a different one. Green screen is a form of color keying, in which an actor or animation is shot against a green background, which is subsequently easily identified and removed by the computer. We will learn more about this in later chapters, but green screen doesn't work with sand animation because all the tonal variations are dependent on the pure light coming through the varying depths of the sand and a green light would contaminate the imagery.

There are two main problems to overcome in color keying sand footage and they work in opposition. One is the ubiquitous "halo," which is the glow of light around the edge of the grains of sand. The second is the holes that appear in the interior shading of an image when the color key is pushed too far. 84

If you push up the threshold of the color key to get rid of the halo, the keying starts to eat away at the center of the image, but if you only focus on keeping the center intact, the halo will run out of control. Because of this, color keying works best on footage that has shading on the darker side. With the right settings, it can be an easy solution for some footage, but it does not work in every situation.

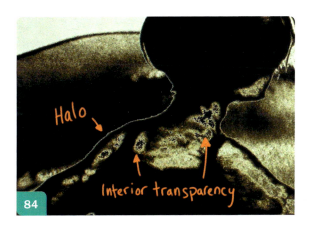

### Exercise

### Applying a Color Key Effects Stack

In After Effects, set up a composition with the foreground and background layer. In Figure 85, I've already made a Garbage Matte for my foreground sequence and placed it over the background. (I've left off the white underlayer of the Garbage Matte so you can see it more easily.) 85

1. Search for the Linear Color Key effect and drag it onto the girl layer. 86 This applies the effect to the layer. Use the eyedropper to select the white area around the girl as the Key Color. Use Matching Tolerance and Matching Softness to refine the matte a bit, but you won't be able to get it perfect at this stage. You can see it's

## Fluid Frames: Animated Sand and Other Powders

looking a bit rough, with a little bit of a halo and some holes in some unwanted places. **87**

2. Now search for the Refine Soft Matte effect and apply it to the layer. First, make sure Calculate Edge Details and Decontaminate Edge Colors are checked. Now you can play with the settings to refine the interior of the image and the blending of the edges. Go back to the Linear Color Key settings and make finer adjustments to Matching Tolerance and Matching Softness as well. There is no magic number for any of these settings, they will vary depending on your footage, so spend some time fiddling until it looks good. **88**

3. You can also adjust the Curves on a layer to compensate for any final areas that might still need a bit of help. Search for Curves in the Effects and Presets panel and apply it to the layer. **89**

   The curve you see is a graphical representation of the black and white spectrum and by clicking on it you can enhance certain points along the spectrum. You can brighten the whites and darken the blacks to create a cleaner key.

4. Once you've found a combination of effects, you can save the entire stack as a preset to use on other footage. Select all the effects in the Effects panel. Then choose Animation > Save Animation Preset. To load the preset on a new footage sequence, select the footage layer and choose Animation > Apply Animation Preset.

87

88

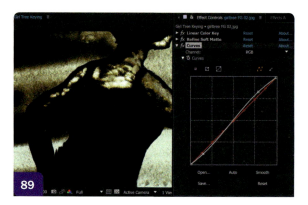

89

> "If I know a shot needs to be composited, I create dark outlines for the foreground layer, so that the compositor can strip the halo back into the dark areas and hopefully create a composited image that looks seamless."
>
> – Marieka Walsh

Animated Sand and Other Powders  Chapter 4

Paint Bucket works well if you have a large blank area and a solid edge. Color keying works if the inside of your image has some shading and no white pixels. These effects won't work in every situation. Take the animated egg, which we used for the Garbage Matte exercise. It has a lot of white in the center and some undefined edging. I want to composite the egg on this painted background. 90 91

90

91

Even the most precise refinement in the Color Key effects stack leaves me with some odd-looking blurry spots because there is too much white in the center. Using the Paint Bucket leaves too much white in the shadow area and not enough around the edge of the egg. 92 93 I will need to use an animated mask around the footage.

92  *Color Key effects stack.*

93  *Paint bucket effect.*

Fluid Frames: Animated Sand and Other Powders

### Exercise

## Animated Masks

1. Create a new composition with the painted background layer under the HATCH Garbage Matte composition. (You can also use the composition you created in the garbage matte exercise). Set the blending mode on the HATCH layer to Multiply. This will help us see what we are doing. **94**

2. Use the Pen Tool (G) and draw a mask around the egg using Bezier points. **95** Use more points than you think you'll need at the bottom and top of the egg, because those are the areas that will be changing shape. You will be glad to have them when you start animating. The edge of the mask should be just a little bit inside the edge of the sand.

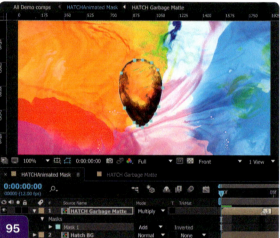

3. Bring up the Mask Feather (F) property and soften the edges just a bit. I used 10px for this 1920x1080 composition. Now turn the blending mode back to Normal. **96** Don't worry about the missing pixels around the edge. We'll take care of those later.

4. Go to the first frame of the timeline. Select the Mask Path (M) and click the stopwatch icon next to the property to set a keyframe. The keyframe should appear as a diamond.

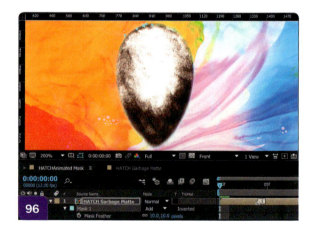

Animated Sand and Other Powders  Chapter 4      107

5. Right-click on the keyframe and select Toggle Hold Keyframe. This means that the position of the mask points will not move until the next keyframe. 97

6. Now, scrub through the footage one frame at a time and move the mask points on each new frame to match the movement in the sand. I find it's easier to turn off the mask while doing this so I can see the edge of the sand. Stay just a little bit inside the outer edge and don't be overly precise. We will eventually multiply a second layer over this one to bring the details on the edge back. 98

7. Go back to the beginning of the footage. Select the HATCH layer and duplicate the layer (Ctrl D). On the new layer (which should be the topmost layer), change the blending mode to Multiply. Open the mask properties (Ctrl M). Select the mask by clicking on it, then delete it (Delete). Now the fine sandy details on the edge of the egg are back, but the center is solid! 99

# 108 Fluid Frames: Animated Sand and Other Powders

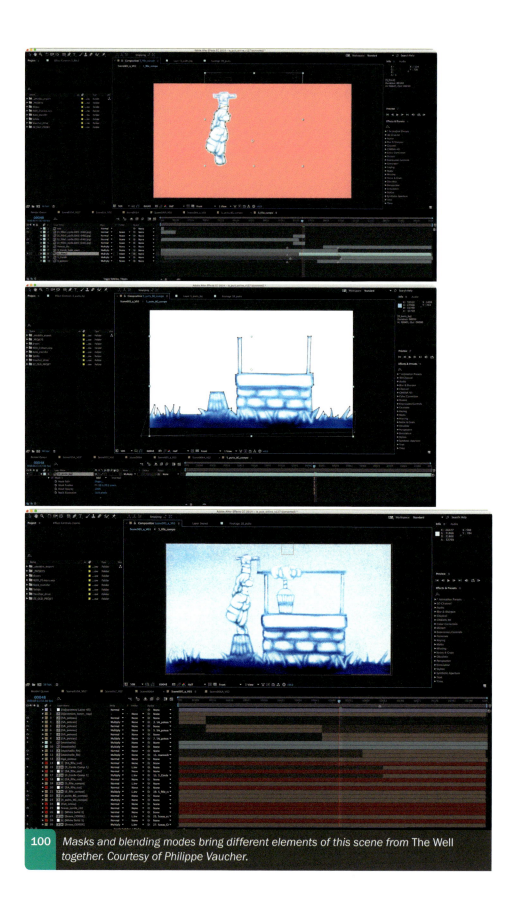

**100** *Masks and blending modes bring different elements of this scene from* The Well *together. Courtesy of Philippe Vaucher.*

Animating masks is really only practical if you have a relatively simple shape (like an egg) or only a few frames to go through. Rotoscoping mask points can be extremely tedious, but allows you to add many more layers to your scene. It is a great idea for background elements that either do not move or move very little. Philippe Vaucher uses a combination of masks and blending modes to composite his salt layers in *The Well*. 100

Working with salt proved to be a particular challenge because salt does not have the dark blacks of sand and it could not be layered over a dark background. Vaucher had to work with very light gradients behind the characters to get a natural blend of the layers.[16]

One final compositing alternative, which is the most precise but also the most time consuming, is to create an alpha channel or Luma Matte *Sequence* in Photoshop, using the original footage as a base. Essentially, this is just rotoscoping every frame to create a pure black and white layer which can be loaded into After Effects and designated as transparency information for the main layer. Sometimes this can be more efficient than animating a complicated mask, especially if you can arrange a sequence of filters to batch process each frame into black and white in Photoshop, which is

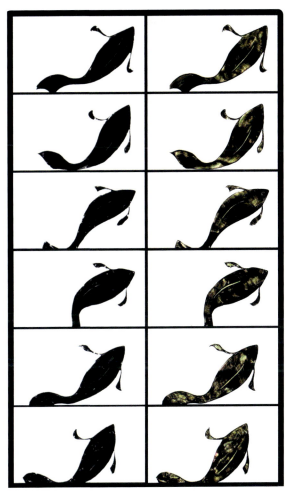

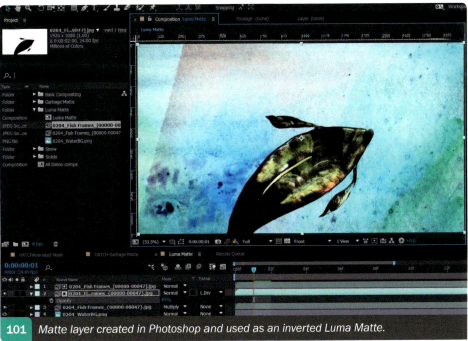

101 *Matte layer created in Photoshop and used as an inverted Luma Matte.*

what I did with my footage. However, I found that each frame had to be cleaned up individually to fill the small gaps in the center of the image.

I did this for many scenes in *A Tangled Tale*, and then imported the new sequence and used it as a Luma Inverted Track Matte for my original animation. **101**

I also added an underlayer with a Multiply blending mode to retain the edge, similar to what we did with the Paint Bucket effect.

There are several ways you could create a transparency layer, either as a separate sequence or embedded into each frame as an alpha channel, but the Luma Inverted Track Matte is the one I found worked best with my particular footage. While revisiting every frame of my animation to create a separate layer was certainly the most time consuming of all the processes I tried, it looked the best in the end. The journey to finding the right combination of compositing techniques was entirely trial and error. Every sequence will be unique and require a specially tailored solution. These compositing techniques are your assets for working with sand footage and just like the tools in a handyman's toolbox, each is best used for specific situations.

## Adding Color

Sand has traditionally been a black and white medium, because it is shot as a silhouette. Before digital workflow, the only way to add color was by using colored sand or lighting gels and filters. The computer has opened up a world of color for sand animators by offering numerous avenues to variegated vibrancy.

## Exercise

### Hand Tinting in Photoshop

Hand tinting is one option for coloring sand footage. It is time consuming, but the results are beautiful. In this method, once you have shot and processed your sequence in black and white, you must revisit each frame with the eye of a painter. The simplest approach to tinting is to open each frame in Photoshop, color it, save, and move onto the next frame. Opening and closing hundreds of files for a sequence is not the most efficient workflow, however. Below is a method of tinting I've developed while working on *A Tangled Tale*. It uses the Timeline and Video Layer features in Photoshop.

1. Open your frames as an image sequence in Photoshop. Choose File > Open (Ctrl O), then navigate to your folder and select the first frame of the sequence. Check the box that says Image Sequence. **102** Set the appropriate frame rate. For the sample footage, it is 12fps.

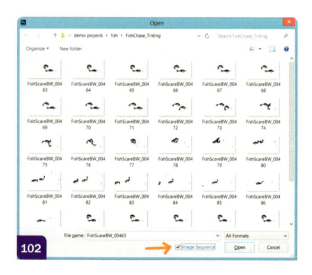

Animated Sand and Other Powders  Chapter 4        111

103

104

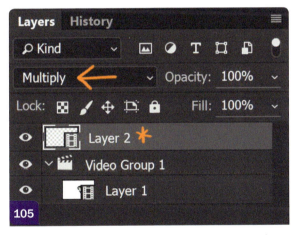

105

2. Open the Timeline Panel (Window > Timeline). The Timeline panel is Photoshop's interface for working with frame-by-frame animation. Make sure you are in Video Timeline and not Frame Animation. 103

Use the panel options to Enable Timeline Shortcuts Keys so you can navigate between frames with the left and right arrow keys. You can also enable and adjust onion-skin settings and make other helpful customizations in this panel. 104

3. I always create a new video layer to work on, so I am not painting directly on the footage. Make a new video layer (Layer > Video Layers > New Blank Video Layer). Place this layer above the footage layer and make sure it is selected. Set the blending mode for the layer to Multiply. 105

4. Now select the Brush tool and choose a brush for your painting. My personal preference is the flat camel brush, or some other textured brushes. Set the Brush mode to Multiply and the opacity to 15%. This means that the brush will only multiply color value on the lighter pixels in the image, leaving the black pixels black. And the low opacity will allow you to blend colors like layers of watercolor. 106

106

## Fluid Frames: Animated Sand and Other Powders

5. Make sure you have the blank video layer selected and paint away! I like to put my color swatches within easy reach and I will frequently change the brush size and opacity. **107**

6. When you are finished, go to File > Export > Render Video and export your colored frame sequence into a new folder. You can export the combined video layers, or you can turn off the original sand layer and just export the color with an alpha channel and combine the two later in After Effects. This might give you some more flexibility for complex compositing. Never overwrite the original footage, in case you need to make changes.

7. If you want to tint the black part of the sand image, set your Brush mode and layer blending mode to Screen. This will add color to the black pixels only, leaving the white untouched. Experiment with other brush modes and textures as you go.

### Exercise

### Tints and Filters in After Effects

Another way to add color is through applying various color effects in After Effects. Here's a quick way to turn sand into snow!

1. Import the Gnome footage from the sample files. Interpret the footage at 8fps and create a new composition. **108**

2. In the Effects and Presets panel, search for Invert. Drag the Invert effect onto your footage. Magically the sand becomes white with a slight hint of blue on a black background. Snow! **109**

3. To make our footage a little cooler, I'm going to add a blue photo filter. Search for the Photo Filter effect and apply it to the Gnome layer. In the Effects Controls panel you can choose the color and density of the filter. **110**

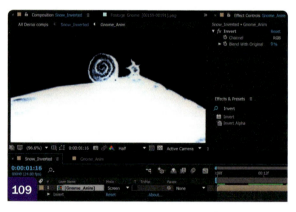

Animated Sand and Other Powders  Chapter 4

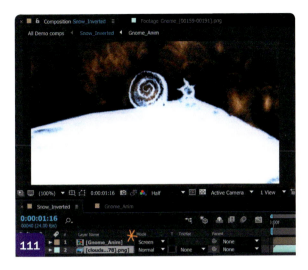

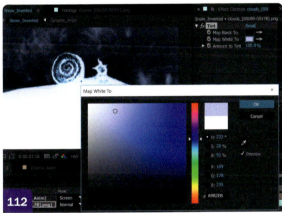

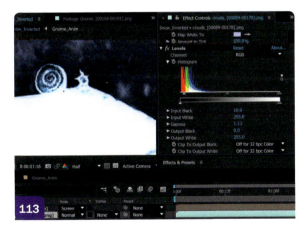

4. Let's add a little more ambiance. I have a cloud sequence I made using a staggered mix on some sand textures. Import this layer and interpret it at 24fps. Place this layer behind the Gnome layer and set the Gnome layer blending mode to Screen. **111**

5. The brownish-yellow color isn't exactly saying snowstorm to me, so I'm going to change the colors to something more frigid. In the Effects and Presets panel search for Tint. Drag the Tint effect to the Clouds layer.

6. Now in the Effect Controls panel, click on the white box labeled Map White To. Select a light shade of blue. This assigns a new color value to the image linked to the black and white value. Now the clouds are looking a little more wintery. **112**

7. I want to enhance the color in the clouds a bit so I'm also going to adjust the levels on the layer. Search for the Levels effect and drag it on the Clouds layer. You'll see a histogram graph in the Effects panel. By sliding the little triangle tabs under the histogram you can adjust the contrast in the clouds, punching up the white and deepening the darks. The middle tab adjusts the mid-tones in the image. **113**

## 114  Fluid Frames: Animated Sand and Other Powders

8. I have a few more effects to show you that may come in handy, so let's keep playing with this footage. Select the top layer with our snow gnome. Apply the Tint effect to the layer by searching for it in the Effects and Presets and dragging it to the layer. **114**

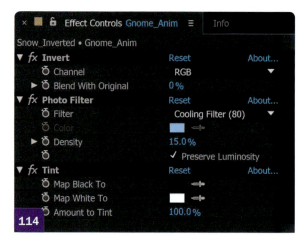

9. Now click on Map White To and move the selector ring around the color palette. All the sand is changing colors. I settled on a bright pink. Now click Map Black To and choose a different color. The background is now green and since our blending mode on the layer is set to Screen, it is now blending with the cloud layer below it. **115**

Our scene isn't so naturalistic anymore, but it's certainly colorful. Using the Tint effect on footage is a great way to make a base layer for more complicated hand tinting, or just add some psychedelic flair to your sand. **116**

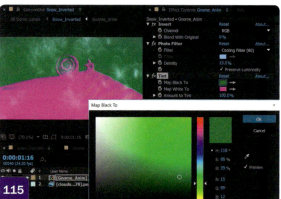

After Effects has a plethora of color-correcting effects beyond these basic ones. You can stack them, combine them, and even animate them. **117** Your sandy animation is no longer confined to a black and white world. With the experimental frame of mind, we can bring them into a new world of color.

## Combining Sand with Other Animation Techniques

### Case Studies from Commercial Projects

When you go to the beach, sand gets everywhere! For the lovers of sandy animation, it's no different; sand creeps its way into all sorts of projects. Having an experimental frame of mind means thinking beyond the obvious applications of the material and finding new contexts for it. With this digital tool-kit, you can combine sand with other artistic projects, bringing a completely new aesthetic to your animation.

For the past several years as a freelance animator, I have been trying to incorporate sand into many of my commercial projects. Now that your brain is full of the possibilities that sand can offer, look at these images from various productions. Can you figure out how they were made?

**117** *The many layers that went into this scene in* A Tangled Tale.

# Fluid Frames: Animated Sand and Other Powders

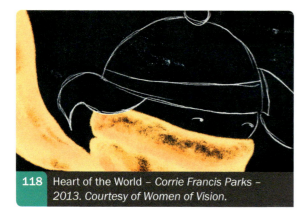

118 Heart of the World – *Corrie Francis Parks – 2013. Courtesy of Women of Vision.*

### Heart of the World 118

We had limited time and budget for this animated Christmas greeting for non-profit Women of Vision so it made sense to do some simple hand-drawn animation for the main character (see Figure 119). However, I wanted to create a magical scarf that whisks the character away, so I animated the scarf with sand, used the Tint effect and some hand tinting in Photoshop to make it a vibrant, glowing orange. The snowy environment around the character was simply inverted sand and created some unity of texture for the piece. 119

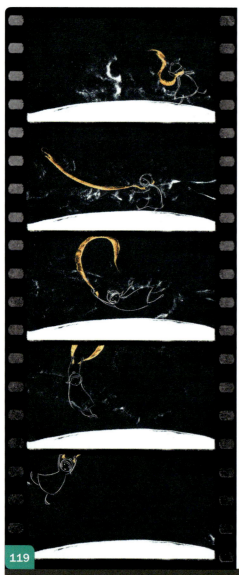

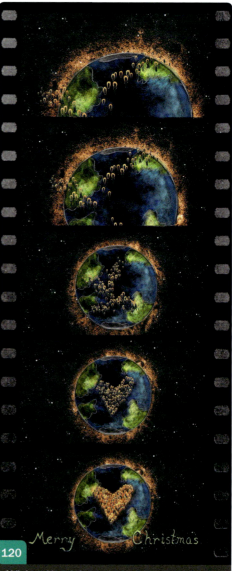

Heart of the World – *Corrie Francis Parks – 2013. Courtesy of Women of Vision. Hand-drawn animation combined with sand.*

Figure 120 show the final scene from the same project. I took inspiration from Chinese sky lanterns for the gathering of women from around the world. Like in the beginning of the piece, each woman was hand-drawn and had a magical orange scarf made of sand. I applied a stack of glowing effects to the scarves, and the women gathered into the shape of a heart for the finale. The background was several layers. The Earth was a layer of colored paint with a layer of sand texture on top with the Soft Light blending mode. I made a cycle for the orange glow around the Earth and a layer of twinkling stars. At the end, I added color and a cycling sand texture to the text. **120**

### Three Scenarios in Which Hana Sasaki Grows a Tail **121**

Sand plays a significant visual role in this book trailer about a town that gets covered in volcanic ash. **122** The majority of this piece was hand-drawn, but the texture of sand seemed ideal for creating the "heavy, golden ash" that rains down on the town. I animated all the drawn parts of the scene first and then used that animation as a reference in my frame capture program to animate the ash in the street. To make the smoke coming out of the volcano seem far away, I used a series of rolling cross-dissolves and a combination of blending modes and After Effects color effects to create the transition between scenes.

### Vezo **123**

This documentary about sustainable fishing in Madagascar had several points where sand animation transitioned into live action footage. **124**

**121** *Ash covers a small town in Japan in this book trailer for* Three Scenarios in Which Hana Sasaki Grows a Tail. *(Three Scenarios – Corrie Francis Parks – 2013.)*

**122** *Several layers of sand with various blending modes created this blanket of heavy golden ash. (Three Scenarios – Corrie Francis Parks.)*

**123** *Composited scene from Vezo. Courtesy of Nomadic Pictures.*

124  *An animated transition back to the live action sequence. Courtesy of Nomadic Pictures.*

In this scene, a man throws an offering into the sea from his boat. After animating the underwater sequence, I shot a separate layer of the offering filling the screen as it sank, and the bubbles in the middle became a way to transition back to live action. I used the sand footage as a Luma Track Matte on the underwater scene so that as the dark sand cleared, the animation cleared with it. I rendered out a frame sequence with an alpha channel and the director was able to place the animation over his live action footage and create this beautiful, complex wipe.

## Notes

1. Bächler, Rolf. Email interview. July 10, 2014.
2. Bächler, Rolf. "Obituary: Ernest 'Nag' Ansorge." ASIFA Switzerland, N.p., 13 Jan. 2014, Web.
3. Cakó, Ferenc, Email interview, 17 June 2014.
4. Cakó. 17 June 2014.
5. Cakó, Ferenc. "The Painter of Sand: An Interview with Ferenc Cakó." Interview by János Palotai. FILMKULTÚRA. n.p., June 2001. Date accessed: Apr. 22, 2015. http://www.filmkultura.hu/regi/2001/articles/profiles/cako.en.html
6. Korejwo, Aleksandra. "My Small Animation World." Animation World Network, 1996. Date accessed: Apr. 22, 2014. http://www.awn.com/mag/issue1.2/articles1.2/korejwo1.2.html
7. Vaucher, Philippe. Personal interview. Sept. 21, 2014.
8. Meléndez, César Díaz. Telephone interview. May 21, 2014.
9. Ibid.
10. Walsh, Marieka. Telephone interview. May 16, 2013.
11. *Making of the Hunter*. Dir. Marieka Walsh, Vimeo, Feb. 7, 2012.
12. Walsh, Marieka. Telephone interview. July 7, 2014.
13. Walsh, May 16, 2013.
14. Vaucher, Sept. 21, 2014.
15. Walsh, Marieka. Email message to the author. Feb. 15, 2015.
16. Vaucher, 21 Sept. 2014.

*Thomas Parks.*

# Chapter 5
# The Transforming Painting

**The Life of a Painting**

**Notable Pioneers in Painted Animation**

    Oskar Fischinger
    Witold Giersz
    Caroline Leaf
    Clive Walley
    Alexander Petrov

**Exploring the Technique**

    Exercise: Motion Painting

**Setting Up Your Studio**

    Your Painting Surface
    Different Types of Paint
    Lighting

**Things to Have in Your Studio**

    Exercise: Finger Painting Portrait with Sponge Transition

**Digital Approaches to Paint-on-Glass**

**Green Screen**

    Creating the Layers
    Exercise: Compositing the Roller Coaster of Luv

**Moving Beyond the Glass**

**Additional Exercises**

## The Life of a Painting

Have you ever wanted to step into a painting and see what the artist's world is all about? Painted animation is as close as we come to that experience. Brush strokes come alive, colors combine in a dynamic palette, and we find an intimate connection with the artist.

The best way to approach this technique is to think of the image as one painting that is continuously transforming before our eyes. Rather than having to make thousands of individual paintings, we allow that painting to come to life frame-by-frame by manipulating one image continuously. **01**

Just as each skilled painter will learn the basic skills of painting and then develop them into a favored style, so each animator will combine the fundamentals of painting and animation in a unique way. The painted animation of Caroline Leaf looks nothing like that of Alexander Petrov or Clive Walley. However, all three start in the same place – with a sheet of glass and a palette of paints under the camera. This chapter will put you on the starting block and where you end up is part of the adventure. **02**

One thing I do hope – I do hope you like to paint! Whether you have years of formal training or are entirely self-taught, animating with wet paint will present some new challenges for the painter. You must add a new dimension to your work – time.

Consider how a painting develops. Do you start with drawings and sketches? Make a color study? Do you like to work on canvas, gessoed paper, or wood panel? Do you build up layers of paint, mix colors on the canvas, or apply paint precisely in pure colors? Any of your painting preferences can be transferred to your animation practice.

Painted animation has the most developed history of all these fluid frame techniques. Painters eagerly embraced animation early on as a natural extension of their art. Once animation became an established form of artistic expression, animators adopted the idea of using paint under the camera to achieve stylistic and conceptual goals. Let's look at five animators from the archives of painted animation. Each had a different motivation for adopting painted animation into their creative process.

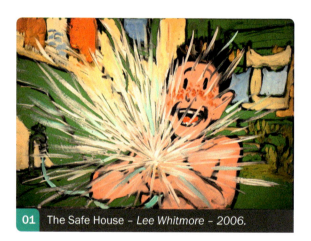

**01** The Safe House – *Lee Whitmore* – 2006.

**02** A Tale of Longing – *Xin Li* – 2012.

## Notable Pioneers in Painted Animation

### Oskar Fischinger

We met Oskar Fischinger earlier, coming of age in the avant-garde film culture of 1920s Germany. An artist exercising the experimental frame of mind, Fischinger had a long career as an animator and painter, working both in Germany and the USA. In 1947 he brought the two worlds together in a unique film commissioned by the Museum of Non-Objective Painting in New York. **03**

In *Motion Painting No. 1* (1947), Fischinger paints on sheets of Plexiglas mounted vertically in front of the camera, recording a frame after each brush stroke. The development of the painting is buried in the final artwork and the film is an excavation tool of sorts for uncovering the layers of artistic thought. Part way through the film, the Plexiglas became so loaded with paint that Fischinger decided to place a new sheet in front and continue. Over the course of the 11-minute film, he ended up doing this a total of six times.[1] The shapes build and overlap but rarely move as an entity around the screen. The colors start light and airy, and the brushwork takes a pointillist approach. A composition of overlapping spiral pathways brings the canvas into darkness and then rectangles laid like bricks bring us back into light. 04 05

The painting continues to evolve with these visual motifs until the music brings us to the climactic ending. Throughout the film, Fischinger moves from one idea to the next, building directly overtop of what is already there, so the history of the painting is always present in our memories.

Richard Whitehall observes, "*Motion Painting No. 1* is devoid of dramatics. It is about conception and growth, the birth and realization of a form and an idea."[2] *Motion Painting No. 1* was innovative in its attempt to document the process of painting at a time when the general population was still fixated on the results of an artist's endeavor. Fischinger himself felt that the work was the culmination of all his previous animation experience.

> [The painting,] without any concession, develops its own possibilities. The unknown, unlimited and unborn possibilities of a creative mind, through this technique developed in *Motion Painting No. 1*, [find their] natural, clear way to let the visual expressions flow without any restrictions or chains and reveal the secrets and beauty of art in its purest and most direct way.[3]

Fischinger chose the Brandenburg Concerto No. 3 by Bach as the soundtrack for the film, but kept the relationship between the visuals and music loose. In his notes on the film, Fischinger uses the

03 *Still from* Motion Painting No. I *by Oskar Fischinger, 1947, © Center for Visual Music.*

04 *Oskar Fischinger in his Los Angeles studio with Plexiglas panel from* Motion Painting No. I. *Photo by Lou Jacobs, Jr., © Fischinger Trust, courtesy Center for Visual Music.*

05 *Still from* Motion Painting No. I *by Oskar Fischinger, 1947 © Center for Visual Music.*

analogy of a winding path along a river to explain how the music and the visuals work independently as two artworks in close proximity:

> The film is in some parts perfectly synchronized with the music, but in other parts it runs free – without caring much about the music – it is like a pleasant walk on the side of a river – If the river springs, we on the side do not necessarily spring to it – but go our own free way – sometimes we even go a little bit away from the river and later come back to it and love it so much more – because we were away from it.[4]

Other artists have built upon this method of progressive motion painting. Clive Walley pushed the idea further in *Divertimento No. 3* (1994), using a specially designed camera rig that allowed him to have an infinite number of receding layers, thereby eliminating Fischinger's problems with the paint building up. **06**

Patrick Jenkins also utilized the idea in his tribute to Canadian painter, Kazuo Nakumura, *Inner View* (2009). "What I basically did was recreate each Nakamura painting, frame by frame, adding a little stroke of paint and taking a frame. I wanted to have the experience of making his paintings myself."[5] **07**

Fischinger's idea to add the dimension of time to the painting process bridged the gap between painting and animation, and, like the underpainting in a masterpiece, remains at the foundation of all painted animation. Let's not forget him and his important work as we dig deeper into the world of painting under the camera.

**06** In Clive Walley's Divertimento No. 3, 1994, a painting recedes continually back as time progresses forward. (Divertimento No. 3 Brushwork – Clive Walley – 1994.)

**07** Inner View – Patrick Jenkins – 2009.

## Witold Giersz

Witold Giersz began working with traditional cel animation at Cooperative of Animated Cartoons in Bielsko, Poland, in the 1950s. An animator with a truly experimental frame of mind, Giersz wished to free the color in traditional cel animation from the confines of the outline and focus solely on the transforming shape. **08** **09**

In *Little Western* (1960), Giersz paints patches of color directly on cel without any outlines. The lively cowboys are constructed with loose brush strokes and are very aware of their painted nature. One cowboy dips his finger into another cowboy's painted chest, using it like a brush to draw a rope across the screen. Later, the blue cowboy collides with a yellow cowboy to reform as a larger green cowboy. Though Giersz was not working directly under the camera for this film, being able to manipulate the paint itself rather than confine it within a drawing eventually led him to painting directly under the camera.

*Koń* (*Horse*, 1967) was Giersz's first film primarily animated with wet paint under the camera, though Giersz did use his cel technique in a few shots for the sake of efficiency. It is quite likely the first paint-on-glass film in the world to be widely shown in festivals.[6] Telling the story of a warrior's attempt to capture a wild horse, the prominence of the material is evident from the opening title, in which paint spreads across the screen in thick patches. Giersz deliberately makes no attempt to blend the colors, letting them exist independently in visible brush strokes. **10**

> I was always attracted to [the French Impressionists'] work, especially because it seemed to be three-dimensional, incorporating both convex portions and deep relief ... By drawing in paint with a blade I was able to achieve even deeper relief. I also admired the French painters for putting colours next to each other rather than mixing them: the resulting impression is much more interesting.[7]

While *Koń* feels like an exploration of a new technique, Giersz's later film, *Pożar* (*Fire*, 1975) reaches a new level of painted sophistication. The variation in texture and color is more refined and integrated into the entire scene.

**08** Witold Giersz at work in his studio in 1989. Photo Credit: Romuald Pieńkowski/Polish National Film Archive.

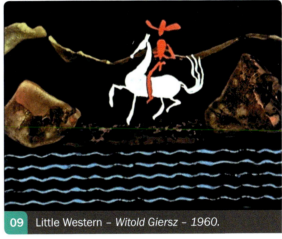
**09** Little Western – *Witold Giersz – 1960.*

**10** Horse – *Witold Giersz – 1967.*

> While painting *Koń*, I learned from some of the technical mistakes in the film. Removing each drawing left a trace so the background around a character pulsated and twitched. Instead of masking this, I decided to use it as an additional effect for a peculiar, lively background. You see it clearly in *Pożar* – the whole frame, the background, not the characters, and their traces, pulsate. It is alive.[8]

Giersz masterfully uses trails of paint, in a way that does not clutter the frame but enhances the sporadic motion of nervous animals as they try to escape the coming fire. In the central part of the film, Giersz delves into abstraction, playing with flashing exposure variations, fiery slashes, and smears of paint. **11** Giersz animated on glass and cardboard, occasionally using a multiplane for special effects like the smoke and raging fire.

In his lifetime, Giersz made over 60 films, always placing a priority on finding new techniques. His most recent work *Signum* (2015), goes back to the very beginning of animated drawings – the Paleolithic caves of Lascaux and Altamira. Using clay and burnt coal as his pigments and stone as his canvas, Giersz takes his vast understanding of animal movement and painted animation into the distant past.

> Hunting scenes were pictured [by Paleolithic artists] as evocatively as possible, with meticulous attention to creating the impression of movement. Today, thanks to the possibilities offered by animation, by hand-painting each phase of movement on the rocks, one is able to fulfill the prehistoric artists' dream and animate their paintings.[9] **12**

By taking yet another step into uncharted territory, Witold Giersz continues to create from an experimental frame of mind, finding new (or perhaps ancient) approaches to painting under the camera.

## Caroline Leaf

We met Caroline Leaf and her sand films in the previous chapter. You may be noticing that animators practicing from an experimental frame of mind are rarely satisfied doing things the same way every time. They are constantly looking for new ways to build upon the techniques they have mastered. After making several films in sand, Leaf was looking to try something new:

**11**  Fire – *Witold Giersz* – 1975.

**12**  Signum – *Witold Giersz* – 2015.

When I moved into the paint, it was only because I wanted to work with colors and colored sand had been too laborious. I was looking for something that was as close to sand as possible and wet paint was the answer for me . . . I never actually felt that I was using different techniques because they were all fluid animation.[10]

Adapted from a story by Canadian author Mordecai Richler, Leaf's film *The Street* (1976) transports us to a Jewish neighborhood in Montreal, where a nine-year-old boy and his family exist in orbital fashion around the dying grandmother in the back room. The boy wavers between anticipation of finally getting his own room, and guilty resentment at his grandmother's tenacious refusal to pass. Leaf's morphing transitions and architectural mutability elicit the feeling of one uneventful day blending into the next, both visually and narratively. She uses her fingers to smear and reform the paint from scene to scene, leaving us ungrounded in space and time, with only bits of overheard dialogue and minimal narration to keep us moving forward to the anticipated passing of the grandmother. **13**

Critic Ron Blumer describes the film in this way:

The visual information comes at us not in distinct, separate bits, but rather as a flowing whole. The individual drawings in fact are wholly unremarkable, if anything crude and childlike. The interest and beauty of her technique lie in the movement, in the spaces between the frames.[11]

Transitioning to paint gave Leaf a new textural palette to play with, allowing more control over the linear aspects of the image and more freedom in the visual design. In one scene, to convey the frenetic pace of the mother restlessly overworking herself, Leaf transforms a mixing bowl of rapidly spinning batter into the daughter's hair being combed, the floor being scrubbed, laundry wrung out, and, finally, back into the spinning batter again. While she retains a muted color scheme similar to sand, Leaf uses color to pull certain characters into the foreground of our attention. It is evident in the simplicity of the character design and color that Leaf is not concerned with the formalities of the painting tradition. Her medium is a means of storytelling exclusively and she adheres to no tradition or influence. Perhaps this is what makes *The Street* feel so authentic and timeless. **14** Having won numerous festival awards

**13** The Street ©1976 National Film Board of Canada, All rights reserved.

**14** The Street ©1976 National Film Board of Canada, All rights reserved.

and an Academy Award nomination in 1977, it remains one of the most widely shown paint-on-glass films in the world.

## Clive Walley

Welsh painter Clive Walley was concerned that the art of painting was being eclipsed by the emerging popularity of film and television. His solution was to infiltrate the enemy camp by bringing painting to the moving image. "The point of making film for me was to save painting from the depredations of film. I hoped eventually to have a way of painting which moved, and which could somehow be as immediate as actual painting."[12]

Walley has an engineering background and worked for many years as a builder, so embarking on a major construction project was a natural extension of his artistic exploration. He built a rostrum camera rig with layers of glass slotted into a rotational chain, allowing the layers to move continuously downward while new ones are placed at the top.

> I always felt with Oskar's wonderful piece [*Motion Painting No. 1*] that he kept getting stuck for space on the picture surface. I wanted to remove the history of the work in a satisfying, mechanical way to keep the road ahead unobstructed, so I built the now well-known rig.[13]

Each layer of this "king of all multiplanes" is spaced about one inch apart and can be completely removed and replaced at another level. The entire rig can also move up or down as a unit and the camera can move along the X, Y, or Z axis. With this sort of flexibility, Walley is able to expand his paintings into infinite space. **15**

But for Walley, painting is naturally a four-dimensional medium. The passing of time as a painting forms is inseparable from the finished work, as are the layers of paint applied. The multiplane rig pulls apart the layers we would normally see compacted on a single canvas. It dissects a painting both dimensionally and temporally. After working with "The Rig" for several years, tinkering and modifying it with each new project, Walley embarked on a six-part series of abstract explorations: the *Divertimenti*.

Each "divertimento" explores a different aspect of painting through diverse methods of brushwork, color choices, camera movements, and specially commissioned music and sound design. In *Winds of Change (No. 1)* we encounter fluttering flicks of paint dancing through a landscape of abstract shapes. *Love Song (No. 2)* trips our emotional heart-strings through color, shape, and music. **16** In *Brushwork (No. 3)*, Walley nods to Fischinger as he records rapid brush strokes painted by an invisible hand, burying the history of the painting as it physically recedes into the past. *Life Study (No. 4)* reveals a vast textural diversity situated in what appears to be infinite space at a microscopic scale. In *Slap-Stick (No. 5)*, **17** the paint pops and bubbles as it moves through underground tunnels of negative space, changing color and shape with each turn.

**15** *Clive Walley with "The Rig." Courtesy of Clive Walley.*

The Transforming Painting  Chapter 5   127

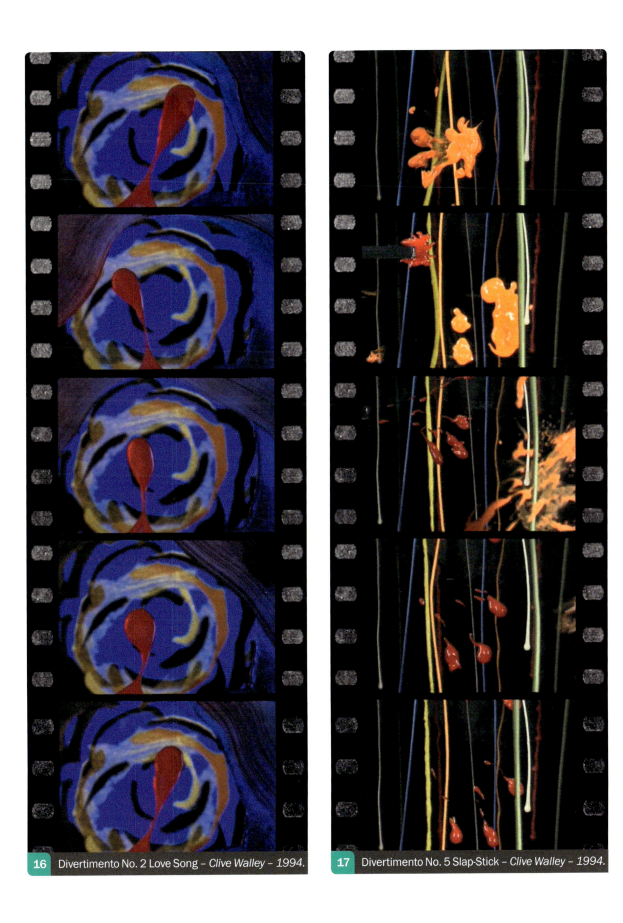

16  Divertimento No. 2 Love Song – *Clive Walley* – *1994*.

17  Divertimento No. 5 Slap-Stick – *Clive Walley* – *1994*.

*Dark Matter (No. 6)* is tonal, transitioning between black and white several times, reminding us that film is an illusion of light.

Walley's films are not mere documentations of a static painting. Rather they invite us to journey with the paint as it searches for a place to settle in the composition. Seeing the texture and liquidity of the paint blown up on the screen brings us intimately close to the material. Walley applies animation fundamentals like squash and stretch, anticipation and follow-through, and easing to make the paint come alive and engage our attention.

Even in its most non-representational formations, the paint has undeniable personality under Walley's masterful hand.

> I was working at a time when gestural painting was still just about viable in the art world. The Americans who took over this tradition of painting from the Europeans weren't shy about the "personality" in their paint. I wanted to take up their endangered tradition and help to point to its revelatory relations with the human body, and hoped I would revivify painting in general at the same time.[14]

Later in this chapter we will examine some of the specific animation techniques Walley uses in this series. A prolific filmmaker, Walley created dozens of films, branching out into live action and, most recently, installation, but always staying intimately connected to his material: the paint.

## Alexander Petrov

In 1989, a new approach to paint-on-glass swept through the festival circuit, gathering awards and glowing reviews. It was Alexander Petrov's *The Cow* (1989), and to use the words of his future producer, Pascal Blais, "It was like seeing a Rembrandt come to life."[15] Working on a backlit sheet of glass with translucent oil paint, the Russian animator varies the thickness of the paint, manipulating not only the color but also the luminescent quality coming to the camera. Watching Petrov work, you will note the deft flicks and dabs of his fingers that sometimes seem more precise than the finest brushes. "Working directly like this with my fingers is faster; it's the shortest route from my mind to the image I am making."[16] **18**

After the critical success of *The Cow*, which received an Oscar nomination in 1990, Petrov was able to further develop his paint-on-glass technique with *The Dream of a Ridiculous Man* (1992) and *The Mermaid* (1996), the latter also nominated for an Oscar. With the help and encouragement of Canadian animator Martine Chartrand, Petrov then partnered with Pascal Blais Studio in Canada for his most well known work *The Old Man and the Sea* (1999). **19**

Based on Ernest Hemingway's story of an aging fisherman's battle with a giant marlin, the real character in the film is the sea, which is both a comforting presence and the old man's antagonist. This 20-minute epic is full of moving water and oceanic expanses of paint. Petrov filmed ref-

**18** *Alexander Petrov with the storyboard for* The Old Man and the Sea. *Courtesy of Pascal Blais Studios.*

erence footage and studied water movements intently in order to convey the depth and breadth of this moody character. To accurately animate the rocking fishing boat on the restless water, he and his son Dimitri made a wooden model of the boat and filmed it from many angles to use as reference. *The Old Man and the Sea* was the first animated film released on the IMAX. Each fingerprint and brush stroke would be magnified on the immense screen, so Petrov had to more than double the size of his paint-on-glass surface, to nearly 30 inches. Thanks to funding and production assistance from several partners,[17] Petrov was able to take full advantage of live video playback and a motion-controlled camera to guide and aid the animation. With only the light and movement to focus on, Petrov reached new heights of painted reality in this richly detailed film. **20**

Petrov's painting style is decidedly within the bounds of romantic realism. Thus, when the refined

**19** *The* Old Man and the Sea *– Alexander Petrov – 1999. Courtesy of Pascal Blais Studios.*

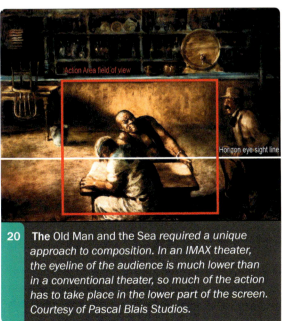

**20** *The* Old Man and the Sea *required a unique approach to composition. In an IMAX theater, the eyeline of the audience is much lower than in a conventional theater, so much of the action has to take place in the lower part of the screen. Courtesy of Pascal Blais Studios.*

**Animated Anecdote** Though Petrov relied on the computer to control the camera movements, the director of photography and motion control camera operator, Serguei Rechetnikoff, was known to double check every calculation and frequently correct the computer. Says producer, Pascal Blais, "The computer wasn't accurate enough for IMAX. It was accurate enough for 35mm, but when it came down to IMAX sometimes it would square off a digit or two. He would change these figures. He was more precise than the actual computer... His log book is an art work that you could frame and hang in a museum."[18] **21**

**21** *Petrov and director of photography Serguei Rechetnikoff, with the custom built IMAX animation camera. The camera was so tall the crew had to cut a hole in the ceiling of the house they were working in so the column would extend to the second floor. Courtesy of Pascal Blais Studios.*

images melt into abstractions of color and light during scene transitions, it is all the more surprising and dazzling. Often they became the artist's favorite parts of the film:

> It's enough to create expressive strokes, creating dynamic movement. This expressiveness beautifies the movement, and I sometime stop and admire the individual frames when I edit the film, because the image that is created in this quick, stream of consciousness way, possesses a unique strength inside.[19] 22

22 *Alexander Petrov at work. Courtesy of Pascal Blais Studios.*

Working 10–12 hours a day, six days a week, Petrov and his team were able to produce 50 seconds of animation a month. Even at that rapid pace, it took two and a half years to make the 29,000 frames that make up the film. All the hard work paid off in 2000, when he finally stepped on to the stage to accept his Academy Award. He has since made another Oscar-nominated film, *My Love* (2006), as well as several commercial works in his signature style. Working with his son, Dimitri, and the occasional group of students and apprentices, Petrov continues to incorporate new technology to make the paint-on-glass technique more versatile.

## Exploring the Technique

### Exercise

### Motion Painting

Before we get into all the variations of applied technique, let's start with a warm-up exercise. Taking inspiration from Oskar Fischinger, we will make a motion painting. You can use whatever painting style and technique feels most comfortable. All you need is a top light setup and a camera to record your brush strokes as they build into a painting. You can use any type of paint and painting surface. The idea is to document how a painting comes into being from an animator's perspective, frame-by-frame.

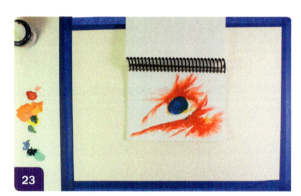

1. To begin, draw a few concept sketches on paper. This will make getting those first strokes on the blank canvas a little easier. However, as you work on the painting, also let the process direct you. If an idea pops into your head while you are painting, follow it and see where it leads. You may end up with a completely different painting than you intended.

2. Do a small color test on a scrap piece of paper. Use this to adjust the lights and exposure settings on the camera. If you start with just the white canvas you may find the image underexposed once it is covered with paint. **23**

3. Begin by taking two seconds of the empty canvas as a lead-in. This will give you the option to dissolve in or add a title later.

4. Now, start your painting. Start with one stroke, or the beginning of a stroke, then take a frame. Continue adding strokes and taking frames. **24**

   To think like an animator, you must break down your painting strokes into frame-sized movements. Where you might normally apply a large, sweeping stroke with one swift gesture of your arm, you must now paint that same stroke in increments. Pointillism, growing lines, and expanding shapes work very well under the camera. Remember that the secret to good animation is in the timing and spacing. What happens between the frames will determine how the animation unfolds.

5. Continue working on your painting, recording frames as you go. Below are some things to consider as you work. **25**

   *Think of the paint as having personality.* Is it tentative or confident? Energetic or languid? Allow your own attitude to run down through your arm and into the movements you use to apply the paint.

   *Vary the timing and spacing of your strokes to create changes in speed.* One common pitfall with painters is that we have a tendency to apply uniform strokes so that movement always goes at the same steady speed. Ease in and out of different stages of the painting. Develop a rhythm, making some moments in the painting happen fast, taking only a few frames, while others meander slowly along. Work in some pauses where little or nothing is happening so the viewers can have a moment to catch up with the flurry of visual activity.

   *Work with the entire frame.* You are the choreographer of this painting. Movement will draw the viewer's eye and you have control over which part

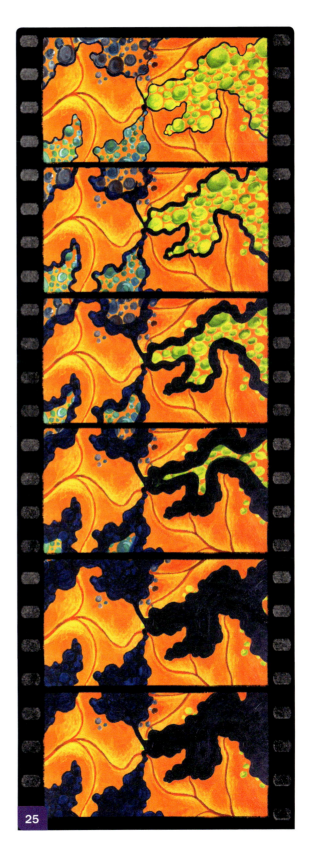

25

of the painting is moving. You can work around the entire canvas so movement is everywhere, or focus on one precise area. Lead the viewer through the painting.

*Work with your materials.* If using acrylics, let the paint dry and come back to apply new layers, allowing the texture to build. If oils, push globs of wet paint around the canvas incrementally, taking frames as you go along, leaving trails as part of your design. You can even use watercolor and allow the spreading drying of the paint to become part of the motion. Try using sponges or your fingers to apply the paint with different textures.

*Above all, enjoy the process of painting.*

6. Once you are done, export and process your frames. Then try playing it with different musical tracks. Remember Fischinger's analogy of a meandering path along the banks of a musical river. At some points, our motion painting will come quite close to the flow of the music and at other points we will be off on our own visual adventure in the distance. Without any planned syncing, our minds will naturally bring together the two independently created works into moments that coincide perfectly.

## Setting up the Studio

So, that wasn't so intimidating, was it? Now that we are all warmed up, let's examine the diversity of choices when it comes to painting under the camera. Creating fluid, animated motion with wet paint can be accomplished in many ways. As we progress, we'll take a closer look into the working methods of the pioneering and currently practicing artists that have made this such a diverse technique.

### Your Painting Surface

Glass is the most common surface for painting under the camera – so common that the technique is frequently referred to as "paint-on-glass." Glass allows for both top lighting and backlighting. It also allows you to isolate certain layers with a multiplane. However, the paint does not always adhere well to the perfectly smooth surface of the glass. You'll find it wants to squish out from under your brush or fingers leaving inconsistent patches. If you are going for full, even coverage rather than a translucent look, this can be frustrating. Some artists use Plexiglas to avoid this problem because it has a more porous surface than glass.

Another approach is to tape an acetate cel to the glass surface and paint on the acetate, also a more porous surface. An additional benefit to the cel is that by making a hinge out of a piece of tape, you can also place a reference drawing underneath the acetate as a guide and fold it back before shooting each frame. **27** Also, working on acetate allows you to save the final frame of a shot as a finished painting – just take off the cel and let it dry.

> **Animated Anecdote**
> 
> *Using cels was a favored technique of French-Canadian animator, Martine Chartrand. Early in her career, she traveled to Russia to study with the great master Alexander Petrov and brought a stack of cels. When Petrov saw the convenience of being able to slip a reference under the cel, he immediately adopted the idea into his process.*

26  *Sheila Sofian animates on opaque Plexiglas because the paint adheres to it better.*

The size of your canvas should be whatever is comfortable. A small working area requires less paint and less time to fill the space with imagery, but will limit the amount of details you can create. **28** A larger area allows broader painting gestures, and more room to create textures and details in the paintings. **29**

Many artists have developed useful modifications to their workspace. Animator Patrick Jenkins started painting on Plexiglas for his film *Labyrinth* (2008). He then moved to boards covered with white and black linoleum, again because the texture on the linoleum helped the paint adhere to the surface. Jenkins made further customizations to his painting surface so he could work at an easel:

> For ergonomic reasons, I had special panels made so that I could take the paintings off the stand and animate in a more comfortable position. The panels have registration holes on the back that are placed over the holes in the animation stand so that everything lines up.[20] **30**

**27** Martine Chartrand animates on sheets of thin Plexiglas. Martine Chartrand ©2006 National Film Board of Canada. Photo Credit: Caroline Hayeur. All rights reserved.

**28** Caroline Leaf working on The Interview (1979). Caroline Leaf ©National Film Board of Canada, All rights reserved.

**29** Lynn Smith's working surface at the NFB. The large area allowed her to add many details in the faces and expressions. Photo credit: Irene Blei.

## Fluid Frames: The Transforming Painting

**30** Pegs on Jenkins's camera stand match holes on the back of his linoleum board, enabling him to paint more comfortably. Courtesy of Patrick Jenkins.

When working on the painted sequences in *The Sound Collector* (1982), Lynn Smith invented a way to get a perfect black background: she draped a piece of black velvet under the glass. Unlike most black fabrics or paper, which still reflect a small amount of light, the tiny fibers that make velvet velvety keep the light from bouncing back to the camera. The gentle curve of the fabric is essential, acting like a black hole that absorbs all the light, delivering a consistent, beautiful black.

> Back [when I was working on *The Sound Collector*], the technicians in the NFB lab asked how I was able to achieve such a rich, dark, black. They were amazed that it was almost as black as the 35mm frame lines.[21]

To replicate this in your studio, drape a piece of black velvet in an even curve from the sides of the glass, creating a smooth bowl-shape about three to six inches underneath the center of the glass. **31**

With this method, there is no longer any need for black paint, which can quickly muddy any other colors on the surface. Smith uses this technique for line work as well as backgrounds:

**31** Lynn Smith's camera stand: you can see the draped velvet through the glass. Also note the black curtain against the wall to minimize reflected light, and the anti-fatigue mat on the floor. The stand was built by George Perkins in 1972 and recently modified for a digital camera. Courtesy of Lynn Smith.

**32** Robbe Vervaeke's large-scale painting easel. Courtesy of Robbe Vervaeke.

When I needed a black line, I would just draw a line in the paint with a wooden cuticle stick or Q-tip and that revealed the black from the velvet below the glass. This was read by the camera as a black line.[22]

To show just how customizable you can make your working surface, let's look into the studio of Belgian animator Robbe Vervaeke. At the beginning of his first painted film, *Erszebet* (2008), Vervaeke started with a traditional 12-field surface under a rostrum camera. After seeing the first tests projected on a big screen, he felt the small brush strokes were not narrating the story effectively. Taking a recycled window pane he mounted it upright on a metal easel and began painting much bigger. **32**

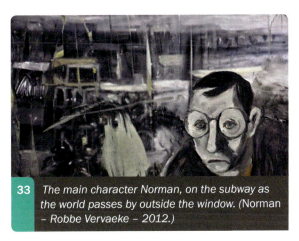

**33** *The main character Norman, on the subway as the world passes by outside the window. (Norman – Robbe Vervaeke – 2012.)*

> I want to feel my wrist while I'm painting. Animators get educated in 12 field, so they automatically start with that size, but it's not always appropriate. It all depends on what you want on screen when you project your film . . . When I made that glass plate I could put my lighting wherever I wanted and that created that unique, greasy feel you've got in my films. In my films, the lighting comes from everywhere, which makes the painting a three-dimensional object.[23]

Vervaeke refined and expanded his setup with the film *Norman* (2012), adding multiple layers and lighting variations. **33**

The bold brush strokes propel the animation forward with an appropriately heavy hand for this film on obsessive voyeurism. Vervaeke uses the two layers to his advantage, frequently positioning his characters in front of windows so the glass he is painting on doubles as the window pane in a scene. The large scale of the painting surface also highlights the architecturally robust background paintings by Brecht-Jan Verschuere. **34**

**34** *Brecht-Jan Verschuere painting one of the backgrounds for* Norman. *Courtesy of Robbe Vervaeke.*

In different scenes, Vervake moves the background panel to create a pan or changes the lighting so it casts moving shadows on the painting. In one scene after a car wreck, he paints Norman behind an actual shattered pane of glass. **35**

By moving things around in his studio, Vervaeke breaks through the two-dimensional plane of the cinema to a more theatrical setting where the paint takes the spotlight.

**35** *Shattered glass in front of the painted animation. (Norman – Robbe Vervaeke – 2012.)*

## Different Types of Paint

There are the water-based paints and oil-based paints. Both are used under the camera and have specific advantages and drawbacks.

Water-based paints, like tempera or gouache, are the choice of Caroline Leaf, Patrick Jenkins, Sheila Sofian, Lee Whitmore, Michaela Müller, and Lynn Smith. These paints are water soluble and easy to clean up. Gouache and tempera can be applied in a thick, opaque layer, or can be very thin and translucent. However, being water based, they dry out quickly, especially under hot studio lights. Several drops of glycerin mixed into the paint will keep it from drying too quickly. Glycerin is usually in the first aid section of most drugstores. **36**

Lynn Smith also uses gouache for her paint-on-glass films. She prepares her gouache according to these principles:

> Water plays an important part in maintaining the right consistency. The key is finding the right proportion between the paint, the water and the glycerin. If you use too much glycerin, or too much water, some line work can fill in. And if there is not enough glycerin, of course, the paint dries. The paint and the water and the glycerin need to be stirred together before being applied to the surface onto which you will be animating. The paint does not need to be continually stirred, but you may need to dabble some glycerin on the paint that is on your palette if you find the paint is beginning to dry.[25]

> "The paint is an actor – in a very subtle way, of course, but it does act."[24]
> 
> – Robbe Vervaeke

Sheila Sofian suggests experimenting with brands, because each brand will have different qualities:

> I use the cheap tempera poster paints. I find that sometimes the chemistry varies depending on the colors I get. So there are times I have bought paint that doesn't work out, where it's completely translucent. It does not become opaque. It's always a challenge to try to find the perfect kind of paint in the right colors that work for me.[26]

Oil-based paints are used by Alexander Petrov, Martine Chartrand, Xin Li, Robbe Vervaeke, and Clive Walley. Painters who are used to managing the studio practice attached to oils will find they are easy to manipulate under the camera. **37**

**36** Painting with gouache and glycerin.

**37** Robbe Vervaeke's palette on either side of his painting. Courtesy of Robbe Vervaeke.

> **Animated Anecdote**
> 
> In her film *The Street*, Caroline Leaf used gouache and black ink. To keep the paint from drying she mixed in a substance called Colorfloat, something cel painters used to use to keep their paint from cracking on flexible acetate cels.

As with any oil painting, make sure you have a well-ventilated studio, especially if you are using any sort of turpentine for cleaning. Though not as problematic as water-based paints, oils can also dry and lose their malleability over the long process of animating a scene, especially when used in a thin layer on a light box, so it is common to add some sort of lubricant. If you are working on a backlit surface, the grease must be translucent to preserve the vibrancy of the paint.

Martine Chartrand uses a clear grease called Superlube in a 1:1 ratio with the paint and Alexander Petrov has adopted her recipe as well. When I made *Ash Sunday*, a top lit film, I added a little bit of petroleum jelly to my oils, which gave a very sticky consistency that could be mounded into little piles. Robbe Vervaeke works quickly and finds he does not need any additives to his paint, only a little linseed oil to retain the liquid quality.

While you may be able to push the wet paint into new positions each frame and reuse certain portions of the painting, you will inevitably be wiping away stray bits and adding fresh paint to new areas. If you are using more than one color, the different colors will mix and contaminate each other and must be removed. To prepare for this, mix up plenty of your colors, keeping them in covered jars or containers so you will have a consistent palette to work from and not run out halfway through a scene.

> **Animated Anecdote**
>
> *During her animation apprenticeship with Alexander Petrov, Martine Chartrand used his recipe, mixing oil paint with a few drops of black grease. The resulting colors were darkened and sometimes dried and became unworkable. Upon her return to Canada, Chartrand tried many different oils and greases, determined to find a better solution. In 1996, she went to repair her bicycle and the repair man showed her Campagnolo Crystal 7, a clear bicycle grease. When it was mixed equally with the oil paint, the colors kept the brightness, the paint was easy to work with, and never dried! She passed on her discovery to Petrov when he came to Canada to make* The Old Man and the Sea. *After Campagnolo stopped producing this product, Chartrand repeated her experiment and now uses Superlube. The recipe has been passed on to many animators through Chartrand and Petrov since.*

## Lighting

Painting under the camera works well with either top light or backlight. Top light brings out the dimensional quality of the paint and allows for brilliant color. Among artists that work with top light are Lynn Smith, Caroline Leaf, Lee Whitmore, Patrick Jenkins, Robbe Vervaeke, and Sheila Sofian. You can apply the paint quite thickly so it completely covers the working surface, or you can allow the background to show through as a base color. **38**

With top lights, you may notice the highlights shining off the wet paint, frequently on the outer part of the frame where the paint is at a slightly different angle to the light. To some degree this can be resolved by adjusting the light placement, or by adding a diffusion sheet or graduated filter in front of the light. However, many artists accept the highlights as an integral part of the material, keeping the audience aware of the wet, pliability of the paint. **39**

**38** *Top lighting provides vibrant even color. (The Safe House – Lee Whitmore – 2006.)*

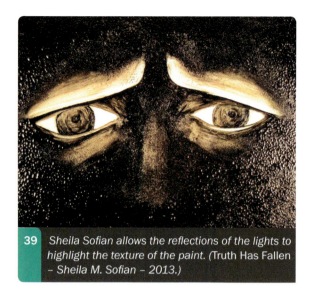

**39** Sheila Sofian allows the reflections of the lights to highlight the texture of the paint. (Truth Has Fallen – Sheila M. Sofian – 2013.)

**40** Backlighting provides beautiful contrast in Petrov's The Old Man and the Sea – 1999. Courtesy of Pascal Blais Studios.

One problem with top lighting is the shadows from the paint cast through the glass onto the surface below. If you cannot eliminate shadows by adjusting lighting, try animating on opaque Plexiglas, linoleum panel, or a thin sheet of acetate.

For backlight you will need translucent oils or very thin gouache or tempera. Most paints are opaque to some degree, so again, experiment with brands. The more light that comes through, the more vibrant the color. **40**

Artists that work backlit include Alexander Petrov, Martine Chartrand, and Xin Li. The setup is the same sort of light box you would use for sand animation. Like sand, the thickness of the paint becomes a part of your palette, allowing you to render dark to light with only a few colors. And don't forget you also have the option to combine top and backlight to get the particular benefits of both methods.

## Things to Have in Your Studio

Painting under the camera is a rhythm of applying and removing paint. The tools you use for each part of the dance will contribute to the overall style of the film. To apply the paint, you can use brushes, your fingers, sponges, or really anything that might seem useful. I find oil brushes are great, even with the water-based techniques, because the added glycerin makes the paint more viscous. Using your fingers gives you a wonderful connection to the surface and the paint, with great potential for blending and smearing the colors. You can also use rubber stamps, different types of sponges, or woven cloth to create textures in the paint. **41** A pointed stick, like a cuticle stick or a kebab skewer, lets you draw lines in the paint. **42**

Have plenty of paper towels and rags on hand for removing paint and wiping your fingers and brushes. Patrick Jenkins buys Q-tips in bulk and goes through hundreds for a scene. The precise, linear quality of his animation shows a particular attention to cleanliness. **43**

In *Conversation with Haris* (2001), Sheila Sofian used a large, wet sea sponge to dab away the paint a little bit at a time. Images decompose before our eyes, symbolizing the devastation caused by the Balkan War. **44**

The Transforming Painting  Chapter 5

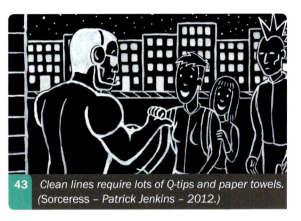

43  *Clean lines require lots of Q-tips and paper towels. (Sorceress – Patrick Jenkins – 2012.)*

41  *Lynn Smith used a checkerboard stamp to make the table cloth in this scene from Soup of the Day. Soup of the Day ©2013 National Film Board of Canada, All rights reserved.*

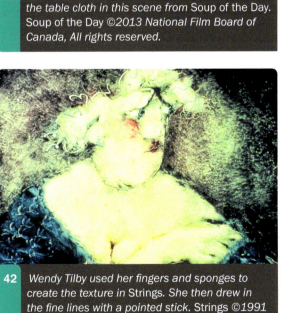

42  *Wendy Tilby used her fingers and sponges to create the texture in Strings. She then drew in the fine lines with a pointed stick. Strings ©1991 National Film Board of Canada, All rights reserved.*

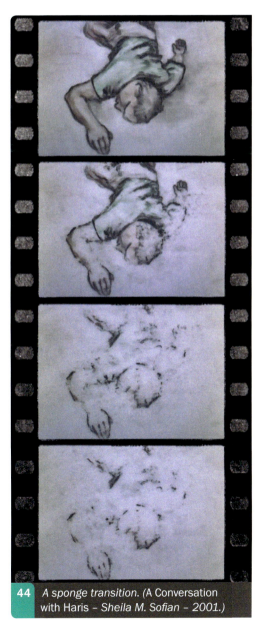

44  *A sponge transition. (A Conversation with Haris – Sheila M. Sofian – 2001.)*

Sofian finds all sorts of unusual ways to transition out of her scenes, sometimes wiping across the frame with a dry brush to smear the image away, sometimes saturating the tempera with water so it melts before our eyes.

### Exercise

## Finger Painting Portrait with Sponge Transition

In this exercise, we will animate a simple portrait breathing in and opening its eyes. We will work monochromatically so we don't have to worry about colors mixing and we will paint mostly with our fingers, so prepare to get messy!

In addition to a standard top lit camera set up, you will need:

- Plenty of paper towels and Q-tips
- Paint mixed with a non-drying agent. I'll be using gouache with glycerin for this exercise, but you can also use oils.
- A large bowl of water
- Artist's sponge.

1. Set the frame rate to 12fps.

2. Choose your favorite color. Start with a 1:2 ratio of glycerin to paint and a few drops of water. If you find the paint is drying too quickly, add a few more drops of glycerin. **45**

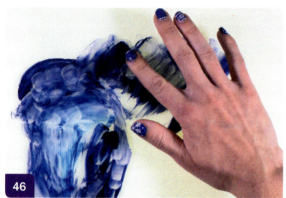

3. Dip your fingers into the paint and spread it around the glass. Enjoy getting messy and get a feel for the viscosity of the paint. **46** If it feels too thick and sticky, add a few drops of water. If it seems to be drying and flaking in parts, add more glycerin.

4. Create a face from the shoulders up with eyes closed. You will probably need to paint and repaint several times as you get used to the material. **47** **48**

The Transforming Painting  Chapter 5    141

Maintaining an experimental frame of mind means not getting too attached to our own work. If something's not working, just smear it out and start again. It may take a little time before you get used to how the paint moves under your fingers and on the glass. Eventually, you will begin to understand how to apply and move the paint into the shapes you want. Remember that this is only the first of many variations of this figure that we will be creating so it does not need to be perfect. Work with a very simple, stylized design, if that makes it easier. **49** If you feel like you need to use a brush or Q-tip to work in some fine details, don't hold back. **50**

5. Once you have an image you are pleased with, take a frame. **51**

We will hold on this position for six frames. If you wish you can create an evolving hold. Lightly touch the wet paint, or gently run your finger along the textures you've created. Focus on just a few areas of the image – the eyes, the face, the skin. Too much movement in an evolving hold can be overwhelming. Take a frame and repeat until you reach six frames. The subtle shimmer in the texture will give the painting a feeling of life that anticipates our first movement.

49

50

51

6. To anticipate the action of opening her eyes, my lady will take a deep breath. Breathe in and observe what your body does. Your chest moves out and up and your head lifts slightly. This is the movement we want to replicate in our animation. Here's a quick sketch I did with a timing chart to plan out the movement. **52**

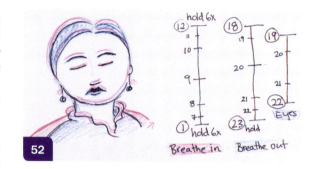

Notice I eased out of the first position and into the second, taking six frames overall for the breath in. Animate this action. Draw the outline of the next frame in the existing paint with a pointe, then work the existing paint out to that guide line. Drawing in a guide before we completely destroy the existing image gives us something to aim for as we push the paint around. **53**

7. Now we will hold again for six frames before breathing out and opening the eyes. If you used an evolving hold at the beginning, make another one here. Note on my timing chart the breath out takes only four frames and starts one frame before the eyes start to open. Offsetting complementary actions (like the breath out and the eyes opening) makes a more dynamic movement.

The Transforming Painting  Chapter 5     143

54

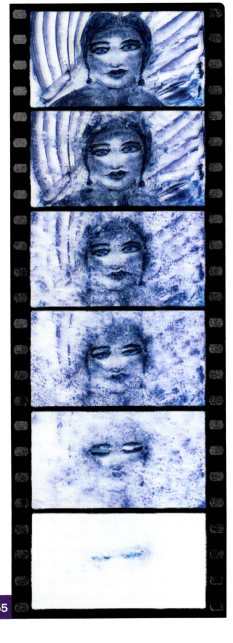

55

8. At the end of the animation, I create another hold, just to give the movement a sense of finality. Since she is wearing dangly earrings, I also have to finish the overlapping action, which takes me a full 16 frames! Whew! I am sort of regretting those earrings, but once they are animated, they do add a bit more personality to the action. 54

9. If you wish to continue animating on this image, by all means carry on. Try tilting the character's head or changing the expression. Once you have finished animating, we will disintegrate the image using Sheila Sofian's sponge dabbing technique.

10. With a damp sponge, gently dab the image working from the outside in. (If you have an evolving hold at the end of your sequence, you must continue that for the first several frames of the sponge transition, otherwise it will look like your animation stops abruptly.) If you are working with oils and water doesn't dilute them, try spraying a few squirts of glass cleaner on the image as you dab away. Take a frame and continue dabbing, taking frames as you go. Work your way into toward the eyes, so they are the last part of the image that disappears. 55

> **#ProTip** *Finger painting is fun. To keep your skin from absorbing all the chemicals from paints, rub on a skin protectant. It acts like an invisible glove to protect your skin from absorbing oil-soluble materials. Your hands will thank you at the end of the day.*

## Digital Approaches to Paint-on-Glass

Many of the compositing techniques discussed in the chapter on sand animation are also applicable for paint-on-glass. Of course, many of the same challenges translate into this technique as well. Though not as problematic as in sand animation, the "halo effect" will sometimes be apparent in painted footage, more often with feathery brush strokes. Transparency between layers is also a challenge, particularly with backlit footage, so the same compositing techniques will come in useful here. **56**

**56** *In this shot, Xin Li used After Effects to animate a painted layer of water and smoke and to animate the subtle movement of the receeding ship. (A Tale of Longing – Xin Li – 2012.)*

Painting allows for a fully robust color palette, but it is also ideal for manipulating colors in post. Patrick Jenkins used color shifting to create a wild strobe effect for this transformation scene in *Sorceress* (2012). **57**

Inverting footage, replacing colors, and experimenting with blending modes on your painted footage broadens the possibilities of what the paint can achieve.

## Green Screen

One additional compositing technique which we haven't discussed yet is keying with a green screen. Green screen techniques are commonly used in every aspect of motion picture production, from special effects, to stopmotion animation, to your daily weather forecast. The computer is able to analyze the image and remove every pixel that has a certain color value, making that part of the image transparent. Then we can place whatever background we want behind it and add additional layers to the animation. The color to be removed can really be any color, but a bright, pure green is generally the most effective. This is some green

**57** *This strobing transformation was achieved through various color shifts applied to the individual frames in post. (Sorceress – Patrick Jenkins – 2012.)*

**58** *Green screen set-up for paint-on-glass.*

fabric I got at the craft store. Nothing fancy here. It's all in how you set it up. 58

We want an even, consistent color in our green backdrop so the computer doesn't miss any pixels that need to be removed. The farther you can get your painting surface from the green backdrop, the more diffuse any shadows will be. Here my glass is about six inches above the green backdrop. If you look closely, you can see a little bit of diffused shadow from the painted image and the edges of my glass.

If that becomes a problem in the compositing, I can eliminate that completely by lighting the green backdrop separately with an additional light and using a bigger piece of glass that extends beyond the green fabric. However, I did a test shot before I started animating and found that the slight shadows here did not affect the keying so I'm not going to worry about them.

One additional way to smooth out the green backdrop is setting a shallow depth of field on the camera. This means the painted image close to the camera will be in sharp focus while the green backdrop will blur slightly. This will smooth out any texture from the cloth and soften any subtle shadows I wasn't able to eliminate with lighting.

To get a good composite, we must apply the paint quite thickly so all the green is covered. Any slight hints of green coming through the center of our painting will become transparent. The edge of the painting is especially important. A clean smooth edge will composite much better than something rough or feathery. And, of course, we are restricted in our choice of colors. Any greens or yellows that are close to the color of the green screen will be affected by the keying process and may disappear altogether. So, there are limitations to this technique, but if we can work within them, we can add numerous moving layers to our work.

## Creating the Layers

Working in layers requires some careful planning so everything will come together seamlessly during compositing. Let's take a look at what goes into the scene of a theme park romance. 60

Here I have painted my background. I used Lynn Smith's black velvet backdrop to get the rich black behind the paint. 61

#ProTip *Another approach that eliminates all shadows is to paint directly on the green surface.*
*Robbe Vervaeke uses a large sheet of green glass as his painting surface. He bought this giant glass sheet from a company that designs modern bathrooms. You could also paint on an acetate cel that is taped to a piece of glass or linoleum that is spray-painted green.* 59

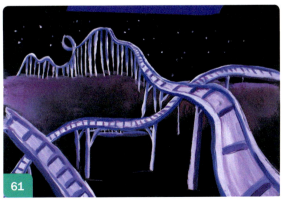

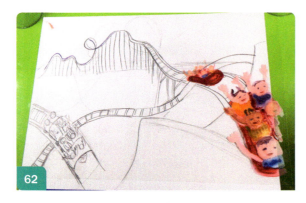

Next, using an animation guide under a cel, I animated the roller coasters zipping along the tracks. I folded back the guide before shooting each frame so the roller coasters will be on a green background. **62**

Now for the main part of the animation. Here are the two characters having their tête-à-tête against the green background. **63**

Finally, I animated the seat of the car the couple is in. This one I did using the black velvet again because I liked the way the thin red paint looked with the black behind it. I've made a strong outline so I can use the Paint Bucket effect on this sequence. **64**

Let's head over to After Effects with all these separate layers to bring them together.

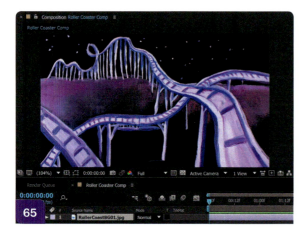

### Exercise

## Compositing the Roller Coaster of Luv

1. In After Effects, create a new composition at 1920x1080 24fps and import all the assets for the scene. Interpret each frame sequence at 12fps by right-clicking on the sequence and choosing Interpret Footage.

2. Drag the background image into the composition. **65**

The Transforming Painting  Chapter 5    147

66

3. We'll start with the animation of the roller coasters in the background. Place the FarCoaster sequence over the background layer. To remove the green screen, we will use After Effects powerful Keylight plug-in, which comes bundled with Adobe CC. **66** You can find this by searching in the Effects and Presets Panel and drag it onto the roller coaster layer.

4. Click on the color swatch in the Keylight effects panel and use the Eye Dropper to select the green screen color. Poof! Magically it disappears! We're done, right? **67** **68** Well, not quite.

5. If I turn off the background layer, I can see there is quite a bit of "garbage" still in the image. This is from some inconsistencies in the lighting and residue on the glass. We need to clean this up. **69**

67

68

69

6. First, let's make a quick Garbage Matte and set a few keyframes to get rid of anything outside the path of the roller coaster. **70**

   That takes care of a good deal of the garbage, but there's still a little bit around the coaster. I can minimize this by adjusting the *Keylight* settings, particularly the *Screen Gain* and *Screen Balance*. **71** Now things are looking much better!

7. Now load in the NearCoaster sequence. You can copy and paste the Keylight effect from the first layer onto the others by selecting the effect, Copy (Ctrl C), then selecting the new footage and Paste (Ctrl V). This gives you a starting point, but you will still need to adjust the Gain and Balance settings specifically for this layer.

   > **#ProTip** *There are quite a few tutorials online for fine-tuning difficult footage with Keylight, including using Key Cleaner and Advanced Spill Suppressor. If you are having trouble getting a good key, start digging in the online resources. For the most part, Keylight will do a great job.*

8. Add the Kiss sequence and copy and paste the Keylight values to this layer and begin your fine-tuning.

9. You will notice in the Kiss sequence that the Gain and Balance settings need to be pushed quite far to get a clean key because the paint is a bit too thin on the characters' faces and the hair has some feathering. This is a case where adding the Advanced Spill Suppressor effect is very useful. Search for it in the Effects and Presets panel and apply it to the layer.

10. When using the Advance Spill Suppressor in combination with Keylight, set View > Intermediate Result. This disables Keylight's native spill suppressor, which otherwise interferes with the Advanced Spill Suppressor effect. **72**

70

71

72

The Transforming Painting  Chapter 5

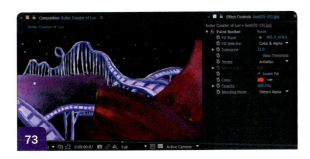

Once the Advance Spill Suppressor is applied, readjust the Gain and Balance until the footage looks good. Always scrub through the footage to see if any frames need additional adjustment.

11. The Seat layer was the simplest to paint, but I have the most complex plans for it in post. Position the frame sequence above the background roller coasters but behind the kissing couple. Then use the Paint Bucket effect outlined in Chapter 4 to remove the black background, since Keylight only works with color value information. 73

12. Drag the footage into the composition and position the first frame of the sequence so the first frame of movement on the seat matches the first frame of movement on the couple. We will extend the first frame of the footage using Time Remap to fill the first two seconds. Right-click on the layer and choose Time> Enable Time Remapping (Ctrl Alt T). This places two time-based keyframes – one at the first frame and one at the last frame. 74 Now we can grab the beginning of the footage and drag it back as if it had infinite frames.

13. Now we will add a little bit of movement to the foreground, as if the couple's car is just going over the top of the first rise on the roller coaster. First, I'll parent the Seat layer to the Kiss layer using the Whip Pick Tool (click and drag). 75 Now they will both move together as I set some keyframes for the position and rotation on the parent layer, making it slowly go over the edge. 76

6. The nice thing about having animation on separate layers is we can adjust the timing in other places too. With the NearCoaster sequence, I can move its start point later in the timeline to have it swish by just as the couple moves in for the kiss, adding a little bit of romantic tension. **77**

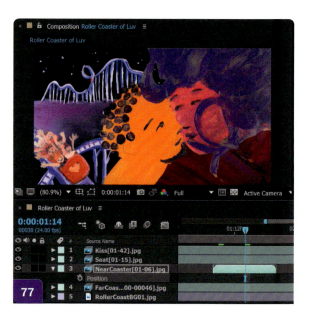

Now we have a fully composited scene with all our layers working together. Green screen work can be very rewarding and efficient, but it does have its limitations. Whether you are working in-camera on a multiplane or compositing layers in the computer, separating and coordinating the different parts of a scene require careful planning and attention to digital details.

## Moving Beyond the Glass

As we think about what digital workflow can bring to under-the-camera animation, Clive Walley deserves a closer look. Walley brought a new dimension to painting with his highly engineered, multiplane rig. His films have a feeling of 3D space that is captivating. Working in virtual environments, we now have the opportunity to expand upon this idea further. While extensive 3D animation is well beyond the scope of this book, a closer look at some of Walley's techniques may inspire you to pursue this avenue of exploration on your own. With 3D software, you can essentially recreate "The Rig" digitally, by placing your abstract painted elements, shot on a green screen or otherwise composited, in a virtual space where you can animate the camera, lighting, and layers. Walley's films seem spontaneous, but they required meticulous planning and detailed exposure charts to keep the camera moves and lighting shifts on track. Ultimately, there were physical limits to what he could do. The wonderful thing about working digitally is that the 3D environment becomes an open canvas for experiments in camera and lighting techniques. Let's take a closer look at some of Walley's films for inspiration, thinking first about how we can recreate them digitally, which will then lead us to how we might build upon his ideas and take them into a yet unexplored dimension.

The vivacity in Walley's films is due largely to the sense that the camera is a character itself. It scrambles through Walley's abstract environment, chasing the dancing paint. In *And Now You* (1991), the viewer is taken on a journey through a network of painted tunnels. The film is a point-of-view shot moving through the environment, much like the aesthetic of a video game. **78**

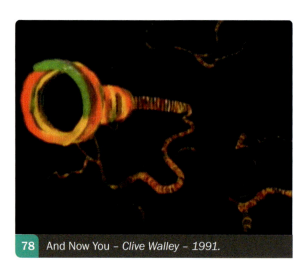

**78** And Now You – *Clive Walley* – 1991.

The illusion of endless, twisting tunnels comes from Walley stacking circles of paint on the rig and incrementally bringing them toward the camera. The circles change their shape and color, and we encounter painted oddities along the way. `79`

To replicate these effects with a hybrid technique, I created a series of painted circles on a green screen. I then keyed out the background and stacked them using After Effects 3D. In Figure 80 you can see the layers spaced out with two lights (offset to provide some variation). Each circle was the same size when I painted it, but After Effects 3D gives the impression of perspective. I can create keys to move the layers along the X, Y, and Z axes, just as Walley moved the stacked panes of glass under the camera on his rig. `80` `81` Or I could build a complete virtual environment and animate the camera through the layers themselves. The virtual camera in a 3D program becomes a viewpoint without the limits of physical space. We can do a truly infinite pull back, or 360° rotations that give us new perspective on the painted world in a virtual space.

Walley's paint is sometimes slurpy and wet and at other times a rigid entity. In this segment of *Divertimento 1: Winds of Change*, he created sequences of brush strokes with a palette knife on a sheet of glass. After they dried, he could peel them off the

**79** And Now You – *Clive Walley – 1991.*

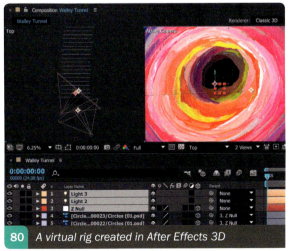

**80** *A virtual rig created in After Effects 3D*

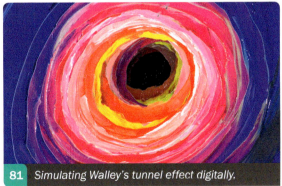

**81** *Simulating Walley's tunnel effect digitally.*

# Fluid Frames: The Transforming Painting

**82** *Walley frequently used dried paint strokes like cut-outs. (Winds and Change – Clive Walley – 1994.)*

glass to animate like cut-outs. Replacing each dried stroke with a new shape every frame, created a leaf-like fluttering effect. **82** Walley also animated other dried paint elements under the camera, like the levers and wheels in this shot. **83** In a digital space, you would create a series of painted strokes as Walley did, capturing them on a green screen background for easy compositing, and then use them as animated elements in your composition. You could add in some animated cycles and moving sequences of paint strokes as well. The digital space becomes a blank canvas for collage with any painted elements you can create. Mix up your paint and start playing under the camera, then take that attitude of spontaneity into your 3D program as you work with the elements imported from the real world. Animate the lights, wrap your painted sequences around modeled shapes, use repetition and cycles to your advantage, change the colors. **84**

Bringing together the digital and physical worlds of artistic creation is the new frontier of animation. There are endless possibilities for an artist that wants to get their hands dirty in the experimental frame of mind. As we wrap up this chapter on painting under the camera, I hope you have an expanded view of the possibilities of this beautiful art form. Here are some additional exercises to use as a jumping off point for further exploration.

The Transforming Painting  Chapter 5

**83** Winds and Change – *Clive Walley* – 1994.

**84** A paint splat collage created by shooting on green screen and compositing in After Effects.

## Additional Exercises

- Use a sponge or brush to animate textures and color evolving across the frame. Note how the repetition of the same brush stroke or sponge dabbing frame-after-frame brushwork creates a natural evolution in the imagery. **85** **86**
- Cover the glass surface with a painted texture and then draw a linear-style animation in the texture by scratching away the paint with a wooden stick or a Q-tip.
- Animate a gradually morphing color by adding a little bit of one color to an abstract texture every frame.
- Animate a walk cycle on a green screen background. Use a set of reference drawings slid under the glass or a cel, or use the Reference Footage function in your frame capture program. Then animate a panning background and composite it behind the walking character.

## Fluid Frames: The Transforming Painting

85  *In* The Orange Umbrella, *I created the evolving painted texture, purely as an abstract exercise. Then I created a cut-out character and animated him in After Effects to interact with the painted environment.* (The Orange Umbrella – *Corrie Francis Parks – 2009.)*

86  The Orange Umbrella – *Corrie Francis Parks – 2009.*

## Notes

1. Moritz, William. *Optical Poetry: The Life and Work of Oskar Fischinger.* Bloomington: Indiana University Press, 2004, p. 128.
2. Whitehall, Richard. "Bildmusik: Art of Oskar Fischinger Exhibition Catalog." Center for Visual Music: Fischinger Research Pages: Fischinger Notes. Long Beach Museum of Art, 1970. Date accessed: Jan. 17, 2015. http://www.centerforvisualmusic.org/Fischinger/CVMFilmNotes2.htm
3. Fischinger, Oskar. "Fischinger Texts: Film Notes, Excerpt from Unpublished Typescript." Center for Visual Music: Fischinger Research Pages: Texts by Fischinger. Collection of Center for Visual Music, c. 1950. Date accessed: March. 9, 2015. http://www.centerforvisualmusic.org/Fischinger/OFFilmnotes.htm
4. Fischinger, Oskar. "Fischinger Texts: Film Notes, From Fischinger's Writings about Motion Painting No. 1, Found on 8 Narrow Strips of Paper." Center for Visual Music: Fischinger Research Pages: Texts by Fischinger. Collection of Center for Visual Music, n.d. Date accessed: Jan. 17, 2015. http://www.centerforvisualmusic.org/Fischinger/OFFilmnotes.htm
5. Jenkins, Patrick. Email interview. Dec. 4, 2014.
6. In an interview with Michael Sporn, Giersz notes that another Polish animator, Piotr Szpakowicz, was also developing his own approach to painting under the camera, in a

very different style. Giersz, Witold. "Witold Giersz Interview." Interview by Marcin Gizycki. Michael Sporn Animation – Splog. Michael Sporn, May 14, 2010. Date accessed: Mar. 13, 2015. http://www.michaelspornanimation.com/splog/?p=2236

7 Frank, Alison. "Wild Horses: Witold Giersz and the Art of Animation." *Sight & Sound Magazine*. British Film Institute, Apr. 15, 2014. Date accessed: Jan. 17, 2015.
8 Giersz, Witold. Email interview. Mar. 4, 2015.
9 "Opening Screenings." *Etudia & Anima Newsletter* 21. MIĘDZYNARODOWY FESTIWAL FILMOWY, Nov. 22, 2014. Date accessed: Jan. 17, 2015.
10 Leaf, Caroline. Telephone interview. Mar. 26, 2014.
11 Blumer, Ronald H. "Smiles in the Sand." *Cinema Canada* (October, 1976): 21–23.
12 Walley, Clive. Email interview. Jan. 5, 2015.
13 Furniss, Maureen. *The Animation Bible: A Practical Guide to the Art of Animating, from Flipbooks to Flash*. New York: Abrams, 2008, p. 222.
14 Walley, Jan. 5, 2015.
15 Carty, Alyson, and Chris Robinson. "*The Old Man and The Sea*: Hands Above The Rest?" Animation World Network, Mar. 1, 2000. Date accessed: Mar. 13, 2015. http://www.awn.com/mag/issue4.12/4.12pages/robinsonoldman.php3
16 Cotte, Olivier. *Secrets of Oscar-winning Animation: Behind the Scenes of 13 Classic Short Animations*. Amsterdam: Elsevier/Focal, 2006, p. 205.
17 Pascal Blais Studios, IMAGICA Corporation, Dentsu Tec. and NHK Enterprise 21.
18 Alyson and Robinson. "*The Old Man and The Sea*."
19 *Alexander Petrov: The Making of "Mermaid" and "The Old Man and the Sea."* Dir. Alexander Petrov. Panorama Animation Film Studio, c. 2000. Dailymotion.com. Subtitles in English by Niffiwan.
20 Jenkins, Dec. 4, 2014.
21 Smith, Lynn. Email interview. Jan. 5, 2015.
22 Ibid.
23 Vervaeke, Robbe. Telephone interview. Feb. 4, 2015.
24 Ibid.
25 Smith, Jan. 5.
26 Sofian, Sheila, Telephone interview. Feb. 22, 2015.

Poznanie – *David Ehrlich* – 2009.

# Chapter 6
# Clay Painting and Beyond

**Notable Pioneers in Clay Painting**

    Ishu Patel
    Joan Gratz
    A Survey of Techniques

**Exploring the Technique**

    Table and Lighting
    The Clay
    Temperature Regulation
    Tools
    Exercise: Warming Up to the Clay
    Exercise: Clay Compositing

**Moving Beyond the Materials**

    Cut-outs, Drawing, and Further Experimentation

Clay under the camera has the unique quality of being both two dimensional and three dimensional. It can be contained on a two-dimensional plane, acting like a painting, or it can be pulled upward toward the viewer into a high relief sculpture. **01**

Up until the 1970s, clay had been a three-dimensional stopmotion medium, used to animate fantastic creatures and endearing characters in special effects and children's television. Using clay under the camera as a two-dimensional medium was more the realm of the experimental animators. Several artists have made this clay-on-glass or clay painting technique their own. Two animators in

**01** Darling – *Izabela Plucinska* – 2013.

particular, Ishu Patel and Joan Gratz, developed the technique in distinctly different ways, laying the groundwork for current practitioners.

## Notable Pioneers in Clay Painting

### Ishu Patel

In 1977, animator Ishu Patel was working diligently at the National Film Board of Canada. He had just completed his Oscar-nominated short, *Bead Game* (1977), and the producers at the NFB were eager to see what he would do next. But Patel was at an impasse. He wanted to explore the theme of the afterlife, drawing on memories from his childhood in a rural village in India. The unearthly creatures he wanted to animate were too complex for drawn animation and the subject matter too serious for cut-outs. One day, while working in his studio, Patel took a piece of filmstrip he wanted to save and, not having any tape, stuck it to the window with a piece of plasticine. As he was leaving the studio he noticed the bright light outside was pushing through the thinner parts of the clay, illuminating it like stained glass. Patel was intrigued.

"I took a big lump of plasticine home and put it on my light table and all evening I kept thinking, 'This is wonderful! This is it!' I could draw in it really easily and see the light coming though."[1] **02** **03**

Patel's film *Afterlife* (1978) was the result of this happy discovery and the first significant use of backlit clay painting in animation. By varying the thickness of the clay on glass, Patel endows his strange drawings of imaginary creatures with nuanced shading. The otherworldly glow of the colored clay, accentuated by Patel's use of the staggered mix, fits the ethereal exploration of the passing from life to death and beyond. Images of strange creatures, radiating delicate patterns of light, accompany the man's spirit as he journeys toward the next world. **04**

> In the beginning it was hard, because I couldn't really draw certain images I had in mind . . . For two months under the camera, I practiced and practiced and practiced . . . [My producer, Derek Lamb] said, "Don't even make a storyboard. Just go under the camera, take the journey from your head all the way down to wherever you want to go."[2]

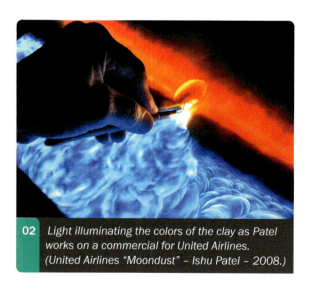

**02** Light illuminating the colors of the clay as Patel works on a commercial for United Airlines. (United Airlines "Moondust" – Ishu Patel – 2008.)

**03** Ishu Patel at work at the National Film Board of Canada. Ishu Patel © National Film Board of Canada, All rights reserved.

Clay Painting and Beyond  Chapter 6

Patel spent a year and a half animating the film, averaging 5–15 images a day. 05

Patel continued working with clay in the film *Top Priority* (1981), using both top light and backlight. The film uses a more colorful palette and the intense backlight mimics the unrelenting heat of the landscape during a drought. 06 Patel found that working with a full color palette presented many new challenges.

> It took a long time. When the character's moving – you have to scrape off the color and put a fresh plasticine there, because otherwise it gets muddy. It was hard. That film was the hardest film I'd ever done.[3]

Patel continued working at the NFB for many years, before transitioning to teaching and starting Studio Image Par Image, which specializes is under-the-camera animation.

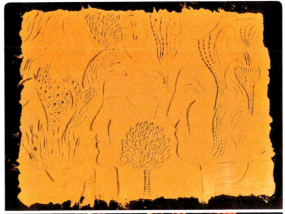

05 *A low relief sculpture and the resulting illuminated image from Afterlife ©1978 National Film Board of Canada, All rights reserved.*

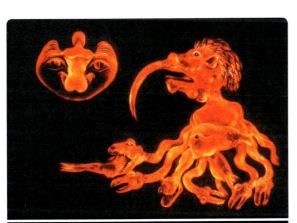

04 *Otherworldly creatures accompany a man in his journey to the next world. Ishu Patel – Afterlife ©1978 National Film Board of Canada, All rights reserved.*

06 *Colored clay in Top Priority ©1981 National Film Board of Canada, All rights reserved.*

## Joan Gratz

Joan Gratz had experimented with animation and painting while in architecture school, but when she got a job at Will Vinton's Portland studio in 1978, her medium became clay. She worked for ten years as a designer and animator for Vinton. While there, she developed her signature clay painting technique, in which she uses her fingers to apply strokes of clay into vibrant, evolving imagery.

> We would mix the colors of the clay at [Vinton's] studio and we would take all those leftover bits of clay together and roll them around and cut them and get these beautiful clay balls with a stained glass quality . . . I think that made me think about [painting with] it.[4] **07**

Gratz paints upright on an easel, adding and removing bits of clay constantly as the image changes. Top light brings out every nuanced color of the clay. After contributing animated clay painting to some of the Vinton Studios films, Gratz formed her own studio in 1987, focusing soley on her specialized technique.

In 1992, Gratz's short film *Mona Lisa Descending a Staircase* won the Academy Award for best animated short, throwing clay painting into the spotlight for a few brief seconds. *Mona Lisa Descending a Staircase* takes the viewer on a visual and auditory journey through twentieth-century art history. Gratz skillfully reinterprets her favorite paintings with the clay, adding her own inside jokes and artistic flair. The true mastery of this film is in the transitions between works. **08** Colors flow off one painting and form into another with their own sense of autonomy. Every frame of the film stands on its own as a work of art, but taken together they become a moving masterpiece. **09**

Gratz is an incredibly prolific artist, despite the time-consuming nature of her technique. She collaborates with other filmmakers, and takes commissions and commercial work, bringing her recognizable visual style to every project. **10**

But being recognizable doesn't mean her work is uniform. With a truly experimental frame of mind, Gratz continues to find new visual aesthetics within her area of expertise. One of the unique characteristics of clay painting is the ability to break into the third dimension. Raising clay up toward the camera into high relief introduces

**07** Kubla Kahn – *Joan Gratz* – *2010.*

**08** Mona Lisa Descending a Staircase – *Joan Gratz* – *1992.*

Clay Painting and Beyond  Chapter 6  161

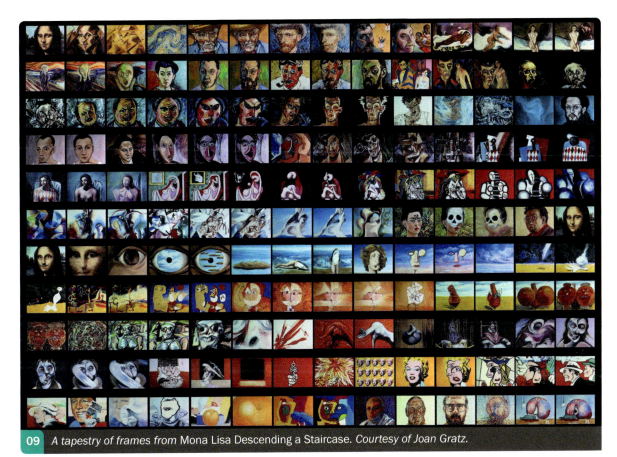

09  *A tapestry of frames from* Mona Lisa Descending a Staircase. *Courtesy of Joan Gratz.*

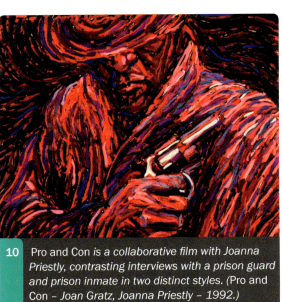

10  *Pro and Con is a collaborative film with Joanna Priestly, contrasting interviews with a prison guard and prison inmate in two distinct styles. (Pro and Con – Joan Gratz, Joanna Priestly – 1992.)*

11  Lost and Found – *Joan Gratz – 2012.*

an unusual visual experience for the viewer, one that is both painterly and sculptural. Gratz's film *Lost and Found* (2012) uses this technique to great effect.

Gratz uses a sandy colored clay that is lit dramatically from one angle to replicate the feeling of a moving woodcut. **11** "Light and shadow are most important," says Gratz, who describes the film as a carved painting. "You're working with depth and texture but not color blocking."[5] Smooth faces and hands rise from the textured background, morph, and are swallowed back into it. The material varies between one and four inches in depth. The glimpses of dimension we can see rising out of the clay hint at a fully formed world hidden behind the veil of texture.

### A Survey of Techniques

An unusual approach to clay on glass is the film *Bitzbutz* (1984) by Gil Alkabetz. The film is a battle between a small white bird and an enormous black monster fighting over the positive and negative space on the screen. As a student at Bezalel Academy of Arts and Design, Alkabetz originally thought to execute his idea with pen and ink, but his teacher, Itzhak Yoresh, suggested working under the camera. He took some scraps of plasticine and made some tests. "Since the plasticine was cheap and old, it broke during the animation, creating 'splatters' around the figure – which I really liked."[6] **12**

Taking the opposite approach to Patel's delicate shading, Alkabetz shot on high-contrast film to achieve the flat black and white look, so the texture of the plasticine is only noticeable around the edges of the image. The result is an uncompromising black and white battle where the consequences of losing are obliteration into the void.

Inspired by Gratz's clay paintings, animator David Ehrlich created several abstract color studies with clay. In *Color Run* (2001), twisted clay strings are absorbed incrementally into a constantly evolving abstract painting. "Using a large rolling pin, I began improvisationally to press various colors together over wood plaques. This was like rolling out dough for a pie, something that I had loved doing for my mom when I was a little boy."[7] The added volume of each clay string pushes the painting outward in a slow-motion explosion of color. **13**

**12** *Silhouette of plasticine shot on high-contrast film creates the two sides of the symbolic battle in Bitzbutz. (Bitzbutz – Gil Alkebetz –1984.)*

**Animated Anecdote**

"One problem was how to animate the small bird, which appeared in white on black. We found that the best way to do it was to animate the whole film in negative, so the bird would be black and the monster white. That made it much more comfortable to animate, since the bird was a piece of plasticine instead of a hole . . . The bird's tracks were drawn with a black felt pen on the glass, and I used the pen's other side to make the monster's eyes."

– Gil Alkabetz

Further exploration resulted in Ehrlich's films *Clayola* and *Clay*, which were exhibited alongside a series of panels from the films at the Hiroshima International Animation Festival in 2008. In these two abstract pieces, Ehrlich draws inspiration from the natural world: "My mind turned first to the way in which flowers swell and burst into radiant color, and then to mountain landscapes bathed in waves of vibrating light."[8] With these sculptural films, Ehrlich was concerned with how animation might be exhibited in other contexts, outside the theater, and how a still artwork might be in conversation with a moving video because of their proximity. **14**

Lynn Tomlinson's film *The Ballad of Holland Island House* (2014) embraces the texture of the clay, using top light to emphasize its dimensional properties. Tracing the story of the last house on an island sinking in the Chesapeake Bay, 400 years of history are represented through a series of transforming vignettes. **15**

The colors mix before our eyes and reform into new scenes, passing in and out of abstraction as they go. Early in her career, Tomlinson used the backlit clay technique, creating commercials for MTV and Sesame Street, but had taken a hiatus from animation for several years to pursue other creative projects. **16**

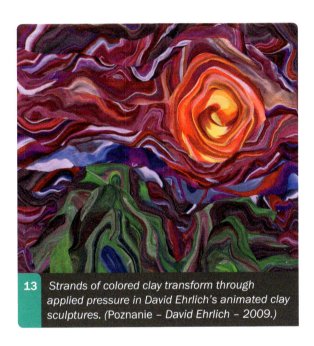

**13** *Strands of colored clay transform through applied pressure in David Ehrlich's animated clay sculptures. (Poznanie – David Ehrlich – 2009.)*

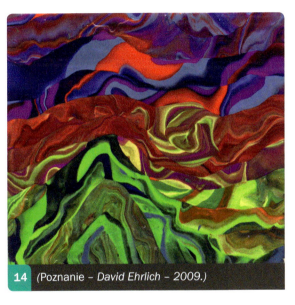

**14** *(Poznanie – David Ehrlich – 2009.)*

**15** *The Ballad of Holland Island House – Lynn Tomlinson – 2014.*

**16** *Backlit clay from The Same Moon – 1995. Courtesy of Lynn Tomlinson.*

# Fluid Frames: Clay Painting and Beyond

The changing technology drew her back, and for *The Ballad of Holland Island House*, she was inspired to change her method to top light. **17** For Tomlinson, a priority was allowing the audience to see the individual bits of clay as they became part of an entire scene. She deliberately leaves the clay unmixed and partially shaped under the camera, giving the film a raw, formative quality. **18**

Polish animator Izabela Plucinska uses a monochromatic color palette and animates in low relief to create atmospheric ponderings on human psyche. In *Darling* (2013), a film about a woman who cannot remember her past, Plucinska works on two layers, sculpting the background and using strings of black clay on a glass layer above to draw characters. **19**

Plucinska lights the blue clay from above to replicate an underwater effect, symbolizing the main character's mental drowning without her memories. The setting is transitory; chairs and teacups rise out of the background when needed and are swallowed when their purpose is finished. In all of Plucinska's low relief clay films, we remain aware that the clay is a single, changing mass under the camera, revealing its stories through transformation.

## Exploring the Technique

### Table and Lighting

If you are planning to do backlit clay painting, you will want a glass or Plexiglas light table, just as you would use for sand or paint-on-glass. Canadian animator Shira Avni animates on a sheet of frosted Mylar (similar to an acetate cel). Because the clay must be very thin for light to penetrate it, stronger lights underneath are more effective at creating a wide tonal range in the image. A dimmable light gives you the option to adjust the intensity of the light for each shot. Backlit clay has the feeling of stained glass and animating this way requires an awareness not only of color but also of managing the depth of the clay so the light can penetrate. **20**

**17** *Tomlinson at work in her studio. Courtesy of Lynn Tomlinson.*

**18** *The Ballad of Holland Island House – Lynn Tomlinson – 2014.*

**19** *Low relief clay in Plucinska's Darling. (Darling – Izabela Plucinska – 2013.)*

Clay Painting and Beyond  Chapter 6    165

20  Shira Avni manipulates the thickness of the clay in her backlit film, *John and Michael*. (John and Michael ©2004 National Film Board of Canada. All rights reserved.)

"I use Jovi Plastelina – it's non-toxic, translucent, odourless, easy to mix and work with, and inexpensive. I don't add to it or modify it other than simply mixing colors together by hand. I mostly use my fingers and occasionally a small clay tool or the back end of a brush for very fine details."

– Shira Avni

21  Top, bottom, and combined lighting schemes for clay.

For top lit work, glass or Plexiglas works well too. Smooth masonite board is another option if you plan to cover it completely with clay. Joan Gratz works upright on an easel while other artists work flat under the camera. If you are working with top lights, position your lights at a 45° angle on either side of your working surface. This will eliminate most of the shadows. Consider adding diffusion or using bounced light to get an even, consistent illumination.

Of course, you could decide the shadows work with your design, as in Gratz's *Lost and Found*. In that case, you will want to light from one side to heighten the relief from the clay. High relief work requires meticulous lighting. Note where the shadows fall and how you can incorporate them into your design.

A combination of top light and bottom light can create a beautiful balance between the glow of backlight and the subtle color of the clay. Set up top and bottom lights as you would for a regular scene and adjust your exposure to account for some of the additional light. **21**

## The Clay

Oil-based modeling clay, which is commonly found at craft stores under names like Plasticine or Plastilina, is the best for clay painting. However, not all plasticine is created equally. Each brand has its own unique formula, so the properties of the clay will vary from brand to brand. Finding the right clay and managing its consistency are part of the art of clay painting. Some clay is drier and difficult to smooth into consistent texture. Other brands are heavily pigmented, making it difficult to keep colors separated. **22**

In general, water-based clay is not used because it dries out over the long process of animating. But we are working from an experimental frame of mind, so the limitations of water-based clay might be an interesting challenge for an adventurous animator. You can manage the fluidity of the clay by dipping your hands in a bowl of water as you work. You might consider allowing the clay to stiffen over time as it dries out and work that characteristic into your production design.

As any good sculptor will tell you, clay isn't ready to use straight out of the package. It needs to be carefully conditioned for the work ahead. For the most part, this just means kneading it with your hands. The clay will soften and become more workable as it warms up. To get more malleability, add a few drops of mineral oil (found in most drugstores). The more you add, the smoother and more workable the clay will become, but too much will make it soupy and sticky. Joan Gratz likes her clay to be the consistency of putty – in-between a solid and liquid. She learnt to mix clay at Vinton Studios, where animators would melt the oil-based clay in a double boiler. Once in liquid form, the clay was just like paint and any color could be achieved from the most basic set of primary colors: "I heat it up with mineral oil and base the amount of oil on the climate temperature and what I'm doing. I'll mix a lot of different colors, and when I'm working I'll also sub-mix a lot of different colors."[9] The double boiler is most effective if you plan to mix large quantities of a color.

For smaller amounts, you can mix colors by kneading two pieces of clay together until they are blended. **23** The same rules of mixing paint apply to clay: dark colors tend to be strong and invasive and a small bit will effectively work

> **#ProTip** *Mineral oil is also useful for cleaning up after a day in the studio. Dab a paper towel in the oil and use it to clean your working surface and clay-covered fingers before washing your hands with soap.*

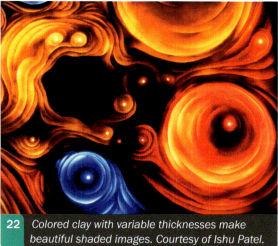

**22** *Colored clay with variable thicknesses make beautiful shaded images. Courtesy of Ishu Patel.*

**23** *Lynn Tomlinson's clay palette. Courtesy of Lynn Tomlinson.*

through a large amount of a lighter color. Start with a light color and add a darker one a little bit at a time until you get the color you want.

Some animators choose to work strictly monotone so they don't have to deal with keeping colors separated. If you want to work with a full color palette, expect to go through a lot of clay. You will need to constantly be removing contaminated clay and replacing it with fresh bits as you animate.

## Temperature Regulation

One thing to keep in mind is the temperature of your studio and how that affects your clay. Plasticine softens and becomes more pliable as it warms up, but gets sticky and difficult to manipulate if it is too warm. If you are working with lights that produce a lot of heat, you will notice the consistency of the clay changes while you work and you may need to do some temperature regulation. This could be as simple as setting up a small fan to blow across the work table and dissipate some of the heat.

## Tools

As with sand and paint-on-glass, your fingers are a great tool. Spreading the clay requires quite a bit a strength, especially if you are trying to get it thin enough for light to come through. You may need to build up your stamina. Joan Gratz uses only her hands to animate:

> I apply the clay with my fingers. I am constantly cleaning off my finger. After a while it gets very sore and I switch to my middle finger, which is less talented. When that is rubbed raw I switch to a third finger or I stop and do something else until my pointing finger has regenerated its skin.[10]

Wooden modeling tools are great for shaping edges and compressing clay. Ribbon tools are helpful for removing clay from precise areas. Potter's needles and other mark-making tools can create texture and line. **24**

Lynn Tomlinson has a wooden modeling tool that acts as an extension of her finger when she

**Animated Anecdote** *Working on film in the 1970s required very bright lights that produced a lot of heat. While working on* Afterlife, *Ishu Patel discovered his clay was turning to soup after about ten minutes on the light table. To solve this problem, he moved the lights as far from the working surface as he could and then set up fans to blow both under and across the table. It was like working in a wind tunnel, but it kept the clay just the right consistency so he could shape it into his tonal drawings.*

**Animated Anecdote** *When Lynn Tomlinson switched to top lighting for* The Ballad of Holland Island House *she no longer had lights underneath the glass warming the clay into a malleable consistency. To solve this, she took a casserole warming plate from her kitchen and put it under her table.*

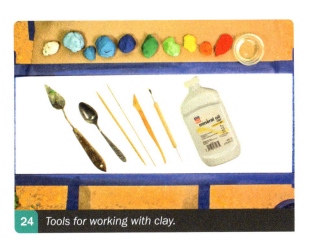

**24** Tools for working with clay.

needs to get into the small details of the clay. Tomlinson also carves stamps out of rubber erasers and uses them to create patterns. Most of all, it is the tactile method of working that attracts her most to clay: "I love that I can use my hands and I don't want to have to use anything that distances me from touching the stuff that I'm moving."[11]

## Exercise

### Warming Up to the Clay

To warm up, we will do a simple, abstract exercise with the clay inspired by David Ehrlich's methods. We will use top light for this exercise.

1. Choose a few colors that will blend well together, some light and some dark. Use sparing amounts of the darker colors since they will overpower the light colors. Take a small lump of each color and condition it for a few minutes, kneading it and rolling it between your hands until it warms up and becomes pliable. You may add a few drops of mineral oil if the clay feels especially stiff. It should have a little bit of resistance, but not feel hard.

2. Roll out a long strip of each color. Then twist them together to form one colorful cord. Roll that cord up into a ball and place it on your working surface. 25 26 27

3. Now the animation begins! Keep a paper towel and a small bit of mineral oil handy so you can clean your hands easily.

4. Take a frame of the ball of clay, then squish it down onto the table a little bit and take another frame. Continue doing this for several more frames until the ball is a flat pancake. Work from the center of the ball and push the clay outward with small pressing motions, letting the natural patterns of color expand. 28

Do this repeatedly, taking a frame each time you work around the circle. It may not seem like much is changing, but be patient. Wait until you have at least three seconds of animation before you play it back.

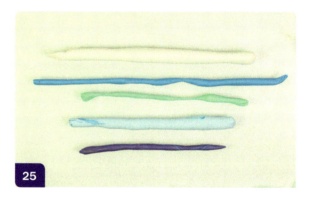

25

26

27

Clay Painting and Beyond Chapter 6    169

28

29

30

5. As you work with the clay, take note of which colors are stiffer than others. Which colors tend to dominate and invade other sections? What colors stick to your fingers and end up contaminating other areas? These observations will help you make decisions for your future projects.

6. As you work your way outward, start adding bits of clay into the center of the pancake to give it more volume. Continue until the patterns are completely covering the frame. **29**

7. Now that the clay is covering the entire frame, we will do a smear wipe. Continue the process of pushing the clay outward each frame to retain the slow expansion. After you expand the clay, swipe your fingers lightly across the clay from one corner to the other several times. This produces a subtle smear across the colors. Don't overdo it. We want the smear to happen gradually across the frame.

8. Take a frame and then repeat, pressing the colors outward, then smear the clay from the corner. Do this frame-by-frame, until the colors have smeared together completely and the original pattern is obliterated. **30**

9. Play back the animation. How do the expanding colors make you feel? What do you think of the smear transition? How might you use these qualities in a future project?

### Exercise

## Clay Compositing

Now that you have a bit of familiarity with the material, we will embark on a longer project, in which we will create foreground and background animation under the camera, and then composite it in After Effects. Several of the techniques from sand and paint-on-glass also apply to clay. In this exercise, I am using a combination of top and bottom light, but you can use any lighting scheme. Since we will be compositing, use the same lighting for both the foreground and the background in this exercise.

## Foreground – Bouncing Ball

1. Choose a color that will stand out against a blue sky and green grass. Roll a small ball of clay then press it to the glass near the bottom of your frame. Shape the clay into a sphere. **31**

2. Create an evolving hold by subtly moving the texture inside the sphere. You can do this with swipes of the finger or pats of your fingertips, depending on what sort of texture you want the sphere to have. Do this for 12 frames. **32**

3. Now it's time to animate the ball jumping up and bouncing three times. You can use my timing chart in Figure 33 as a guide, or create your own. Squash the ball in anticipation for a jump. Then stretch the ball as it springs upward. **33**

   Reshape the ball each frame, paying attention to shading and texture as you animate the first two bounces. The second bounce should go higher than the first, as though the ball is gaining energy.

4. On the third bounce, hold the ball in the air near the top of the frame, stretched out as it speeds upward. Later, we will animate the background rushing behind it to create the illusion of it rocketing up. **34** Create another evolving hold for 12 frames to finish off this sequence.

5. Export the image sequence.

6. Open After Effects and create a new 1920x1080 24fps project. Import the bouncing ball sequence and set the frame rate to 12fps. Insert it into the timeline. We will use this as a timing guide for animating the background.

## Background Layer – Panning Sky

Because we will be following the ball as it rises, we need a background that we can pan in After Effects. I've created a long, vertical expanse of sky with clouds and some grass at the bottom. You can leave the clouds out and just animate a sky background, or a more abstract interpretation of a sky. To handle this unusual aspect ratio, you should work

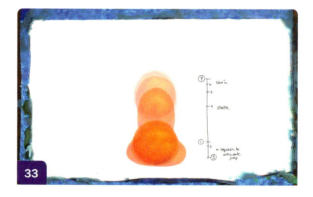

Clay Painting and Beyond  Chapter 6   171

35

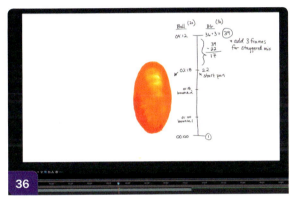

36

37

> **#ProTip** — *If you can't get a long enough image for a vertical pan, you can also create several smaller sky layers and stack them vertically in After Effects.*

lengthwise on your light table to maximize the resolution of your camera. We will rotate and pan the entire image sequence in After Effects. **35**

1. Create your background plate. Be sure to use the same lighting you used for the bouncing ball.

2. As the ball bounces in the foreground, we are going to animate the clouds rolling across the sky using a staggered mix. On the third bounce, we will pan up with the ball. The upper portion of our background plate will only be seen during the pan. That means we don't need to animate it for the first part of this sequence. That will save us a lot of time, but we need to do some math to figure out exactly on which frame to start animating the upper portion of the background.

3. Calculate the total number of frames. Since I'm doing a staggered mix, I'm going to animate the background on threes (and also save some time). The entire sequence of my bouncing ball ends at timecode 00:04:12. This means if I animate the background on threes I will have 36 frames plus an additional three frames to account for the overlap of the staggered mix, so a grand total of 39 background frames (see the Staggered Mixes Exercise in Chapter 3).

4. Find the frame to start the pan. Look at your bouncing ball sequence and find the frame where the ball rockets up the last time. In my sequence, that is at 00:02:18. So, I need 22 frames of just the lower part of the background animated (the part that will be visible). Then I need to animate the remaining 17 frames with the full background moving because the camera will be panning upward over that portion of the image and it will become visible. **36**

5. Now that we've got the timing worked out, let's start animating. Use tools and your fingers to push the clouds out about one millimeter each frame. **37** Then lightly swipe your fingers over the clay in the sky as you did in the warm-up exercise. Or use a tool to create a texture. In this case, I used the back of a spoon. Swipe in the

## Fluid Frames: Clay Painting and Beyond

same direction each time so the movement will be consistent. 38

When we do a staggered mix with the footage, the small movements will blend together dreamily.

6. Work on the lower portion of the image for 22 frames, then start to move the upper section of the image. Continue animating the entire image until you get your full sequence of 39 frames.

7. Export the image sequence, then head over to After Effects for some compositing.

38

> "My students are often surprised at how much slower [clay painting] is than paint-on-glass, but I love the luminosity and depth of the colors, and the sculptural element that comes with the clay"
>
> – Shira Avni

### Compositing the Layers

If you worked through the sand and paint-on-glass compositing tutorials, you will recognize some of these compositing steps. Since clay usually has a clean, defined edge, compositing is a bit more straightforward. You could also shoot your bouncing ball on a green screen and use Keylight to composite.

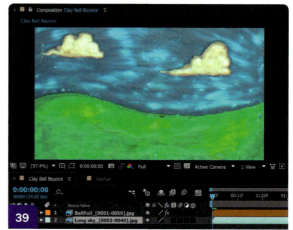

39

1. Open your After Effects project with the bouncing ball footage. Import the background sequence and change the frame rate to 8fps (Ctrl Alt G).

2. For now, turn off the bouncing ball layer. We will start by creating the staggered mix for the background. Drag the background into the composition under the ball and resize, rotate, and position it as necessary. 39

3. Duplicate the layer and shift it three frames forward. Set the Opacity of this layer to 75%.

4. Duplicate again and shift another three frames. Set this Opacity to 50%.

Clay Painting and Beyond  Chapter 6

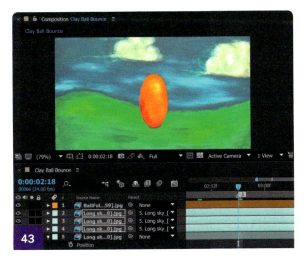

5. Duplicate again and shift yet another three frames. Set the Opacity to 25%. **40**

6. We now have ghosted layers in the mix. Parent the three upper layers to the first layer at the bottom of the stack. **41**

    This way, the movements of the parent layer will transfer to the child layers. When we animate our pan, all the layers of our mix will move as one unit.

7. Select all the layers and shift them back on the timeline so the first frame of the top layer is the first frame of the timeline. Set your work area to the last frame of the bottom layer.

8. Play back the animation. What do you think?

9. Turn on the bouncing ball layer. Since we have a clean edge and the movement is contained within a narrow corridor in this sequence, the Paint Bucket effect will work well for removing the background.

10. Apply the Paint Bucket effect to the layer. Move the Fill Point to a corner where the clay will not interfere with it. Set Stroke to Spread, check Invert Fill, and change the Blending Mode to Stencil Alpha. Now adjust the Tolerance and Spread Radius until you have a clean composite.

11. This looks pretty good, but the edges are a bit too hard to blend believably into the background. We will add the Roughen Edges effect to soften it. Search for this effect in the Effects and Presets panel and apply it to the layer. **42**

12. Set the Edge Type to Roughen, then adjust the Border, Edge Sharpness, and Scale to your liking. The effect is very subtle but makes a difference in how the ball interacts with the background.

## Adding the Pan

1. Now we can use the foreground layer as a timing reference for the pan in the background. We already determined the pan will start at 02:18. Move the time marker to 02:18 and set a position keyframe on the bottom sky layer. **43**

2. Go to the end of the sequence (04:12) and move the background down. A keyframe will be automatically created. **44**

3. Spend some time adjusting the curves on the pan so it eases out of its starting position and hits a constant speed. **45**

4. As a final touch you may want to keyframe some upward motion on the ball and a little Directional Blur so it looks like the camera is catching up to it as it pans upward. Little details like these make the animation that much more interesting and believable. **46**

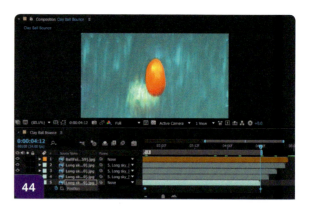

44

45

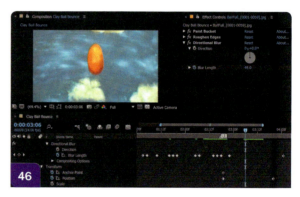

46

> "It's a challenging, slow, painstaking medium with a steep learning curve that requires a surprising level of physical endurance and patience. I had a lot of trial and error, and many reshoots in my films. I guess I am persistent, and also I really love the meditative quality that comes from the physicality of the medium."
>
> – Shira Avni

47 Puffer Girl – *Joan Gratz* – 2009.

From this point on, it is experimentation and practice. Step back from your work and be willing to reshoot until you get it right. As with all these fluid frame techniques, there is no easy road to mastery, it is a process of making and overcoming mistakes. As you come to understand the clay, you will find new ways to capitalize on its strengths and overcome its weaknesses. After decades of doing clay painting the traditional way, Joan Gratz is now using the computer to combine her clay painting with artistically rendered live action footage. **47** She is also digitally multiplying her images and weaving them into moving tapestries. **48** If the pioneer and master of such a technique can still find things to learn from the material, then certainly we will find our own avenues for exploration. **49**

Clay Painting and Beyond  Chapter 6

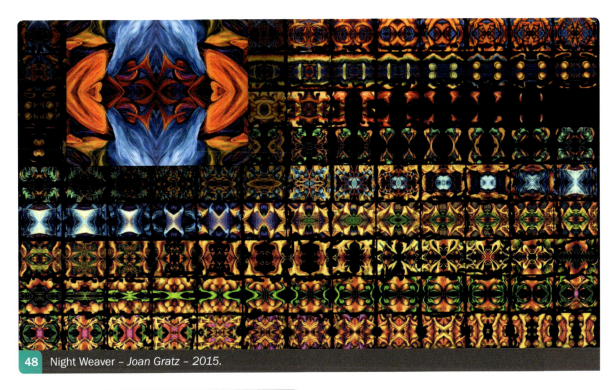

48  Night Weaver – *Joan Gratz* – 2015.

49  The Same Moon – *Lynn Tomlinson* – 1995.

## Moving Beyond the Materials

### Cut-outs, Drawing, and Further Experimentation

In getting to know the artists in this book, you may have noticed that several of them move between various techniques. French animator Florence Miailhe animated with pastel, paint-on-glass, and sand, often combining different techniques in her sensuous films. **50** Caroline Leaf worked in both sand and paint-on-glass; Lee Whitmore has made films with paint-on-glass and drawing with pastels under the camera. Cultivating your experimental

50  *A fluid frame artist is not limited to one method. Florence Miailhe combines sand, paint, and other under-the-camera techniques in her vibrant films. (Au premier dimanche d'août – Florence Miailhe – 2000.)*

# Fluid Frames: Clay Painting and Beyond

frame of mind will naturally lead you to test out new materials and combinations of materials, including other under-the-camera animation. For example, Lynn Smith and Nicolai Troshinsky both use paper cut-outs in combination with fluid frame techniques. The unconventional design of the characters in *Astigmatismo* inspired Troshinsky to include paint-on-glass animation:

The character designer, Gina Thorstensen, made the characters from very liquid ink. That was the last thing I expected, and I liked it so much I decided to add the paint-on-glass technique. In the beginning, I thought I would do everything with cut-outs but I added this new element to the animation just to respect her design.[12] 51

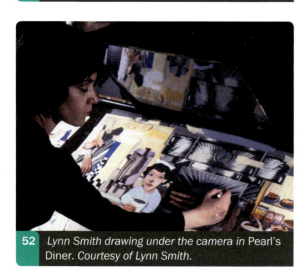

**51** *Character designs by Gina Thorstensen for* Astigmatismo.

With wet paint as their bodies, the two main characters move nimbly with an air of youthful suppleness, distinct from the rigidity of the cut-out world around them.

In some regards, the cut-out medium is a faster medium for working because you can create very detailed, visually rich images without having to redraw every frame. But its limitation is that the paper cannot easily be transformed or morphed. In *Pearl's Diner* (1992), Lynn Smith animates meticulously constructed cut-out characters while drawing some elements of the scene with Caran d'Ache water-soluble crayons. 52

Smith is able to create effects like a blinking neon sign by drawing and erasing under the camera. She creates the multifaceted reflections on the stainless steel backsplash behind the diner's skillet by drawing as well. At one point, she even brings one character's fanciful imaginings to life, transitioning fully into a dreamy drawing sequence. 53

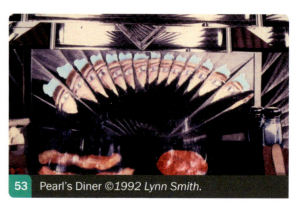

**52** *Lynn Smith drawing under the camera in* Pearl's Diner. *Courtesy of Lynn Smith.*

**53** Pearl's Diner ©1992 *Lynn Smith.*

Drawing under the camera (as opposed to drawing on paper and then filming) involves rubbing out and redrawing each frame, just as one might do with paint-on-glass. With drawing under the camera, we lose the liquidity of the fluid frame materials, but retain the flow of the straight ahead process. The atmosphere of improvisation remains and this is quite apparent in Smith's film *Sandburg's Arithmetic* (1994). **54** The shifting perspectives, flying numbers, and morphing shapes of animals and people flow alongside the rhythmic cadence of Carl Sandburg reading his poem 'Arithmetic.'

Smith draws on several layers of acetate, which enable her to keep certain elements of a scene still, while animating other parts. Backgrounds, animation guides, collage elements, and cut-out pieces could also be slid under the acetate. Smith notes that when using acetate it is important to always have the same number of layers at all times, otherwise there will be noticeable jumps in the exposure as the number of layers changes. **55**

The water-soluble crayons are very easily removed with a small amount of water, and scrape off the acetate with tissue or a plastic knife.[13] The traces left behind by the drawings become more important and accentuated this way. Most artists will deliberately leave the residue of the rubbing as a physical trace of the animation process. In her film *Ada* (2002), Lee Whitmore animates with pastel chalk, finding a balance between her exquisite line drawings and the rough, messy style of the material. **56**

**55** Sandburg's Arithmetic ©1994 Lynn Smith.

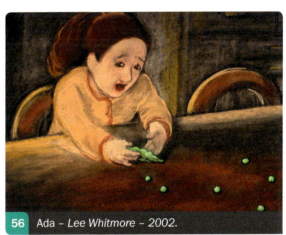

**56** Ada – Lee Whitmore – 2002.

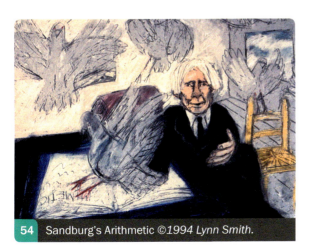

**54** Sandburg's Arithmetic ©1994 Lynn Smith.

**57** *Pulling light from the dark background of the paper, Whitmore creates a room full of atmosphere in Ada, giving us a window into her memories. (Ada – Lee Whitmore – 2002.)*

## Fluid Frames: Clay Painting and Beyond

Originally a traditional 2D animator, Whitmore credits the charcoal drawing films of South African artist William Kentridge as the inspiration for her switch to under-the-camera methods. **57**

In *Ada*, Whitmore's formidable grandmother goes through the daily ritual of shelling peas in the dim dining room of her childhood home. Whitmore first covers the paper with charcoal and then draws back into the blackness with an eraser, adding color with soft pastels:

> I knew the paper would need to be the best quality and be as heavy as I could get in order to withstand the multiple drawings and rubbings out. After experimenting I found a paper I liked the feel of – Saunders Waterford rag paper. **58**

Working under the camera will lead you into a limitless frontier of exploration. The more you work with these techniques, the more comfortable you will become applying them in different contexts thus maximizing the potential for play. Speaking of her discovery of under-the-camera animation, Whitmore explains,

> Perhaps the most interesting thing about this technique is it allowed for – even demanded spontaneity . . . As I drew, ideas for movements and gestures would come into my head, and I was able to respond by immediately drawing them. I felt I had become, in a sense, more like a performance artist.[14]

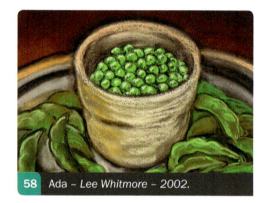

**58** Ada – Lee Whitmore – 2002.

That element of performance is embedded in all the techniques we have covered on our journey through fluid frame animation. It requires preparation and rehearsal, but once we are in the spotlight the best thing is to relax and embody the experience. This is the unique aspect of creating animation under the camera. Embrace it, enjoy it, and allow the animation to lead you to eventual expertise.

## Notes

1. Patel, Ishu. Telephone interview. Oct. 3, 2014.
2. Ibid.
3. Ibid.
4. Gratz, Joan. Telephone interview. Oct. 14, 2014.
5. *The Joan Gratz Retrospective*. Dir. Joan C. Gratz. ShortsHD, 2013. iTunes.
6. Alkabetz, Gil. Email interview. Oct. 17, 2014.
7. *Clay Animation*. Dir. David Ehrlich. David Ehrlich, 2005. DVD.
8. "Clay Paintings by David Ehrlich." Hiroshima: 12th International Animation Festival Hiroshima, 2008.
9. Gratz, Oct. 14, 2014.
10. Ibid.
11. Tomlinson, Lynn. Personal interview. Oct. 13, 2014 at Towson University.
12. Troshinsky, Nicolai. Telephone interview. Feb. 20, 2014.
13. Smith, Lynn. Email correspondence. Jan. 5, 2015.
14. Whitmore, Lee. *Hand-drawn Histories: The films of Lee Whitmore*, 2011. DVD Booklet.

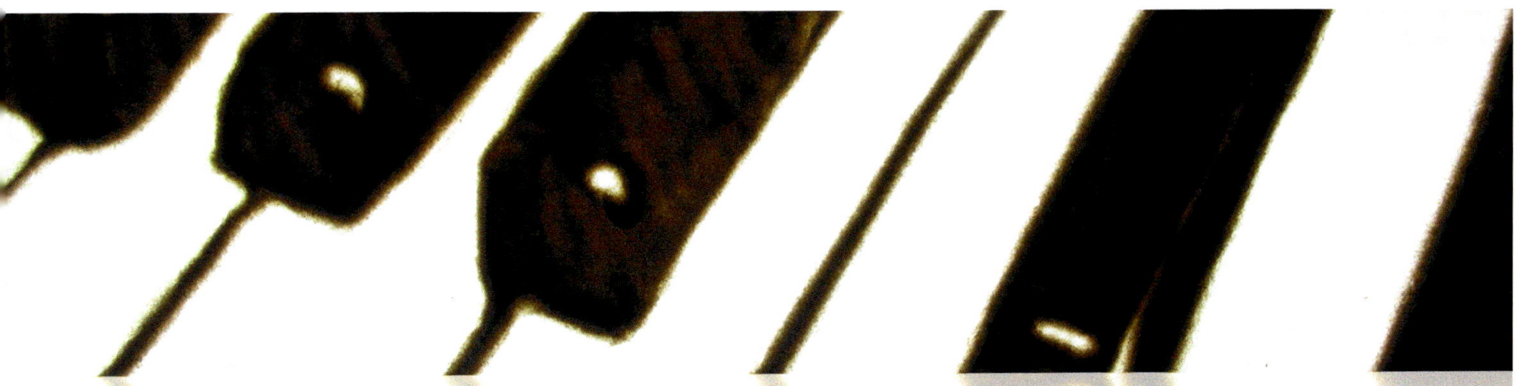

*It Might Be Real – Anna Humphries – 2012.*

# Chapter 7
# Beyond the Frame

**Sound Design and Music**
    The Mix

**Digital Output**

**Getting the Film Out**
    The Process Video
    Film Festivals
    Distribution
    Releasing Online
    Alternative Exhibition

**A Final Word**

No matter what production method you are using, there is far more to an animated film than just the animation. All of the hard work – the conceptualizing, the long hours under the camera, the meticulous scrubbing of pixels in post – may add up to a glorious visual feast, but in order to have that feast enjoyed by the rest of the world, you must plate it and serve it with the same attentiveness you apply to your animation. That means incorporating a robust approach to sound and exhibition into your production plan. **01**

Even though this chapter comes at the end of all the production information, I will emphatically state that you should be thinking about and working on these things throughout your production! Remaining peripherally aware of the external forces that shape your project's reception in the world will ensure that reception will be a grand one. When you step away from the camera for a break, do a little work in the areas of sound design or documentation. When you do finally finish the production, the road to your audience will be clear of obstacles.

> "You need to be able to trust the people that you surround yourself with. Your musician needs to be sure that he's in it for the long haul; that you're not going to drop him. He needs to be able to add and contribute to the visuals in a way or to the story in a way. You need to discuss your content. The same with a compositor; he needs to be involved in every single aspect of the film."
>
> – Robbe Vervaeke

## Sound Design and Music

Sound designers and musicians are artists that have a collaborative role in creating the film experience. Sound will help the audience comprehend some of the visually intense or narratively difficult sections of the film. While it is possible to do some of this yourself, I highly recommend working with others, because they are the experts, just as you are the expert in animation. Collaborating also brings another level of artistry to your film that is outside yourself – your collaborators will, at times, interpret your own work in ways you never expected.

Personally, I like to involve my collaborators as early in the process as possible, even if it is just sharing the storyboards and concept designs. **02**

I think about sound design throughout the production process and let my ideas grow alongside the visuals so I can communicate a clear vision to the musician and designer. Then I let them take the helm and practice their art.

Sometimes it makes sense to have some elements of the sound in place before you start filming – if you are making a music video, for example, or if you have dialogue and need to time the animation precisely. **03**

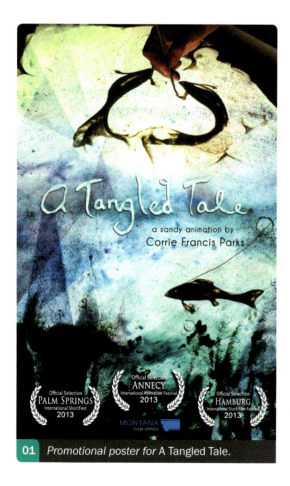

**01** *Promotional poster for A Tangled Tale.*

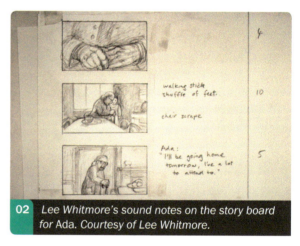

**02** *Lee Whitmore's sound notes on the story board for Ada. Courtesy of Lee Whitmore.*

**03** *Anna Humphries's animation for the music video It Might Be Real. Courtesy of Anna Humphries.*

In other situations, it is fine to wait until the visuals are completely finished and you have achieved picture lock before finalizing sound design and music. With this approach it is the sound artists' responsibility to create the synchronization, so it is important that the visuals do not change once they start work.

In the *Divertimenti*, Clive Walley worked closely with the six musicians – one for each film – allowing each to play a key role in determining the direction on the imagery. Most often, the music was either started or completely recorded before Walley began the animation. In *Divertimento No. 5*, Walley created many of the sounds himself, while collaborating with composer Bryn Jones

> I mostly planned to make a film based on the rude sounds of wet paint . . . So I started by making a track which I largely composed before I knew what the film would be like, and which slurped and spat and farted along in an independently interesting way.[1]

Nicolai Troshinsky linked his sound design in *Astigmatismo* to the film's theme of being lost. He asked sound designer Pierre Sauze to create a soundtrack without any visuals to reference.

> I told him to make me a composition which had space and things happening, but it had to sound interesting on its own, because I was sure that if it sounded interesting on its own then anything on top of it would only be better. And it worked, because he was essentially creating the rhythm of the film.[2]

Michaela Müller works very closely with her sound designer, Fa Ventilato. For her current project they took a field trip together to get ideas:

> The film is about airports, so my sound designer and I went to JFK for one day and we recorded some binaural sound. We were just walking together and not talking much because he was recording. From that material I made a sound sketch. I showed him the animatic with my sound sketch and then we talked about the film and we made a huge plan for each scene.[3]

Though this paint-on-glass film will take years to finish, Müller and Ventilato will continue recording sounds in airports around the world, allowing their plan to develop as the film is created.

A soundscape can be very literal or more surreal for a film. **04** A literal sound design matches visual content with realistic sounds, while a more surreal approach will make use of unusual pairing and symbolic connections between audio and image. For *A Tangled Tale*, I wanted an ambiance that represented both the digital and organic textures in the film. After I had picture lock, I asked my sound designer, Cole Pierce, if he could create an underwater environment

**04** *Despite Michaela Müller's abstracted imagery in* Miramare *the sound design provided a grounding sense of the environment – in this case a rustling cornfield. (Miramare – Michaela Müller – 2009.)*

that brought these two visual aesthetics together. Working from his own field recordings and electronically created sounds, he was able to weave together an ambiance track that expanded in auditory depth as the film progressed. To keep the mixture of sounds from abstracting the environment too much, Pierce synced very subtle watery sounds to the fishes' movements, which anchored the surreal soundscape under the surface. **05**

Music is intimately tied to our emotional response to a film. There were certain sections of *A Tangled Tale* that were visually ambiguous – meaning it was hard to know what the audience was meant to feel at that moment. This is where musician Mark Orton took over. We watched the film together multiple times, discussing the emotional arc of the story and how the audience should feel during each scene. Mark was then able to reflect that emotional narrative in the music he composed. **06**

Additionally, music can serve as an aspect of sound design. Musical effects can sync precisely with a specific movement, just like sound effects. You may develop musical motifs for certain characters or settings in the film. An attentive musician will be thinking not only of the aspects of musical composition, but will understand the journey on which you wish to take your audience. Music paves the way for that journey with incredible efficiency. **07**

Here are some things to think about as you approach the sound and music for your film:

***Au naturel or surreal:*** Do you want a sound design that accurately represents the actions and environment on screen or a more unusual pairing of visuals and sounds? Because our brains like to associate things we hear with things we see, you can get away with a lot when it comes to creating a sound environment. Unexpected pairings or an unfamiliar ambiance can completely change the way the audience interprets the visuals. On the flipside, if your imagery is already quite abstract or surreal, a naturalistic sound design can provide a grounding point for the audience.

**05** *A scene-by-scene music and sound breakdown for* A Tangled Tale.

**06** Composer Mark Orton at work in his studio.

**07** Some of the instruments used in the soundtrack for A Tangled Tale.

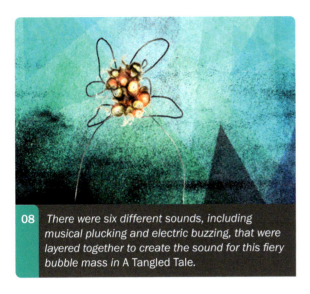

**08** There were six different sounds, including musical plucking and electric buzzing, that were layered together to create the sound for this fiery bubble mass in A Tangled Tale.

**09** When I was working on The Klondike Letters Project in Alaska, I hiked around with this little recorder to capture environmental sounds and interviews with other hikers. I named him Donald.

***Think layers:*** Good sound design is never just one sound. A designer will balance multiple sounds together, like layers in a painting, to create a composition with auditory depth. **08**

***Ambiance:*** The sounds that envelop us – wind in the trees, distant traffic, the hum of electric lights or a computer fan – are sounds we don't pay attention to specifically, but without them the world would seem eerily empty. Bring that fullness to the screen and your audience will be immersed in the experience.

***Be precise, but not overly precise:*** Not everything needs to be perfectly synced. Let the music wander on its own for a while. Our minds will make the connection they want to make and leave the rest. **09**

## The Mix

The sound mix is where all the individual layers of effects, music, dialogue, and ambiance get blended together into the perfect auditory experience. A professional re-recording mixer will work in a special room with speakers set up to replicate the sound balance in a theater. If you have been listening to your soundtrack on headphones up until this point, it will be wildly revealing!

The re-recording mixer is there to create the experience of your film and you know your film better than anyone, so you should plan to be present at the mix and be bold and speak up if something doesn't feel right. Don't worry about using technical language, explain what the audience should be feeling at a particular moment. If an effect needs to reverberate through the halls or if you want to make the floor tremble with the subwoofer, you can do that here.

Communicating ahead of time with the mixer will save lots of time during the actual mix, which can be a lengthy process, sometimes taking days. If there are specific effects that need to stand out, or sounds that should be panned from the left side of the theater to the right, or the front or back, make notes. Put your sound designer in touch with the mixer ahead of time so they can coordinate the types of files and layout of the tracks. A mixer will usually want the music, ambiance, effects, and dialogue on separate tracks so he can blend them in different ways. There can be more than one effect on a layer as long as they are not overlapping. Respect the professionalism of your collaborators and make their jobs as easy as possible! **10**

Not everyone can afford a professional mix, but be wary of doing it yourself. Headphones are fine for editing sound, but when you start to fine-tune levels, at the very least you should do so in a room that has good speakers and multiple channels. Certain wavelengths of sound will be mixed at the wrong level for speakers if you use headphones and you will be disappointed. Your film will likely be shown in different formats – it might play at a festival in a big theater with full surround and then be projected in a classroom with terrible speakers. You don't want your audience to cringe at high-level distortion, or miss half the dialogue because it is on the wrong channel. A well-crafted mix will add a high level of professionalism to your production, no matter where it is shown. **11**

If you get a professional mix, do it in 5.1 or 7.1 surround. Technology is rapidly changing and it may not be long before every online video platform streams in full surround sound and we all have special earbuds that replicate the grandest theater experience on our cell phones. Well, maybe that's still a ways in the future, but it is always easier to mix down a complicated mix than to create one from the basics. You should leave a mix with several versions of your soundtrack, ready for various output. Tell your mixer what formats you plan to output to – DCP, HDCam, or digital – and he or she should be able to provide you with the proper formats.

This is a good checklist of audio mixdowns to get from the mix.

- 5.1 or 7.1 surround sound mix
- 4.0 mix
- StereoLR (which is actually four tracks)
- Stereo mixdown ready for online streaming and standard DVDs

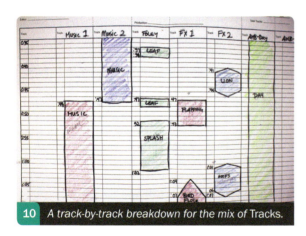

**10** *A track-by-track breakdown for the mix of* Tracks.

**11** *Even though* Soup of the Day *was based on a catchy song, the layered details in the soundtrack, like clinking glasses and restaurant noises, are what bring the story to life.* Soup of the Day ©2013 National Film Board of Canada, All rights reserved.

## Digital Output

The one thing I've learnt over my many years of filmmaking is that formats change. My very first animation, made when I was in high school, was shot with a rickety old VHS deck that could capture one frame at a time. Now I am sending digital files over the internet to festivals across the world. There were dozens of variations on format in between, and after I wrapped production on every film, I had to research what formats festivals wanted. What may have been the standard two years ago was no longer the preferred format now. **12**

There are many, many options for digital output, so you will need to ask yourself, "Where do I want to show my film?" Do you plan to submit to film festivals? Will you only release online? What about TV broadcast or gallery exhibition? Each of these venues requires its own research to determine the best format. Ultimately, when you show your film you want it to be shown in the best possible quality for the venue. Most professional tier festivals, like Cannes, Sundance, and Annecy, will prefer a Digital Cinema Package (DCP) for screenings. This is a specially formatted set of digital files specifically for theatrical projection. Some festivals still accept HDCam tapes (a digital tape in high definition), but the majority of screening venues are moving toward collecting digital files only, because there are no shipping costs involved for the filmmaker or the exhibitor. TV has its own set of specs and each online platform has recommendations for bitrates, compression formats, and sizes.

The best way to research digital output is to pick up the phone and call someone. Call the festival you will be showing at and talk to the technical supervisor. Find out what works best in the theater that will be showing your film.

Then, if you plan to use a professional processing company, call them and describe what you need. Ask for a student or independent discount – most places are willing to support small-budget filmmakers with reduced rates. If you plan to

**12** *An appropriate use of obsolete festival beta tapes: propping up stopmotion sets. Courtesy of Tiny Inventions.*

The technical requirements for the Animafest Zagreb 2014 World Festival of Animated Film:

**Selection preview of the film:** DVD or file with technical specifications: Format: Quicktime or MPEG4; Codec: H.264; FPS: Native; Resolution: Full or Native. Films with dialogues or narration in languages other than English must have English subtitles.

**Screening Copy:** 35 mm, Digital Betacam PAL, HDCAM (PAL), DCP – no KDM encryption key. The Festival reserves the right to refuse a screening copy of dubious technical condition that may cause problems during the screening.

output yourself, read extensively and always test your files before your big screening! Always have a backup version too.

Nearly everything is projected in high definition, and increasingly TV and online streaming is going in that direction. Soon the standard will be 4K and if the trend for higher resolution continues to rise or hits its ceiling, only time will tell. So the best advice is to make your film at the highest resolution possible and always output an uncompressed frame sequence at that top resolution for archiving. A frame sequence is the most versatile, because compression codecs will always be changing, but a sequence of full resolution frames can be dropped into any editing program and output into the format of the day. You could even output to film, should celluloid experience a revival in 50 years. This gives you the full flexibility in the future to upgrade to a higher format, even if right now all you need is a basic 1080p digital file.

**#ProTip** *To archive your After Effects file and collect all the source files in one location, select your composition and go to* File > Dependencies > Collect Files. **13**

**13** Archive everything!

## Getting the Film Out

So now you have your film with a great soundtrack and it's officially done! Bask for a moment in the feeling of completeness, you deserve it . . .

OK, that's enough, the work is not done yet! As with any artistic project, showing your film is the actual culmination of all your hard work. Having your film seen is not about gathering the most views on a particular media platform or winning the Academy Award. Your main concern should be finding *your* audience – the people who will enjoy and appreciate your film specifically. This could be a handful of people with a specialized interest in your subject or technique, or it could be an online audience of millions. It really depends on your film and your objectives. So this is the very first thing to consider. Where is your audience and how do you reach them? **14**

**14** Seek out local opportunities to toot your horn. Everyone loves to read about a homegrown success story.

## The Process Video

An important marketing tool for fluid frame animation is a "Making Of" video that reveals some of the process. Making a film seems like magic, but it's really a lot of hard work. Showcasing the intense artistry and stamina required to make work under the camera will not only be educational, but also add value to the production in the eyes of the viewer. Of course, you can't document the process after the process is complete, so this is something you should be thinking of and preparing for from the very beginning stages of your film. **15**

Look at other artists' process videos to get ideas, as there are several approaches. Marieka Walsh intercut scenes from the film, shots of her working in the studio, and shots of her talking about the meaning and development of the story in *The Making of "The Hunter."* Nicolai Troshinsky made a very detailed video in which he explains some of the technical and theoretical challenges of *Astigmatismo*. César Díaz Meléndez took a show-don't-tell approach, leaving out the explanations and simply cutting together photos of his studio, timelapse footage and video footage captured while working on *Zepo*. Martine Chartrand filmed herself creating one frame of *MacPherson* to show just how long it takes to create one of her painted frames (the video footage adds up to about 20 minutes!). As you are in full production, keep the following in mind so you will have good material to work with when making the process video:

**Document everything.** When we are in the midst of shooting, we don't really want to be bothered to set up a second camera to film ourselves, but this is essential. Get an HD webcam and film yourself working. Take the occasional photo with your hands in the shots manipulating the materials. Take photos of your studio, your camera, and lighting set up, even the cat that kept you company through the long hours. **16**

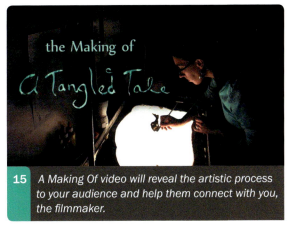

**15** *A Making Of video will reveal the artistic process to your audience and help them connect with you, the filmmaker.*

**Decide what your focus will be.** Will you go into detail on one particular aspect of the production, or provide a basic overview? Is your audience other experimental filmmakers or your parents' friends who think you work for Pixar because you are an animator? The details you reveal will depend both on who will be watching and how much of the process you wish to remain a mystery.

**Think about production value.** Light your studio so you get a good image quality. Put up concept art and storyboards in the background. Have a shot in progress on the light box and make your tools or painting palette visible. It's OK to stage a shot for the sake of educating your viewers. Use a decent microphone to get clear audio of you talking about the film and the process.

**16** *Document your process.*

***Have someone else interview you about your process.*** Have a friend or family member who knows nothing about animation interview you. Then have a fellow animator interview you. They will come up with two very different sets of questions!

***Script it.*** I'll admit, I get a little nervous in front of a camera. For *The Making of "A Tangled Tale"* I wrote down questions for myself and the answers in outline form. Then I recorded the voice-over, using my notes to help me stay on track and cover each topic thoroughly. I also recorded several takes, and picked the best one. Having the answers as an outline instead of fully written out kept me from sounding like I was reading off a page, but I didn't have to come up with something on the spot or memorize what I wanted to say. When I had to be on camera, I did the same thing, and just tried not to look at the notes. **17** It took a few extra takes, but eventually I was able to work out the wording of my answers into something I could use in the film. This process was also very helpful later when it came time for Q&A sessions at festivals!

## Film Festivals

Film festivals are thriving in all corners of the globe. There are many, many festivals that focus specifically on animation, as well as genre-specific festivals. Live action film festivals are adding animation categories, so they are eager for good content. Festivals are a place where filmmakers gather and exchange ideas, network, and interact with their audience. **18**

People who attend film festivals love to hear the stories behind the films. They are interested in the processes and the ideas that go into a production. It's a chance for you to talk about your film, the artistry and ideas behind it and learn from others in kind.

Of course, there are many more films being submitted to festivals as well, and the selection process is highly competitive. With festivals receiving thousands of entries, many charge entry fees to keep the number of entries down and help support the staff needed to catalogue and correspond with all the entrants. Determine a budget for entry fees and be strategic about which festivals you

**17** *Usually I like to be behind the camera, but I'll make an exception for my audience.*

**18** *Ready for the Annecy International Festival of Animated Film.*

**19** *Submitting to festivals that focus on your subject matter is an efficient way to reach an audience that will appreciate your film. (The Ballad of Holland Island House – Lynn Tomlinson – 2014.)*

submit to. Look for festivals that speak to your specific niche or genre. Because *The Ballad of Holland Island House* is based on the effects of climate change, Lynn Tomlinson has had great success at environmental festivals. **19**

Small festivals are less competitive and often a great place to get to know other filmmakers and patrons in a more intimate setting (one of my favorite festivals is in Brookings, South Dakota!). If your film has already gotten into some festivals, and your entry fee budget is getting low, it never hurts to send a polite request for a fee waiver or reduction. The best way to go about this is to briefly explain why your film would be a good fit for that particular festival, and include a link to preview the film. Most often the answer will be "No," but occasionally if the festival is looking for content and yours fits the bill, it will be "Yes!"

Submit to festivals you know you will attend if selected. **20** If you have a friend in that city you can stay with, or can drive yourself there instead of buying a plane ticket, or it's in a place you've always wanted to visit, that's a good festival to add to your list. Festivals in other countries frequently have no entry fee so seek them out. Sometimes these festivals will even provide accommodation and a small expense stipend if you attend the festival.

> **#ProTip** *An electronic press kit (EPK) is something you should have ready before you release your film or submit it to festivals and distributors. It is an information package that contains all the essential details about the film. Here's what you should include in your Electronic Press Kit.*
>
> - *One page of essential information about the film including:*
>   - *Director name and contact information*
>   - *Screening specs (year of production, length, available formats)*
>   - *Log line*
>   - *Brief synopsis*
>   - *Awards or important festival screenings*
>   - *Links to the website and online versions of the trailer and process video*
> - *Three or more stills from the film*
> - *Picture of the director*
> - *Director's biography/filmography*
> - *Press release or articles about the film*
> - *Artist's statement*
> - *Images from the production, a process video*
> - *Video file of the trailer*
> - *Full cast and crew list*
> - *Dialogue list (in case a festival or distributor wants to create subtitles)*

**20** Animators relax and socialize in between screenings at Annecy.

**21** Always read the guidelines and make sure you can deliver the festival requirements by their deadlines. Courtesy of Northwest Animation Festival.

> "The process of making Astigmatismo has taught me a lot of discipline. Between responding to customers and answering festivals, I have to be disciplined. It's not enjoyable to do, but I learned that it is part of the work and has to be done, so that's okay. I spend a couple of days each month doing festival things and then at least a couple of hours every day answering emails and stuff like that."
>
> – Nicolai Troshinsky

When submitting a film to a festival, always read the regulations and double check you have met the submission requirements and are able to provide the required screening format by deadlines if accepted. **21** I keep a spreadsheet of all the festivals I've submitted to or plan to submit to, keeping track of dates, fees paid, acceptances, and screening copies sent.

Once you are accepted by a festival, the festival should, at the very least, give you a full festival pass to attend. **22** It is in their benefit to have filmmakers in attendance interacting with the festival sponsors and patrons. Educate yourself before you go as to who will be there, what films you want to see, which workshops and parties you want to attend. Many festivals will let you bring a guest as well, so you can bring someone from the film crew or a family member or friend. Festivals are networking opportunities though, so your festival companion should be someone who is

**22** Hamburg Kurzfilm Festival.

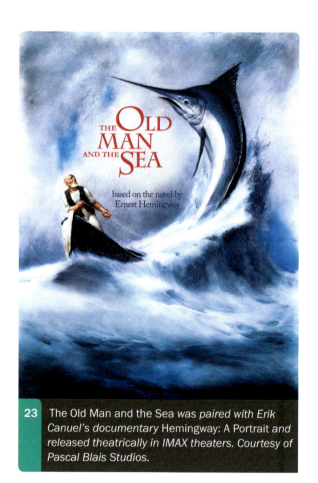

**23** *The Old Man and the Sea was paired with Erik Canuel's documentary* Hemingway: A Portrait *and released theatrically in IMAX theaters. Courtesy of Pascal Blais Studios.*

comfortable experiencing the festival with you but won't keep you from working the crowd. Bring plenty of business cards and postcards to hand out – after all, this is a business trip!

## Distribution

The festival-going audience is small, but focused. They love films and are open to experimental works. The next step up for reaching an audience is television and paid broadcast opportunities. If your film has done well on the festival circuit, you may be approached by a distributor offering to program your film on TV, release it theatrically or with a video-on-demand service. 23 This can be a great opportunity to reach an entirely new audience and you should receive some form of payment in exchange for the right to broadcast. Frequently these arrangements will require that your film not be released online, and there will be exclusions for other distribution forms, possibly on a country-by-country basis. You may have one distributor in France and another in England and another in the USA. These terms will all be outlined in the contracts.

There are scammers out there that will try to make you pay for the privilege of having them shop your film around to different distributors. A marketing agent might take a cut of any profits, but you should never have to pay upfront for someone to sell or distribute your film. Do not sign any legal documents without a thorough analysis by a lawyer! The rights to your film are valuable, so the more rights you give up, the more financial compensation you should expect to get.

## Releasing Online

The biggest audience is the entire connected world and the way you ultimately reach them is through an online release of your film. When planned thoughtfully, an online release will help your film reach more viewers than all of the other methods combined and allow you to interact with them on many levels.

One strategy is to hold a film back from online release while it makes its festival run. Some festivals, and certainly distributors, prefer a film not be online, because it competes with their viewership. I have noticed that festivals are becoming more relaxed with this regulation. If the festival enjoys your film enough to have selected it, they understand the value of showing it in a theater with a big screen and immersive sound. Sometimes all it takes is a polite email to the festival director to allow the film to remain online. Generally speaking, once a film is available online, the options for paid distribution are limited. Frequently these opportunities arise during the festival life of a film, which usually is about two years from completion.

The downside of holding a film back during the festival run is by the time it's over, the film is two years old. You might be fully immersed in another project, there are new films winning awards at festivals and getting press. For a successful online premiere you will need to work extra hard to build anticipation around the release.

The second option is to release your film online as soon as possible, or after it has played a

24 *A successful online release requires a lot of behind-the-scenes preparation.*

few big festivals. Again, you will need to work hard to build anticipation, because if you and your film are not well known via festival buzz, you have to create that buzz yourself. Whether you release your film immediately or wait until after your festival run, the common denominator of success is hard work and planning. **24**

The platform on which you release the film is important. YouTube and Vimeo have different focuses and draw a different audience. Other video-on-demand (VOD) platforms reach a more specific, niche audience. Some of these have a paywall – meaning someone must pay either through a subscription service or a one-time fee to view the video. Other platforms use advertising to generate revenue and you might have distracting ads beside, before or even on top of your video. With a paywall, you will get a share of the revenue, but it will significantly reduce the number of viewers who see your film.

When you do decide to put your film online, make it a party! Build some anticipation by posting the trailer and process video to social media sites a few days before. Recruit your friends and family to be part of your "Online Premiere" team. Ask them to share the video with their networks. Research any blogs or online forums that might be interested in your technique or subject matter. Send out press releases with your EPK, and a preview link so those who write the posts can see the film ahead of time. And be available the day of the release to respond to comments, social media, and email about the film. This is your opportunity to connect with your global audience.

For the online premiere of *A Tangled Tale*, I used Google Hangouts to host a live Q&A on the day of the release. Anyone could send in questions via a chat window or Twitter. My sound designer and composer also joined the Q&A to answer questions about their work on the film. **25** It was a lot of fun to revisit the production with these two artists (who had never met in person) and some fans from around the world.

## Alternative Exhibition

The fine art world is welcoming time-based media with open arms. Can you exhibit your animation in a gallery, project it in a dome or on a building? Could it be turned into an interactive app or game or incorporated into a live performance? Animation

**25** Q&A on Google Hangouts. Questions were submitted via chat and Twitter and we answered them during the live broadcast.

**26** Gallery installation at the Warren Miller Performing Arts Center, Big Sky, MT.

is moving outside the theater, so maybe your audience might be out there in another venue.

Soon after releasing *A Tangled Tale* online, I was invited to create an exhibit for the Warren Miller Performing Arts Center in Big Sky, Montana. `26` Just as I approach each film as a journey for my viewers, I approached the gallery space as a journey for each visitor. The exhibit, installed in a long corridor, revealed the process and artistry of sand animation. I was able to lead visitors through the production of the film, starting at one end of the gallery with the storyboard panels, then taking them through an interactive installation where they could create and project their own sand art. Frame sequences from different scenes were suspended on the walls and at the end of the corridor, the film was projected on the wall. `27`

At the opening of the exhibition, I did a sand animation demonstration and showed several short films before inviting visitors to explore the gallery at their leisure. This exhibition added a new dimension to the viewer's experience of the film because they were able to experience and visualize the artistic energy that went into the film. `28`

## A Final Word

We invest a lot in our work. We spend so much time thinking about the meaning of each plot point, putting ourselves wholly into the creation of every frame, that when it comes time to send a film out to its audience, we want to be with it every step of the way. So remember that while you have created a journey for your viewers, they will travel it individually, with their unique combination of personal history and aesthetic tastes. Like every work of art, once your film leaves the safe confines of the studio, it encounters each viewer on their own terms, regardless of your intentions.

I love asking audiences how they interpret certain parts of my films, rather than just telling them what I meant to say. It is always surprising to hear the perspective of someone else experiencing an idea I have gone through forward, backward, and inside-out. Inevitably I learn something about my own work, when I send the film out to the world and let the audience take over.

But that is not to say you should let your journey end there. Any work completed in the experimental frame of mind is bound to raise new topics of exploration. In this book, we've discovered the haptic techniques of fluid frame animation, and I hope you have some sand, paint, or clay still lingering under your fingernails. You have probably realized by now that I'm a big advocate of learning while animating; there is no better way to understand these materials than by moving them under

`27` *Photo credit: Kevin Fosse.*

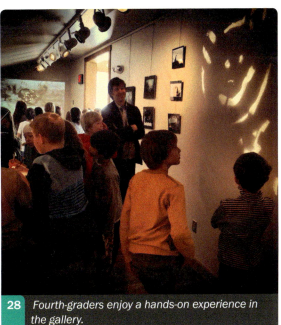
`28` *Fourth-graders enjoy a hands-on experience in the gallery.*

the camera and seeing what happens. The expert advice from the many artists in this book is only there to give you a bit of a head start because all the animation that has been done up until this point is the foundation for the possibilities ahead. The combination of the physical and the digital is barely tapped and all of us are counting on you to take these techniques further. **29**

You know by now that it takes work to create the fluid animation this book encompasses; you will spend long hours under the camera, experimenting and practicing, and just as many in front of the computer refining and expanding your animation. When you reach the end of your own adventurous exploration, be proud of the hard work you put into your fluid frames and push them out into the world to stand on their own. Then bolster up your experimental frame of mind and start something new. **30**

## Notes

1. Walley, Clive. "'The Divertimenti' An Interview with Clive Walley." Interview by David G. Ehrlich. *Animation Journal* 7.2 (1999): 30—51.
2. Troshinsky, Nicolai. "Astigmatismo." Telephone interview. Feb. 20, 2014.
3. Müller, Michaela. Personal interview. March 20, 2014.

**29** It always takes a while to really let go of a project and declare it finished. I made this handy flowchart after finishing A Tangled Tale.

**30** Generations of animators sign the wall at Otis in Hiroshima.

*Corrie Francis Parks.*

# Appendix A
# Case Studies

**Case Study:** Loving Vincent

**Case Study:** Truth Has Fallen

**Case Study:** Trag/Trace/Spur and Up the Stairs

We have explored many materials in the new frontier of animation. Now where do we go? Here are three interviews with directors and artists that are taking fluid frame animation into broader applications.

## Loving Vincent – A Case Study

One surefire way to know that a technique has come into its own is when someone finds a way to make it scalable. At the turn of the twentieth century, animation was in the category of parlor tricks and esoteric entertainment (see works by Blackton, Cohl, Méliès, and, the quintessential example, Winsor McCay's *Gertie the Dinosaur*). It wasn't long, though, until someone took this magical, time-intensive cinematic art form and found a way to production line the process. Registration systems, stylistic uniformity, and, finally, the invention of the cel enabled small studios to take on bigger projects and animation sprouted into the industry it is today.

Now that robust animation industry has its own form of auteur, time-intensive methods. One such method is painted animation – the manipulation of wet paint under the camera, frame by painstaking frame. This form of creating was always a solitary endeavor – a single animator with a unique vision

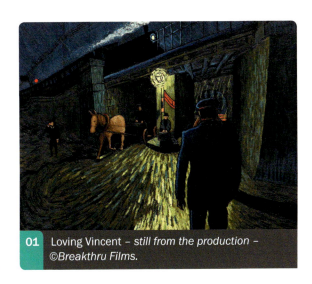

**01** Loving Vincent – *still from the production* – ©Breakthru Films.

in a dark camera room for months, even years, sometimes creating only one or two paintings a day. Certainly, there is no way to mass produce such a technique – every painter has their own style and method and to impose the uniformity that upward scalability requires would be sacrilege. Or would it? Perhaps not if the style was that of one of the most revolutionary and influential painters of the nineteenth century – Vincent van Gogh. **01**

This is the idea behind *Loving Vincent*, a forthcoming feature length documentary/drama on the final years of Van Gogh's life. Every single frame of the film is hand-painted by a team of 60 artists, making it the first mass-produced painted animation film. What has enabled this momentous endeavor is the meticulous planning, research, and artistic orchestration from directorial team Dorota Kobiela (*The Little Postman*) and Hugh Welchman (*Peter and the Wolf*).

I spoke to Hugh just as the studio was ramping up for full painting production in January 2015. At this point, the *Loving Vincent* team had finalized the script, trained the first round of painters, and shot the first live action reference scenes for production.

Corrie Francis Parks: So, your team must be full on into everything right now.
Hugh Welchman: Yes, we started the painted animation on the 12th of January so we shot the live action footage that is the starting point for the animation just before Christmas break. Then we had to get the effects done and the reference animation done on that footage, put them all together so they are ready for the final stage, which is painting. So, it was technically pretty tricky just getting thirteen people up and painting, but now everyone's well into that shot and it's good. They're still freaking out but, you know, it's not so intense as the training.
CFP: So, it's still not an entirely comfortable process for them?
HW: On the other animation films I've worked on, the animators have four or five years of experience as animators. On this film they have four or five weeks of experience as animators. I tell them they're going to get faster, but they don't believe me. They will. They'll eventually see the results, but none of them are professional animators because no animators can paint well enough to be selected for the film. We would have loved to have had some animators but we had 600 applications and around 30–40 of them were professional animators, but their painting just wasn't good enough to be able to do this kind of film.
CFP: You've been involved in several animated films over recent years and one thing I've noticed within the animation industry is that there seems to be a renewed interest in physical materials. I see more films where their physical process of making the film is just as important as the film itself. And now we see all the "making of" videos and the production blogs. Do you see that as being something of a trend and is that why now is a really good time to be making *Loving Vincent*?
HW: That was something that I struggled with quite a lot back in 2002 when I started putting together *Peter and the Wolf*. I was very clear that I wanted to do the film with Susie Templeton. She had a handmade style and I loved it! At the time, everyone wanted to do CG. No one wanted to touch most particularly drawn animation, but also puppet animation. I remember we had a meeting with one executive producer that Channel 4 [A UK public television station] trying to get us to work with and they said, "Yeah, I really like it, but you should do it in CG," at which point me and Susie politely lasted out the few minutes of the meeting and left. So, for me that handmade quality has always been part of the joy.

I trained in live action, so for me it's much more tangible if I can see it. Puppet animation is the same as live action; it's just very slow. You have real lights, you have real actors, you have real cameras, so for me it made a lot more sense. I remember seeing the first *Toy Story* in the cinema and didn't know why everyone was getting so excited. I just never really liked the CG aesthetic. I made a number of CG animations because I was interested and you can't really avoid it. We used the computer a lot in *Peter and the Wolf* and we use it a lot on *Loving Vincent*. I mean we couldn't make films that look so handmade without the infrastructure of digital technology.

CFP: I think that that's what so great about where we are right now. CG and traditional methods are becoming partners rather than two separate fields. I couldn't do the things that I do in sand without After Effects and shooting digitally. I think it's a really fantastic, exciting time for animation because the two worlds are colliding and we get a completely new aesthetic out of it.

HW: And also you can reclaim the art form. There were a bunch of animators who were very highly paid, very well respected, and suddenly they just couldn't get jobs. Now suddenly in 2D you're getting back some of the experience that was there before. Unfortunately, many people retired or had to go into other things during that ten-year gap where no one would touch 2D drawn animation. One of the things that also annoys me is that a lot of the computer animators that we work with can't draw. I think whatever animation film you're making, you should be able to draw. **02**

CFP: So, even with this renewed interest, it's still a pretty crazy idea to think that you can make a feature length film with hand-painted frames. What was it that convinced you that something of this scale was even conceivable, let alone possible?

HW: I think it was very much following my gut rather than following my head. If I rationalized it, I'd still say that this is a completely crazy stupid thing to do. At the same time my gut tells me that what we're doing is inspired and it's going to be brilliant. I literally have that every day – those two things.

It started out as a short film idea from Dorota Kobiela. She came and worked for us for a year, which turned into two years, and in that time we got to learn about this film: painted animation bringing the paintings of Vincent van Gogh to life. We started doing research into Van Gogh and the story of his life and I was just blown away at how popular he is. He's sort of like a rock star! His reach is incredible. I didn't really know anything about art, but still, I could recognize a Picasso or a Salvador Dalí or the *Mona Lisa* or Vincent van Gogh's paintings. It's very distinctive. So, we had no massive ambition to do a feature length painted animation, but we did think Vincent van Gogh's story could be told as a feature film because the audience is big enough.

I didn't really understand what style Dorota wanted to do, so we did the concept trailer. When it started to come together, I literally had the hairs on the back of my neck standing up and I thought, "I have to make this film! This is so different. It's so beautiful.

**02** *One of the painters at work. ©Breakthru Films.*

It's something I would love to put together." So that was the decision point. All animation takes ages to make, so I didn't really start to grapple with how much longer it's going to take to paint this film than if we were dealing with puppets. Right now that's why, from dawn until dusk and very often in the nighttime as well, during my dreams or waking moments, it's what possesses me; 56,800 paintings! Made by a bunch of people who've never animated before! `03`

CFP: How did you select your team of painters?

HW: They're amazingly brilliant artists, especially this group of the first 16 people, who are here now. Eventually, we want to expand it to 60 painters. Out of the 600 people who applied, we asked 300 people to do a three-day audition. So, they had to take three days out of their life and come and do an audition. Out of those 300, we chose 55 for the training and most of them made it through that. At the moment, we've got around 50 trained, but I wouldn't take them all on at once because that would lead to mutiny and despair. I wanted to get the best painters up to speed first and my aim is that they're averaging five to six frames a day – close to half a second a day. So when this group gets up to speed, then we'll bring on the next one. And they'll start off saying, "Oh it's impossible," just like this first group did, but then I can point over to the first group and say, "They're doing it, and it took them 6 weeks to get up to speed."

CFP: That's a good strategy. Did you encounter some of those feelings of being overwhelmed during the training?

HW: The training is six weeks and it's very intensive and they're just trying to get their head around it. Definitely there was a certain pain barrier for the painting and for the animation during the training and for everyone it comes at a different point. Some people get their head around it very fast and have already animated this particular movement and you've got someone next to them, who's also an amazing painter, and they're stuck there for five days. But at some point it clicks. `04`

`03` Loving Vincent – *still from the production* – ©Breakthru Films.

`04` Each painter went through an intensive six-week training course, learning how to animate in Van Gogh's style. ©Breakthru Films.

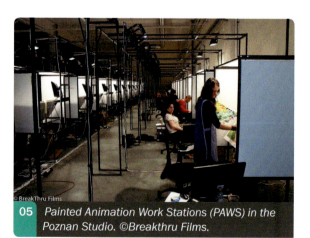

`05` Painted Animation Work Stations (PAWS) in the Poznan Studio. ©Breakthru Films.

We also pay people by the frame, so if someone went really slowly, then we might just say to them, "Look, this is not for you. It's stressing *us* out because you're not earning enough."

So, we'll see. There's been some very beautiful shots started so far. Would you like to go see one?

CFP: Sure! **05**

At this point Hugh was kind enough to pick up his laptop and take me on a mini tour of the Breakthru Films studio, which is in a large warehouse in Gdańsk, Poland. We walked out of the office and down the stairs past a large wall of beautifully drawn storyboards, known as the "Weeping Wall." Then we went past the rows of painting booths known as PAWS (Painted Animation Work Stations). Each booth is home to one painter and is equipped with an easel with an 80x50cm canvas and painting supplies. Soft, white light bounces off three walls, evenly illuminating the painting surface. Behind the artist, mounted on a steel frame, was a projector, which projected reference footage onto the canvas, and a DSLR camera for capturing each frame. On a shelf above the painting were two monitors, which showed the reference footage and the live feed from the camera via the frame capture program Dragonframe. **06**

**06** *Artists use projection and reference footage as a guide for the animation. ©Breakthru Films.*

The crew has spent weeks fine-tuning their PAWS. Everything is bolted down tightly to eliminate any wobbling. Two buttons by the easel are programmed to switch off the projector and take frames so the artist only has to move out of the way once the frame is ready and click the button. The workflow has been streamlined to the ultimate level of efficiency so the painter can focus all of his or her energy on each brush stroke. **07**

Peering into the studio, I met painter Bartok, who was working on a portrait scene of Van Gogh's friend, Père Tanguy. With Van Gogh's famous portrait as a starting point, and reference footage from actor John Sessions in period costume, Bartok was skillfully bringing the man back to life to tell Van Gogh's story. **08**

In this documentary, Van Gogh's life is stitched together by those closest to him – the people whose portraits he painted. Gleaning a mysterious, inconclusive tale from extensive research into his personal letters, Welchman and Kobiela have revealed the broader, empathetic backstory that

**07** *The PAWS are set up to optimize the painter's comfort and efficiency for the long hours of animation. ©Breakthru Films.*

contextualizes the sensationalism of Van Gogh's more notable mental lapses and his enigmatic death, right as his painting career was taking off.

After our tour, we went back up to the office and continued the conversation:

CFP: From what I understand, you have painters that develop the keyframes, which are the first frame of every shot . . .

HW: Our keyframes are actually designs; they're not keyframes in animation terms. The keyframes are used when we can't take an exact replica of a Vincent painting – because his framing wasn't the 1:183 framing or if we've got to go outside of the frame into the next room or if we have an action sequence. So, this group of painters that have been with us since June were doing the keyframes to prepare all those shots.

But certain shots, particularly moving shots, we make people do miniature frames first, from the beginning, middle, and end. So, we might do up to five miniatures before they start the first frame at that size.

CFP: And those are more like the keyframes in a traditional drawn animation; you use them to work out the movement.

HW: Exactly, so they don't get lost in a moving shot.

CFP: Is the entire canvas wet or is the image mostly dry with just the moving bits being wet and changing every frame?

HW: Just the parts that are moving. Of course, if it's a moving shot, then they're repainting it every time because everything is different.

CFP: How much paint do you expect to go through, based on what you've seen so far?

HW: A lot! I can't remember exactly off the top of my head but it's about 5,000 liters. At the moment, because we've only got 13 painters, we operate a kind of serve-yourself system, but when we have more painters that's going to be impossible. Once we've got 50 painters going, it actually will save us money to have a person whose full-time job is handing out paints and checking that people aren't overusing or letting it dry. It's a huge expense for the film.

CFP: So you're not mixing it with bicycle grease like Petrov does to keep it from drying?

HW: No. We were thinking of another substance that Vincent used in his paints, which is why some of his paints have actually sunk after so many years. At the moment, if the painting's dried out over the weekend, they just scratch it off and paint again.

CFP: One of the big problems with working with wet paint is that the colors get all muddied and mixed up when you continue to manipulate them.

HW: We haven't come up with any way to avoid that yet!

CFP: You have a lot of minds working on this problem collectively. Surely you should come up with a brilliant solution!

HW: That would be good, but no. The main thing we've found is that if it gets too muddied, scrape it off, repaint it.

CFP: Tell me about the workflow with shooting the live action on a blue screen and compositing. At one point early on, you had

08  *Actor John Sessions as Père Tanguy. ©Breakthru Films.*

considered doing the reference in CG, but I think live action is probably a better economical and aesthetic choice.

HW: Vincent's paintings are realistic enough, especially the portraits, that you're always going to get more emotion off the human face. And it's a very emotional story. Stylized animation is never going to have that immediate payoff for an audience, so that was really the reason. A lot of the story is told by the portraits and we want to see the emotion on their face. Very early on that was a decision that I made with Dorota, that we should have real actors. I think there's a fusion between the energy of the human being and the energy of the painting. The crowds are going to be CG though!

CFP: When you're shooting the actors, how do you know where to place them? Do you have some sort of system where you can see the keyframe that you developed?

HW: Yep, you see the keyframe, you see the actors, and we do the 3D models and the matte paintings beforehand. We mostly get away with doing matte paintings, but for some environments we have to do 3D models.

CFP: I'm going to play devil's advocate for a moment. Why not just develop a series of filters and plug-ins that replicate Van Gogh's brush strokes and call it good? Why go to all this trouble training painters?

HW: Quite simply, no one has shown me a computer process that looks as beautiful as what we do. If there was, I would've done it. I wouldn't go through this painful, risky process if there was a computer where I could press a button and it would do it or if I could get a bunch of very smart people in a room programming and they could come up with it. The Van Gogh Museum has done some three-dimensional prints of Van Gogh's paintings and even they're not the same.

One thing I always say, which I also said with puppet animation, is that you can feel the passion of the hands on it. You can feel the flare in the drawing line, you can feel the passion of the hands on the puppet – that condensed life kind of thing. It's the same with painting. There's a certain energy you get off real painting that you don't get off a print.

CFP: A lot of artists that work under the camera, and it's generally a very auteur form of animation, say they enjoy the spontaneity of the technique and going with the flow. But on a project of this scale, of course, everything has to be planned and predictable. So is there any room for spontaneity in this film?

HW: In terms of the animators, even in the 13 shots we've got running at the moment, there's a range in terms of individual flair. Much more than you would on a normal film. It's inevitable when you're working with these talented painters. There's one shot that's being done of Vincent holding his ear in the handkerchief, walking along to the brothel to give it to the prostitute. It looks unbelievable, so much better than I thought it was going to be – and that's all the animator. Really, in terms of the way that he's brought out the light, it looks amazing.

CFP: It's the first time something has been done on this scale, and on the one hand it's sort of like mass producing this technique, but it can

09 During full productions, 60 painters could work simultaneously on the film. ©Breakthru Films.

only be mass produced with brilliant individual artists so, like you said, there's no way to discount that aspect. `09`

HW: I experienced the same thing with 2D animation, puppet animation, and CG animation. One of the big challenges of my job is to keep that very special quality over such a big scale, which is one of the reasons why I'm taking it a stage at a time – bringing on a small team of animators, getting them up to a level and not bringing on other people until I feel they're at the right level.

Obviously, the bigger the film, the more authoritarian you have to be, but you have to always try and do that in a nice way. You have to be very strict, but you can't be horrible because that goes against the spirit that you want in a team. It's not like a factory where, if you sack someone for pushing that button, you can hire someone else for pushing that button. Painters of that level just don't exist. I can't just get 60 people who are good at painting to waltz off the street and under a projector and expect it to turn out. They have to become great animators very quickly so my job is to shave off time wasted for stupid things and give them space to concentrate on animating. Even though people will say this is 80% rotoscoping, it's still 20% animation, and the difference between good films and great films is in that 20%. `10`

10  Loving Vincent – *still from the production* – ©Breakthru Films.

## Truth Has Fallen – A Case Study

Any independently produced feature film in animation must, by necessity, be a passion project. When Sheila Sofian read about James McCloskey, who fights to free prisoners who have been wrongfully convicted of murder, little did she know her first interview would take her on a 16-year journey into feature documentary. *Truth Has Fallen* introduces three individuals who have been freed by McCloskey's work. Through their stories of wrongful conviction, imprisonment, and eventual release, the documentary sheds light on the flaws in the American justice system. `11`

An integral part to the film are the segments of paint-on-glass animation, Sofian's specialty. The personal stories of the imprisoned are told through symbolic imagery and artistically emotive recreation, allowing the audience to connect deeply and sympathetically with the subjects. In contrast, the more detached explanation of the judicial misfiring are depicted through live action re-enactments and interviews with experts.

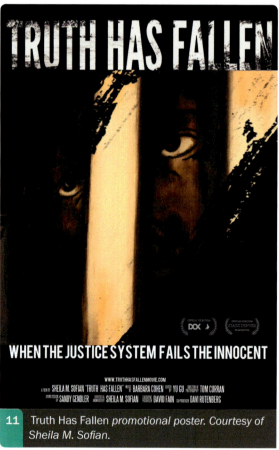

11  Truth Has Fallen *promotional poster. Courtesy of Sheila M. Sofian.*

Sofian is not only the animator, but also the director, researcher, and producer on the film, truly a massive endeavor for one person, but one that was fueled by her deep-set belief that these stories needed to be pushed into the public eye. In February of 2015, as the film was traveling the festival circuit, I spoke to Sofian via Skype to ask her about her technique and the film. **12**

Corrie Francis Parks: Can you tell me about your background and about the first time you started doing paint-on-glass?

Sheila Sofian: Sure, well the first time I tried paint-on-glass was when I was in undergraduate school at Rhode Island School of Design. We had a painting-on-glass assignment in our sophomore year and I eventually decided to use the technique for my senior film, *Mangia*. Caroline Leaf came down to give a presentation, so they let me go to dinner with the faculty and her, and I was able to ask her a lot of questions. She even gave me some paint. She was really generous. So I learned about the kind of paint and tools to use from her, which helped a lot, but it was mostly figuring it out on my own. **13**

CFP: I've noticed that pretty much everybody working in these under-the-camera techniques has just figured it out as they went along. It seems to attract that sort of animator. What did you discover along the way that honed in the technique for you?

SS: There were a couple things I can point to. After I was done with *Mangia*, I talked to Caroline Leaf about it and she was asking about what tools I used. I said "Well, paintbrushes and Q-tips," and she suggested the wooden cuticle sticks. And she also said she mostly uses her fingers, which I honestly hadn't thought about! Ever since then, when I work with my fingers, I find it's so much better because as the paint dries you really get a lot of control over it; you get these really beautiful results. So even though it was just a passing comment, it made a really big influence on me.

Also, later on I read an article in which Wendy Tilby mentioned sponges. So I went out and tried different sponges – In *A Conversation with Haris*, I did a lot of sponge work and I just love it; it's so beautiful. You can create textures that you can't any other way, so now every time I go shopping, I look for different kinds of sponges and different kinds of textures.

CFP: Your work in particular has that textural feel. I can sense the different ways you apply the paint. Tell me a little bit more about the tools you use.

**12** *Sheila Sofian. Courtesy of Sheila M. Sofian.*

**13** *Mangia – Sheila M. Sofian – 1985.*

14    *Sofian's studio. Courtesy of Sheila M. Sofian.*

15    *A motion blur effect created with a brush. (A Conversation with Haris – Sheila M. Sofian.)*

SS: I use Q-tips a lot. And the wooden cuticle sticks. Because I animate on white Plexiglas, every place I press with a Q-tip or stick reveals the white underneath. So if I want a white line I can make fine, very controlled white lines with the stick. When I'm animating, I'll outline the next frame with the stick and then I'll know where everything needs to be. I also will use it for cross-hatching. **14**

    I go through a lot of Q-tips and paper towels. I discovered a big fat paint brush, which I used in *A Conversation With Haris*. I have these faces coming toward the screen, so I'll paint it completely, and at the very end I'll take the brush and just whoosh it across. It makes a bit of motion blur. Then I'll do the next painting fully painted and just destroy it a little bit with a whoosh of the brush. So it looks kind of blurry as the faces come toward you. **15**

CFP: And your work is all top lit?

SS: My very first film was top lit and bottom lit, and I liked the translucency of it, but I also found it very unforgiving. You can see all the bristles in the paintbrush. I find top lit is a little easier for me to control.

CFP: What kind of paint are you using?

SS: I use tempera paints mixed with glycerin. I have a little palate where I put a bunch of paint and I just put a couple drops of glycerin and mix it in. You have to be careful not to do too much because it becomes too translucent. If you don't do enough, then it dries up too quickly, so it's just finding the right consistency that's easy to work with.

CFP: Why Plexiglas and not regular glass?

SS: I really like the way paint adheres to the Plexiglas. I think I have less problems with translucency too. Sometimes when I scratch, the marks don't clear away completely and I have to use Soft Scrub to get a black mark out completely. I've tried clear glass and glass with different types of textured paper underneath it, but then it casts a shadow.

CFP: Your work is also full of rapid transitions that take us from location to location, from scene to scene. How did you develop that way of thinking – it's a very different way than traditional cinematic editing?

SS: I try to plan out how that next scene is going to begin. What I especially like is when it not only moves from one image to the next, but it moves from one moving image to another moving image. I want to push my work more in that direction because I think that's more beautiful. 16

CFP: You've focused on animated documentary pretty much since the beginning of your career. What drove you to documentaries as opposed to telling fictional stories or abstract stuff?

SS: I love documentary, I love animation, and I was attracted to it. I was talking to a friend of mine, Ruth Hayes, and I was telling her about a film that I had started as a live action documentary about battered women. I was sad that it never turned into a film because these people didn't really want to be identified. I just had talking heads in shadows and it wasn't visually interesting. She's the one that said, "Why don't you do an animated documentary?" It's so obvious now, but I never put those two together. So I went back into the film and I did more interviews and it became *Survivors*. After that, I realized it was very natural for me to go in that direction, so I would look for topics that I was passionate about, to keep me going for the years that it took to make a film.

CFP: I imagine that deep investment in your subject matter must be a big part of your motivation. How did *Truth Has Fallen* come to your attention?

SS: It was a newspaper article I'd read. Usually it's something human rights oriented that really makes me want to tell this story or get it out there. That's the sort of thing that fires me up – that really makes me want to go, "Yes, I have to say this!" From the time of the first interview to the time it was finished was 16 years, though the animation production was done in about ten of those years. 17

CFP: Was the length of the process in part due to the nature of the animation, the funding, or were you actually waiting for the stories to develop over time with each of these people that you were focusing on?

SS: With *Truth Has Fallen*, it was just the labor. The film's an hour long and half an hour is animation, so that was about – I think it worked out to about 20,000 paintings. I was originally going to do more live action, and I was unable to get the funding, but ultimately I think it was better that I didn't shoot more live action.

16  Truth Has Fallen – *Sheila M. Sofian – 2013.*

17  Truth Has Fallen – *Sheila M. Sofian – 2013.*

**18** *Interviewing Vincent Bugliosi. Courtesy of Sheila M. Sofian.*

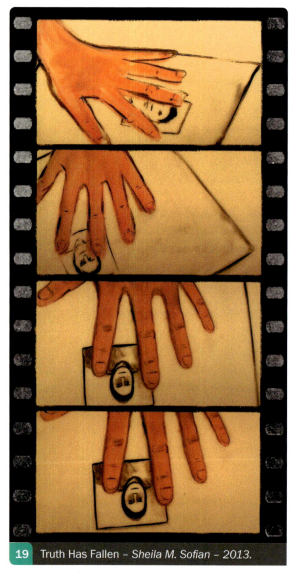

**19** *Truth Has Fallen – Sheila M. Sofian – 2013.*

CFP: Tell me a little bit about the research that you had to do for *Truth Has Fallen*.

SS: That was an interesting process. Originally I read this article about James McCloskey. He's dedicated his life to reinvestigating cases of people he thinks are innocent. I interviewed him, and then he put me in touch with the people that he had helped get released from jail. Those people were so grateful to him they were very willing to help me and to be interviewed. At one point, I hired a producer and she helped me get some heavy hitters, like Barry Scheck, co-founder of the Innocence Project, who's famous for the O.J. Simpson trial, and Vincent Bugliosi, who prosecuted Charles Manson and wrote *Helter Skelter*. **18**

With each interview I learned more that I'd want to take to the next interview and research a little bit more. Just finding out how different the laws were in every single state was really eye opening for me. I had some people that were great resources and allowed me to tap into them.

For example, there's a segment in the film about eyewitness identification. When you look at photographs from a book to identify someone, you tend to do comparative judgments. So if a photo kind of looks like the person you saw compared to the other photos, you will identify it as the person, even if it really isn't the person you saw. The experts I interviewed advocate for the sequential form of eyewitness testimony, where you lay the photographs down one at a time. I had to contact the lawyers to ask, "Well, do you stack them on top or do you remove each one?" because I want to animate the right way. They made themselves available to answer those kinds of questions so I could make sure I illustrated accurately. **19**

CFP: Because in a documentary, a lot is tied up in the little details.

SS: Right, exactly. I want to make sure if it's going to be any form of documentary that I get the facts right.

CFP: Did you have a method for keeping track of all of those details?

SS: When I was in undergraduate school, I did an internship with a documentary film company and they taught me to transcribe all of my interviews and do a paper version of the film. In those days it was more like putting it all on index cards, spreading it on the floor, and figuring out the order. So I always transcribe, which helps me also go through all the information again in my head, even though there were hours and hours of interviews! Then I would just go through and highlight all the things I thought were interesting and related to what I was trying to say in the film. [20]

My first cut was more academic, and I worked with that version for eight years. Then I hired an editor to help me. She had me do a timeline of everything – every person who is featured in the film, a timeline of their cases. Then we went back through the audio and found parts of the story that we thought were important to be told.

My editor went back through a lot of the audio I had not used and she actually resurrected some that I had forgotten about. She made it much better, much more personal, much more energetic and interesting. The only problem was that she added four or five more minutes, which meant another year of animation!

CFP: So it sounds like your approach to the storytelling definitely evolved over the course of the film, especially through the help of your editor. Do you feel like your approach to the animation and the application of the animation evolved alongside?

SS: I will say toward the end I was taking shortcuts. Fatigue was setting in and there's one scene – it was supposed to be much longer, but I just stopped on one frame and shot that for the rest of the sentence because I was like, "I can't animate anymore!"

There was a time when I was feeling like I was surfing a wave, like everything was just coming really naturally and I just felt like, "Oh, I'm really in the flow now and everything's just working out really well!" That was during my sabbatical when I was fully immersed in it and I wasn't having to do other things. [21]

CFP: What does animation bring to the documentary genre? And then specifically, what does paint-on-glass bring to the animated documentary aspect?

SS: I believe that animation allows you to get into the head of the person that's talking, because you're not concentrating on seeing that person and judging that person – your brain isn't working on those things at all. Instead, it's only the contents of their words. I think you can focus more on what it is that they're saying.

I've always thought that paint-on-glass was really a beautiful medium for depicting memories and dreams and so I think, especially when people are recalling events, you can create a more dream-like flow; hook on an image here, and then go over there, and then transition over to this in a very lovely way. When I made *Truth Has Fallen*, I consciously

20  *On set for a live action sequence. Courtesy of Sheila M. Sofian.*

decided that the paint-on-glass animation would be when the people who were in prison were talking. When the expert testimony was there, the audience could be more detached and I could shoot live action. I want you to empathize with people who were in prison, imagining what their experience was like. **22**

CFP: We never see the subjects of the film until the end credits. What sort of reactions have you gotten from people taking that approach? Have people been surprised at what they look like, have been surprised at their stories?

SS: People seemed to be happy to see what they looked like in the end. It's kind of a nice little moment, you know.

CFP: Yes, I felt that too at the end, because I had invested myself into their stories through the animation. At the end we've had this internal experience based on the animation and when we finally see them there's this connection because we've been involved in this emotional, imaginative experience throughout the film.

22  Truth Has Fallen – *Sheila M. Sofian* – 2013.

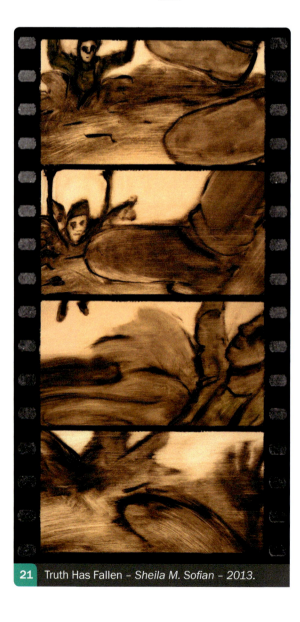

21  Truth Has Fallen – *Sheila M. Sofian* – 2013.

Do you have any final words of advice for new paint-on-glass animators?

SS: Well you know, the most basic mistake everybody makes is when they get Plexiglas or glass is they don't tape it down. They'll be working and halfway through you get this big shake and it's just so distracting, so it sounds really stupid, but just get duct tape!

You know what I love to do? A lot of times I like add water to the surface and just see where it goes, just because I can. If it doesn't work out I don't have to use it. So don't be afraid of experimenting, just allow the paint to tell you what to do next. Sometimes the animation starts to take over and it starts to suggest things to you. So you go, "Well, I'll try that because that looks kind of interesting." You don't have to use everything you shoot, so just allow some time for the paint to tell you what to do next. And don't be afraid of embracing accidents because sometimes those are the coolest things that can happen. Just keep a lot of clean water near you. And don't let your cats walk on top of your painting!

## Trag/Trace/Spur and Up the Stairs – A Case Study

In September 2012, Croatian dancer Zrinka Šimičić Mihanović, Swiss animation artist Michaela Müller, and New York based sound artist Fa Ventilato joined together to create a multimedia performance produced in cooperation with the Zagreb Museum of Contemporary Art. Each artist brought their individual artistic expertise to the empty space, resulting in a 30-minute experience of bodily movement, projection, and sound: *Trag/Trace/Spur*. Further development led to a second version of the performance, *Up the Stairs, Behind Doors, Out the Window*, at the Student Center of Zagreb in 2013. The second performance series included four additional guest artists. 23

As an animator, Müller is known for her award-winning paint-on-glass film *Miramare*, which premiered at the Cannes Film Festival in 2010. Bringing paint-on-glass into live performance presented some new problems for Müller, both creative and technical. I visited Müller in her Brooklyn studio in March of 2015 to ask her about the performance and its development. 24

Corrie Francis Parks: Can you tell me a little bit about that first performance? How did you develop it with your collaborators, Zrinka Šimičić Mihanović and Fa Ventilato?

Michaela Müller: A few years ago, when I was in Zagreb painting *Miramare,* I took classes in contemporary dance. There is a very good scene in Zagreb for contemporary dance and of course I met some very good dancers. We talked about possibilities for collaboration. I always had the wish to connect animation and dance.

23  Trag/Trace/Spur. *Photo credit: Jasenko Rasol.*

A few years later the Museum of Contemporary Art in Zagreb gave us one corner of the exhibition space to realize this idea. It had three walls and the front was open, where we could put seating for an audience. **25**

I brought in sound artist, Fa Ventilato, who also worked on *Miramare*. He's very fun to work with because there is no place he will not go to experiment. Together, we developed this performance which was about leading up the stairs – it's called *Trag/Trace/Spur*. We tried to interactively develop something which would naturally incorporate an animation. We did twenty minutes of improvisation – Zrinka was dancing and I was painting with her, but I was also recording frames of the painting like stopmotion.

CFP: So you were painting live and recording a stopmotion film?

MM: Yes, it was very funny, because I had to think about the animation in two ways. What I was painting was directly projected in the space where she was dancing, so we tried to have a communication between my painting and her dance. But I also was recording frames with a foot pedal. **26**

Immediately after the performance, as a second ending, we watched the film I recorded together. The film functions like a reminiscence of what you lived through when you watched the performance, but it is much faster. The dance might take place in one corner for ten minutes and I was painting in the same corner, but then it is only ten seconds of the recorded film and the dancer is gone. So I had to think of both the film and of interacting with the dancer. That was my challenge.

And, of course, each performance is different, and it did not always work. But what was interesting was that the films only worked in the performance space. The film is projected on the three walls and the floor – if you would watch the film afterwards in a theater, it wouldn't make sense because it's not in the three dimensions.

24  *Michaela Müller. Photo credit: Corrie Francis Parks.*

25  *The performance space in the Museum of Contemporary Art, Zagreb. Photo credit: Christian Nobel.*

26  *Müller recorded frames throughout the performance with her toes so she could play back the animation at the end of the dance. Photo credit: Jasenko Rasol.*

CFP: So the film really only works in the context of the performance, both as a function of the memory of the performance and also an interpretation of the space. I can understand how it's very site specific, that you can't take it and show it somewhere else because it's about that particular space.

MM: We were invited to the Animateka Festival in Ljubljana and did it at the closing ceremony. There we did it in a huge theater – it was a very different space, and it did not really work as nicely as in the gallery space. In the gallery you felt like you are in the cave exploring the painting on the walls and you discover art. It was very intimate.

CFP: How were you communicating with the dancer and the musician, since you were all improvising together?

MM: Zrinka is in the projection. She cannot really see what is around her, so she had to develop skills to feel it somehow. She's very talented. And Fa had a sound library, which we recorded together. He made sounds which could trigger our reaction, so we tried to build something together. During the performance he created a live soundtrack, made only from sounds mixed together and when the film was played at the end, he did music. So it was a clear separation of the soundtrack for each part of the performance. **27**

CFP: How did the piece change over the course of those several performances?

MM: We thought it would change much more. We had some things we returned to. There was what we called "the fire," only it was more like a mood, and these moods would come back almost each time, maybe not in the same order, and sometimes something was very long and sometimes we went through it faster. In the end, after one week, we came to some limits. It needed more experimenting, but we felt during the performance we could not experiment so much.

CFP: Because there was an audience?

MM: Because there was an audience, yes.

CFP: Did you feel like you gained more confidence in the motions of the paint and in how you all were relating to each other over multiple performances? By the last performance did it feel different making it than the first one?

MM: It certainly felt different because I never did performances, so it was my first time on the stage being watched – I was very shy. It was also the first time I did something with improvisation. (Zrinka and Fa are very experienced with improvisation.) I was a bit nervous each time and less toward the end, so I gained confidence. We have not performed enough for me to say if the confidence is because we were getting better or because I got more used to it. **28**

We came together again a year later in a different space, and there we had other guest artists included and it was much more complicated. That one was called *Up the Stairs, Behind Doors, Out the Window*.

CFP: *Trag* developed into that piece, but they both have the idea of exploring a space, moving through a house. Where did that idea come from initially?

**27** Trag/Trace/Spur. *Photo credit: Christian Nobel.*

MM: With *Up the Stairs*, Fa and I were in New York and Zrinka was in Zagreb. We thought we would like to develop something before we met to rehearse and improvise, so we started with a basic element of life: the house. Then we read books and talked and we had a common web-based notebook where we contributed brainstorming ideas based on the topic of the house. I think that was a good way to find a starting point, but maybe a bit too broad. **29**

When we met, we started with props and a blanket made up like a tent and we projected on the tent. We had a colleague who is a curator and she came to have a look and said she's so tired of blankets on stage. If we do that she would find it very boring. So we skipped the blanket and we skipped all the props. **30**

Before the performance, we went through the audience and asked people questions about their house. For example, we asked them, "Which is your favorite room in the house and why?" "What would you like to eat tonight?" or "What's your favorite childhood memory at home?" Then Fa took the answers and tried to weave them into the sounds and to connect them with the idea of our house. So each performance we explored a different house.

CFP: How did you prepare for those performances, both the first one and the bigger one with more people involved? Did you ever rehearse together? Did you rehearse on your own?

**28** Up the Stairs *performers (left to right): Ema Abadžieva, Tanja Minarik, Michaela Müller. Photo credit: Jasenko Rasol.*

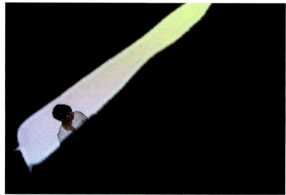

**29** Trag/Trace/Spur. *Photo credit: Jasenko Rasol.*

**30** *Dancer Zrinka Šimičić Mihanović.* Trag/Trace/Spur. *Photo credit: Jasenko Rasol.*

MM: Yes, all of that! Also, I build my tools. I tried to find transparent tools, like a transparent squeegee and plexi sticks for the paintbrushes, so they would not be seen.

CFP: That's one of the things I'm very curious about. You are using a live video feed, but I never see your hand when you're doing the painting!

MM: Yeah, that's a big problem. I fight with it. You can see the hand if you look, but I have long plexi sticks which I stick on the brush so I can keep the hands out of view most times. **31**

CFP: It must be harder to paint like that.

MM: Yes, but it's rather abstract, so I can push the color around quickly. It's hard because my painting field was very small and then projected so big. One little brush stroke was already covering the figure of the dancer.

So we had about two weeks to get together and find out what we wanted to do. We did rehearsals every evening for two hours to prepare. When I think back on those two pieces, the second one with the guest artists didn't find shape or a final form. It is a process, and it stayed a process. **32**

CFP: Do you think that that's a factor of the different space that you were in or the different people, because there were more people that you were collaborating with?

MM: What was it? It probably was more than one factor. I think it's much more difficult working with more people because you have to get to know each other to improvise together. But they were also all very good artists. Our initial goal was to shift focus off the dancer at times, and make it more multimedial and less theatrical, but maybe because it was only one dancer, the audience always had to look at the dancer, so we didn't really get that.

CFP: That's a big challenge to divert the audience's attention away from a live person on a stage . . .

MM: . . . unless she's sleeping!

CFP: I can see how you were trying to do that by covering her up in darkness with the paint or the way that she laid down on the floor and was still for a while and just didn't do anything – sleeping, like you said. But the audience is always aware there is somebody there in that darkness. You just have that awareness. That's a big challenge.

MM: I think it worked much better the first time when we were in the white space in the gallery because you could see the three of us all really well. We were all in the light. In *Up the Stairs*, it was more like a black stage for the dancer where everybody else was outside. People could see me and Fa, but they would not watch us. There were many things

**31** *Michaela Müller. Trag/Trace/Spur. Photo credit: Jasenko Rasol.*

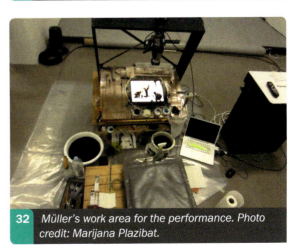

**32** *Müller's work area for the performance. Photo credit: Marijana Plazibat.*

to explore in such a short time, that's why I think it stayed in the process and didn't find its final place. **33**

CFP: Now you are working on a new short film, and you are working on projections for an opera in Belgrade as well. Do you feel like you are pursuing two separate things or do they come together?

MM: I think they must interact but I don't know how. I love the theater as a very direct, collaborative art and I also love the fact that when it's over, it's gone, which is the opposite of film. I always thought that the gesture of painting and the abstract element of paint are a great contribution to opera. I think painting is emotionally like music and singing. I've always wished to be part of an opera with paint animation and I hope this project will be realized. **34**

Painting an animated film on glass, on the contrary, is a very lonely work in the dark. It takes years to accomplish. Here I have a clear storyboard that shows me the way.

CFP: Well it sounds like you have some really interesting projects going on. Thank you so much for sharing your process.

MM: Somehow they come at the right time. When I think one has ended, somewhere some other project shows up.

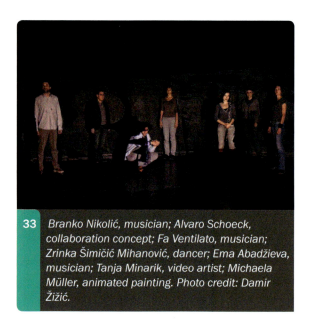

**33** *Branko Nikolić, musician; Alvaro Schoeck, collaboration concept; Fa Ventilato, musician; Zrinka Šimičić Mihanović, dancer; Ema Abadžieva, musician; Tanja Minarik, video artist; Michaela Müller, animated painting. Photo credit: Damir Žižić.*

**34** *Dancer Zrinka Šimičić Mihanović. Trag/Trace/Spur. Photo credit: Jasenko Rasol.*

*Corrie Francis Parks.*

# Appendix B
# Artists' Profiles

### Gil Alkabetz

**Where he calls home:** Kibuz "Mashabei Sade," Israel; Stuttgart and Potsdam, Germany

**Fluid frame technique:** Clay on glass

**Fluid frame film:** *Bitzbutz* (1984)

Bitzbutz – *Gil Alkebetz – 1984.*

**#ProTip** *Since the stories in each film are different from each other, their visual language differs too. I usually don't use a style I already used in a previous film for a completely different story. That was also the case in* Bitzbutz *– first I had a story, and it took me some time to get to the flat black and white look, and even more time to decide about the technique.*

**Find out more:** www.alkabetz.com

### Nag and Gisèle Ansorge

**Where they called home:** Lausanne, Switzerland

**Fluid frame technique:** Sand

**Fluid frame films:** *The Ravens* (1967), *Fantasmatic* (1969), *Anima* (1977), *Sabbath* (1991), and many, many more.

**Find out more:** http://www.swissfilms.ch/

Sabbat – *Nag and Gisèle Ansorge – 1991.*

## Fluid Frames: Artists' Profiles

### Shira Avni

**Where she calls home:** Montreal, Canada

**Fluid frame technique:** Clay on glass

**Fluid frame films:** *John and Michael* (2004), *Tying Your Own Shoes* (2009)

*Shira Avni ©2006 National Film Board of Canada.*
*Photo credit: Caroline Hayeur.*

**#ProTip** *Practice and expect to rework shots – it's not a quick technique to learn. Plan out your shots very well but leave room for some improvisation – sometimes the "happy accidents" lead to the most beautiful work. Let yourself be swept up by the meditative process and your work will reflect the joy of the process.*

Find out more: www.nfb.ca/explore-all-directors/shira-avni

---

### Ferenc Cakó

**Where he calls home:** Budapest, Hungary

**Fluid frame technique:** Sand animation

**Fluid frame films:** *Ab Ova* (1987), *Ad Rem* (1989), *Ashes* (1994), *Song of Sand* (1995)

*Ferenc Cakó. Photo credit: Szabolcs Bánlaki.*

**#ProTip** *Have a well thought-out working process and endless patience; don't rush it.*

Find out more: http://sandanimation.tumblr.com/

Artists' Profiles Appendix B

## Martine Chartrand

Where she calls home: Montreal, Canada

Fluid frame technique: Oil paint on glass

Fluid frame films: *Black Soul* (2000), *MacPherson* (2012)

*Martine Chartrand ©2006 National Film Board of Canada. Photo Credit: Caroline Hayeur.*

**#ProTip** *From Petrov, I learned to question my animation: "Why is this scene so important? What is this thing that you shouldn't have moved because it's not working or it's not important?" He inspired me to be like Sherlock Holmes on my own work – to find the problems and question them so I do not put not too much energy on a scene that I don't need.*

Find out more: www.martinechartrand.net

## David Ehrlich

*Clay painting. Courtesy of David Ehrlich.*

Where he calls home: Springfield, Vermont, USA; Beijing, China

Fluid frame technique: Clay on wood panel

Fluid frame films: *Etude* (1994), *Taking Color for a Walk* (2002), *Color Run* (2001), *Clay* (2008), *Poznanie* (2009)

Find out more:
http://www.awn.com/animationworld/david-ehrlich-excavation-flawed-soul
http://www.iotacenter.org/visualmusic/historysearch
http://blog.sina.com.cn/davidehrlich

## Oskar Fischinger

*Still from* Motion Painting No. 1 *by Oskar Fischinger, 1947, © Center for Visual Music.*

Where he called home: Germany, USA

Fluid frame technique: Paint on Plexiglas

Fluid frame film: *Motion Painting No. 1* (1947)

Find out more: http://www.centerforvisualmusic.org/Fischinger/

## Fluid Frames: Artists' Profiles

### Witold Giersz

Where he calls home: Konstancin, Poland

Fluid frame technique: Oil paint on glass, drawing under the camera

Fluid frame films: *Horse* (1967), *Fire* (1975), *Signum* (2015)

Find out more: http://culture.pl/en/artist/witold-giersz

Witold Giersz. Photo Credit: Romuald Pieńkowski/Polish National Film Archive.

---

### Joan Gratz

Where she calls home: Portland, USA

Fluid frame technique: Clay on glass

Fluid frame films: *The Creation* (1981), *Mona Lisa Descending a Staircase* (1992), *Puffer Girl* (2009), *Kubla Kahn* (2010), *Lost and Found* (2012), *Night Weaver* (2015), and many more

Lost and Found – *Joan Gratz* – 2012.

 *I'm not that critical of myself. I don't look at something and think, "Oh, I could've been better." It just is whatever it is. I think that saves a lot of time.*

Find out more: http://www.gratzfilm.com/

---

### Anna Humphries

Where she calls home: London, UK

Fluid frame technique: Sand

Fluid frame film: *The Oyster Murders – It Might Be Real* (2012)

It Might Be Real – *Anna Humphries* – 2012.

#ProTip *My philosophical bit of wisdom would be to keep on moving forward and just enjoy the medium that you're working with. Because you can't go back, you've got to keep on going, so just see where it will take you. Don't worry about the past mistakes, just keep on going until you've made something useful.*

Find out more: http://anna-mation.co.uk

### Artists' Profiles  Appendix B

Patrick Jenkins. *Courtesy of Patrick Jenkins.*

### Patrick Jenkins

Where he calls home: Toronto, Canada

Fluid frame technique: Gouache on linoleum panel

Fluid frame films: *Labyrinth* (2008), *Inner View* (2009), *Sorceress* (2012)

**#ProTip** *Try some metamorphoses, transforming one thing into another. That's what paint-on-glass does well. Don't disguise that the imagery is made up of paint and brush strokes. That's part of the charm of paint-on-glass animation! It's painterly!*

Find out more: www.patrickjenkinsanimation.com

---

Tunnel – *Maryam Kashkoolinia – 2012.*

### Maryam Kashkoolinia

Where she calls home: Tehran, Iran

Fluid frame technique: Sand on glass

Fluid frame films: *Tunnel* (2012), *When I Was a Child* (2014)

**#ProTip** *Be patient and forbearing, and be aware that sand is not a group work; it's better to be an individual work. The script should be reasonable length and it should make sense for the sand technique. For example,* Tunnel *was a story about digging, so it seemed reasonable to choose sand for the film.*

---

On the Beautiful Danube. *Courtesy of TV Studio of Animation Films Ltd. Poznan.*

### Aleksandra Korejwo

Where she calls home: Poland

Fluid frame technique: Salt

Fluid frame film: *The Swan* (1990), *On the Beautiful Blue Danube* (1993), *Carmen Suite* (1994–96), *Jubilee Concerto* (2011)

Find out more: http://www.imdb.com/name/nm1018305/

Fluid Frames: Artists' Profiles

### Caroline Leaf

Where she calls home: London, UK

Fluid frame techniques: Sand, paint-on-glass

Fluid frame films: *The Owl that Married A Goose* (1974), *The Metamorphosis of Mr. Samsa* (1977), *The Street* (1976), *Interview* (1979), *Sand or Peter and the Wolf* (1969)

The Street ©1976 National Film Board of Canada, All rights reserved.

**#ProTip** *I like limitations. They give you energy to help you make choices. If you said to me, "Come up with a story," I would flounder. And choosing the story was not easy. But once I'd found something that was open enough, I could put my own ideas into it.*

Find out more: http://www.carolineleaf.com/

---

### Xin Li

Where he calls home: Harbin, China; Melbourne, Australia

Fluid frame technique: Oil paint on glass

Fluid frame films: *The Umbrella* (2011), *A Tale of Longing* (2012)

The Umbrella – *Xin Li* – 2011

**#ProTip** *Animation is like a special language. Sometimes, you can speak your emotions; you can tell people what you think. But sometimes a certain emotion, you can't express, like the deeper emotions in the heart. I think animation or filmmaking is a way to express this emotion, and also let people evolve and communicate with each other.*

Find out more: www.xinlianimation.com

---

### César Díaz Meléndez

Where he calls home: Madrid, Spain

Fluid frame technique: Sand animation

Fluid frame films: *No Corras Tanto* (2009), *Atormenta* (2009), *Zepo* (2014)

Zepo – *César Díaz Meléndez* – 2014.

| #ProTip | *Keep your mind out of the way and you can improvise when you are moving the sand. Like in* No Corras Tanto, *I would draw and look and think, "Oh, it look a little like a face, now I'll make a face." Feel free to do what the sand is telling you. I think it's not very difficult. People think you move it grain by grain, but for me it is just like drawing. It is easier for me to draw in sand than with a pencil. I'm more free.*

Find out more: https://vimeo.com/cesarlinga

Matières à rêver – Florence Miailhe – 2009.

### Florence Miailhe

Where she calls home: France

Fluid frame techniques: Gouache on glass, pastel under-the-camera, sand

Fluid frame films: *Hamman* (1992), *Schéhérazade* (1995), *Les oiseaux blancs, les oiseaux noirs* (2002), *Conte de quartier* (2006), *Matières à rêver* (2008), *Méandres* (2013)

Find out more: http://www.imdb.com/name/nm0583939/

Michaela Müller. Photo credit: Corrie Francis Parks.

### Michaela Müller

Where she calls home: New York, USA

Fluid frame techniques: Gouache on glass

Fluid frame films: *Miramare* (2009), *Trag/Trace/Spur* (2012)

| #ProTip | *While making* Miramare, *every day, when I went to bed and again when I woke up in the morning, I stayed there with my eyes closed and tried to watch the film in my mind. I had the storyboard but then I tried to learn the film by heart, to watch it and feel it, that's how I was able to improvise under the camera when I started to paint.*

Find out more: www.triboje.com

Fluid Frames: Artists' Profiles

### Corrie Francis Parks

Where she calls home: Baltimore, USA

Fluid frame technique: Sand on glass

Fluid frame films: *Ash Sunday* (2001), *Tracks* (2003), *A Tangled Tale* (2013)

*Corrie Francis Parks. Photo credit: Thomas Parks.*

**#ProTip** *Don't let uncertainty about where you are going keep you from starting. I often don't know how my films will end until very late in the production. I let the work develop as I become familiar with the materials and techniques I'm using and often that leads me to an interesting twist or resolution to the project.*

Find out more: www.corriefrancis.com

### Ishu Patel

Where he calls home: Kingston, Ontario, Canada

Fluid frame technique: Clay on glass

Fluid frame films: *Afterlife* (1978), *Top Priority* (1981)

*Afterlife ©1978 National Film Board of Canada, All rights reserved.*

**#ProTip** *When I came to the NFB, most films were very complex three-dimensional drawings, with sand and paint-on-glass. But I didn't want to do that; I wanted to do drawings like I did when I was a boy from the village, when I had no idea of anatomy and perspective and drew everything linear. So, I would break all the cinematic rules; you make up your own rules, but you have to know about the rules first. As long as you know how to draw properly, you can decide what kind of drawings you create.*

Find out more:
ishupatel.com
ishupatelphoto.com

Artists' Profiles  Appendix B

Alexander Petrov. Courtesy of Pascal Blais Studios.

### Alexander Petrov

**Where he calls home:** Russia

**Fluid frame technique:** Oil paint on glass

**Fluid frame film:** *The Cow* (1989), *The Dream of a Ridiculous Man* (1992), *Mermaid* (1996), *The Old Man and the Sea* (1999), *My Love* (2006)

**Find out more:** http://www.imdb.com/name/nm0678154/

Darling – Izabela Plucinska – 2013.

### Izabela Plucinska

**Where she calls home:** Baltimore, USA

**Fluid frame technique:** Clay

**Fluid frame films:** *Darling* (2013), *Breakfast* (2006)

**Find out more:** http://www.izaplucinska.com/

Lynn Smith. Photo credit: Irene Blei.

### Lynn Smith

**Where she calls home:** Montreal, Canada

**Fluid frame techniques:** Gouache on glass, drawing under the camera with water-based crayons, cut-out animation, and any combination of them all

**Fluid frame films:** *Soup of the Day* (2013), *Sandburg's Arithmetic* (1994), *The Sound Collector* (1982), *Pearl's Diner* (1992), *This is Your Museum Speaking* (1979), *Siena* (1999)

 **#ProTip** When beginning a new project, deciding the right technique may require some testing.

You will need to allocate a reasonable amount of time (at the very least: a full day – hopefully more). And you will want to devise some tests that you believe will uncover the range of possibilities inherent in the technique you are considering.

But testing is not just the time to try out specific ideas. Testing is also a time to make mistakes. This is because in the mistakes, you may discover something you did not know you were looking for. Plan definite experiments, and at the same time do not be afraid to have some fun by trying out some impossible ideas. Very Important: Document your entire exploration by recording everything.

## Fluid Frames: Artists' Profiles

Find out more: https://www.nfb.ca/explore-all-directors/lynn-smith?language=en

On method:

http://www.pyramidmedia.com/homepage/search-by-title/humanities/film-studies/lynn-smith-method-detail.html

On *Sandburg's Arithmetic*:

http://www.pyramidmedia.com/homepage/search-by-title/humanities/sandburg-s-arithmetic-detail.html

The Shout It Out Alphabet from A to Z:

http://www.pyramidmedia.com/homepage/search-by-title/animation/shout-it-out-detail.html

### Sheila Sofian

Where she calls home: Los Angeles, USA

Fluid frame technique: Tempera paint on Plexiglas

Fluid frame films: *Mangia!* (1985), *Survivors* (1997), *Conversation with Haris* (2001), *Truth Has Fallen* (2013)

Truth Has Fallen – Sheila Sofian – 2013.

**#ProTip** Sometimes the animation starts to take over and it starts to suggest things to you. So you go, "Well, I'll try that because that looks kind of interesting." You don't have to use everything you shoot, so just allow some time for the paint to tell you what to do next. And don't be afraid of embracing accidents because sometimes those are the coolest things that can happen.

Find out more: www.sheilasofian.com

### Wendy Tilby

Where she calls home: Calgary, Canada

Fluid frame technique: Oil paint on glass

Fluid frame film: *Strings* (1991)

Strings – Wendy Tilby. ©1991 National Film Board of Canada, All rights reserved.

**#ProTip** Paint on glass is very forgiving. In other words, if where you start and where you are going are clear, you can get away with a lot of fudging in-between.

Find out more: http://www.tilbyforbis.com/

## Artists' Profiles Appendix B

### Lynn Tomlinson

Where she calls home: Baltimore, USA

Fluid frame technique: Clay on glass

Fluid frame films: *The Ballad of Holland Island House* (2014), *Cauldron* (1994)

Lynn Tomlinson. Courtesy of Lynn Tomlinson.

**#ProTip** *Remember each frame is only being glimpsed for a tiny fraction of a second, so embrace the smear and the smudge! Let your images stretch and distort during transitions. Looseness can create more expressive and smooth animation.*

Find out more: www.lynntomlinson.com

### Nicolai Troshinsky

Where he calls home: Madrid, Spain

Fluid frame technique: Paint-on-glass with cut-outs

Fluid frame films: *Astigmatismo* (2013)

Astigmatismo – Nicolai Troshinsky – 2013.

**#ProTip** *For me, when I am doing creative work, it's important I don't know everything. If I become too good, it becomes mechanical. I vary techniques because if you don't know it, you have to figure it out. So there is a challenge, a tension in the art-making process. So, when I finish something, I learned a lot along the way. And if I do the same thing again, it will start to feel like work.*

Find out more: www.astigmatismo-shortfilm.com

## Fluid Frames: Artists' Profiles

### Philippe Vaucher

**Where he calls home:** Montreal, Canada

**Fluid frame technique:** Salt and sand on glass

**Fluid frame films:** *Wuji* (2008), *Cumulus* (2011), *The Well* (2013)

*Philippe Vaucher. Courtesy of Philippe Vaucher.*

**#ProTip** If I'm doing a long hold, I like to tap the glass to animate the sparkle or shimmer in the salt. This tapping gives it just this slight, natural vibration and by tapping the glass and not the image, you don't run the risk of seriously damaging the shape when you touch it.

**Find out more:** www.philvaucher.com

---

### Robbe Vervaeke

**Where he calls home:** Ghent, Belgium

**Fluid frame technique:** Oil paint on glass

**Fluid frame films:** *Erzebet* (2008), *Norman* (2012), *Fighting Pablo* (in production)

*Robbe Vervaeke. Courtesy of Robbe Vervaeke.*

**#ProTip** Never forget that we're making films, not shots, so you need to be able to kill the shots in order to make a good film. We threw out the first version of the *Norman*, actually about eight months of work, because it wasn't working. You need to be able to cut something. If you can't, don't start a film.

**Find out more:** www.robbevervaeke.com

### Clive Walley

**Where he calls home:** Frome, United Kingdom

**Fluid frame technique:** Paint-on-glass

**Fluid frame films:** *Y Rhaeadr* (1982), *Quartet* (1987–89), *And Now You* (1991), *Adagio* (2002), *Divertimenti* (1994), *Light of Uncertainty* (1998)

*Clive Walley. Courtesy of Clive Walley.*

**#ProTip** One thing the rig succeeded in doing was to produce a very direct and quick test bed for visual ideas. I occasionally showed students how you could just tear up stuff and throw it in, on different layers, adjust the lights, and in seconds you were transported to a possible new film.

**Find out more:** http://www.red-wharf.com/clive_walley.htm

### Marieka Walsh

**Where she calls home:** Sydney, Australia

**Fluid frame technique:** Sand animation

**Fluid frame films:** *The Hunter* (2011), *The Crossing* (2016)

*Marieka Walsh. Photo credit: Kurt Sorensen.*

**#ProTip** I've been doing a lot of work in both salt and sand and I'm a bit in love with salt; it's so ghostly. I'm also loving that the sand leaves trails in the salt you can't clean up; it's a messy and uncontrollable element in my very tightly controlled shot and I like that.

**Find out more:** www.mariekawalsh.com.au

## Fluid Frames: Artists' Profiles

### Lee Whitmore

Where she calls home: Sydney, Australia

Fluid frame techniques: Gouache on glass, pastel under-the-camera

Fluid frame films: *Ada* (2002), *The Safe House* (2006)

Find out more: www.leewhitmore.com.au

*Lee Whitmore. Courtesy of Lee Whitmore.*

# Index

References to figures are in *italics*.

3D animation 150; with Adobe After Effects 151, *151, 152, 153*

Abadžieva, Ema *212, 214*
*Ab Ova* (Ferenc Cakó) 79, *79*
abstract transitions 89, *89*
abstract work 22, 27
acetate cels 31, 132, 136, 138
action: anticipation of 49, 57, *57*; follow-through of 57, *57*; lines of 49, *56, 57*; overlapping action 57–58, *57*; secondary action 58, *58*; timing the action *54*, 55, *55*
*Ada* (Lee Whitmore) *8, 25*, 44, 177–178, *177, 178, 180*
Adobe After Effects: 3D effects 151, *151, 152, 153*; animated masks exercise 106–110, *106–107, 108, 109*; archiving and collecting files *186*; blending modes 100–101, *100, 101, 108*; CC Wide Time effect 66–69; clay compositing exercise 169–175, *170–174*; Color Key Effects Stack exercise 103–105, *103–105*; compositing the Roller Coaster of Luv exercise 146–150, *146–150*; composition for Vaucher's *The Well 94*; Ease Out and Ease In features 63, *63*; and exploration of medium 20; familiarizing oneself with 6; Garbage Mattes exercise 98–99, *98–99*; layering 64, *64*, 91; Master Null 62–63, *63*; Motion Blur 63, *64*; Paint Bucket effect exercise 101–102, *101–102*; staggered mix *65*, 66; and *A Tale of Longing* (Xin Li) *144*; and *A Tangled Tale* (C. F. Parks) 94–95; tints and filters exercise 112–115, *112–114*; zooming and panning 62

Adobe Bridge 91
Adobe Lightroom 37, *90*, 91
*The Adventures of Prince Achmed* (Lotte Reiniger) 15, *15, 16*
aesthetics: animated transitions 60–61, *61*; in-camera vs out-of-camera 58–59, 93–95; drawn camera moves 59, *59*; hand of the artist 61–62, *61*, 94; leaving trails 59–60, *60*; *see also* animated movement principles; digital toolbox

After Effects *see* Adobe After Effects
*Afterlife* (Ishu Patel) 65, 158, *159*, 167
Alexeieff, Alexander, *Night on Bald Mountain* (Alexander Alexeieff and Claire Parker) 15–16
Alkabetz, Gil: on animating films in negative 162; artist profile 215; *Bitzbutz* 162, *162*, 215; on stories and styles 215; on storyboards and endings 25
alpha channel (or Luma Matte Sequence) in Photoshop 109–110, *109*
*And Now You* (Clive Walley) 150, *150, 151*
Animafest Zagreb (World Festival of Animated Film Zagreb), 2014 technical requirements *185*

animated masks exercise 106–110, *106–107, 108, 109*
animated movement principles: animated movement principles, development of 48–49; animating on twos (or double-framing) 50, *50*; anticipation (of an action) 49, 57, *57*; arcs of motion 55, *56, 57*; easing 51, *51*; follow-through (of an action) 57, *57*; holds and cycles 52; lines of action 49, *56, 57*; overlapping action 57–58, *57*; secondary action 58, *58*; squash and stretch 49, 55, *55, 56*; staging 52–55, *52, 53–54, 55*; timing and spacing 49, *49*, 51; *see also* aesthetics; animation; digital toolbox
animated transitions 60–61, *61*
animatics 25
animating on twos (or double-framing) 50, *50*
animation: under-the-camera 1, 5; and digital technology 1–2; and experimental frame of mind 1–4; fluid frame animation 6–7; and "haptic" materials 1; history of 11–17; *see also* animated movement principles; under-the-camera animation
Annecy International Animation Festival 16, *16*, 77, 185, *188, 189*
Ansorge, Ernest "Nag" and Gisèle: artists' profile 215; *Fantasmatic 4*; *Les Corbeaux* (*The Ravens*) 17, *17*, 77, *77*; *The Little Boy Who Stole the Moon* 77; photograph

# Index

of 77; sand animation 3, 76–77; *Smile (3)* 77
anticipation (of an action) 49, 57, *57*
anti-fatigue mats 42
aperture 40
archiving, in Adobe After Effects *186*
arcs of motion 55, *56*, 57
artist's hand 61–62, *61*, 94
artists' profiles: Alkabetz, Gil 215; Ansorge, Nag and Gisèle 215; Avni, Shira 216; Cakó, Ferenc 216; Chartrand, Martine 217; Ehrlich, David 217; Fischinger, Oskar 217; Giersz, Witold 218; Gratz, Joan 218; Humphries, Anna 218; Jenkins, Patrick 219; Kashkoolinia, Maryam 219; Korejwo, Aleksandra 219; Li, Xin 220; Meléndez, César Díaz 220; Miailhe, Florence 221; Müller, Michaela 221; Parks, Corrie Francis 222; Patel, Ishu 222; Petrov, Alexander 223; Plucinska, Izabela 223; Smith, Lynn 223; Sofian, Sheila M. 224; Tilby, Wendy 224; Tomlinson, Lynn 225; Troshinsky, Nicolai 225; Vaucher, Philippe 226; Vervaeke, Robbe 226; Walley, Clive 227; Walsh, Marieka 227; Whitmore, Lee 228
"art that moves" 48; *see also* animated movement principles
*Ash Sunday* (C. F. Parks) 5, *5*, *33*, 137
Association Internationale du Film d'Animation / International Animated Film Association (ASIFA) 16, *16*
*Astigmatismo* (Nicolai Troshinsky) 20, *21*, 31, *31*, 39, *39*, *54*, 55, 176, *176*; process video for *187*; and sound design *181*
audiences: reactions of 193–194; targeting of 179, 186; *see also* exhibition
*Au premier dimanche d'août* (Florence Miailhe) 175, *175*
Avni, Shira: artist profile 216; on clay painting 172, 174; frosted Mylar 164; *John and Michael* 165; *Jovi Plastelina* 165; pace of work 43; on preparations for long shot 43; on process and "happy accidents" 216; working with backlit clay 43
*The Awakening* (Waldemar Mordarski) 78

Bach, Johann Sebastian, *Brandenburg Concerto No. 3* and O. Fischinger's work 121–122
Bächler, Rolf 76
Back, Frederick 64
backlighting 32, *32*, 33, 34, 40, 42, 137, 138, 164
back-up, external storage drive 36
*The Ballad of Holland Island House* (Lynn Tomlinson) *2*, 45, 70, *71*, 163–164, *163*, *164*, 167, *188*, 189
Barbin, Pierre 16
Bartosch, Bertold 15
Batchelor, Joy *16*
*Bead Game* (Ishu Patel) 158
Benson, John, animated transitions 61
beta tapes 185
*Bitzbutz* (Gil Alkabetz) 162, *162*, 215
*Black Soul* (Martine Chartrand) 44, 45
Blackton, James Stuart 12, 195; *Humorous Phases of Funny Faces* 13
black velvet, use of for painting animation 134–135, *134*, 145, 146
Blais, Pascal 128, 129
blending modes 100–101, *100*, *101*, *108*, 109
blending stumps, as tools for sand animation 88
Blumer, Ron 125
*Bottle* (Kirsten Lepore) *2*
bounced light 33, *33*, 34
brushes: for painting animation 138; for sand animation 87, *88*
Bugliosi, Vincent 206, *206*

Cakó, Ferenc: *Ab Ova* 79, *79*; artist profile 216; *Fészek (Nest)* 79; live sand animation performance 80, *80*; sand animation 79–80
cameras: in-camera vs out-of-camera 58–59, 93–95; drawn camera moves 59, *59*; mechanical animation cameras 49; sketching with 23; *see also* digital cameras; digital toolbox; lenses; under-the-camera animation
Canada: National Film Board of Canada (NFB) 16, 64, 158; NFB English Animation Studio 78
Cannes Film Festival 185, 209
Canon: Digital Single Reflex Lens (DSLR) cameras 35–36, *36*, 38, 40; EF 85mm f/1.2 lenses 39
Canuel, Erik, *Hemingway: A Portrait* 190
*Carmen Habenaro* (Aleksandra Korejwo) 80
*Carmen Torero* (Aleksandra Korejwo) 7
case studies: *Loving Vincent* (Dorota Kobiela and Hugh Welchman) 195–202, *197–202*; *Trag/Trace/Spur and Up the Stairs* (Michaela Müller et al.) 209–214, *209–214*; *Truth Has Fallen* (Sheila M. Sofian) 202–209, *202*, *205*, *206*, *208*
cat protector *42*
CC Wide Time effect, with Adobe After Effects 66–69
cel animation 49, 123
CG (computer graphics) 2, 196–197, 200–201
Chak Pur tool, for sand mandalas 88, *88*
chapter overview 6–8
Chartrand, Martine: acetate cels on glass 31, 132; animating on Plexiglas *133*; artist profile 217; backlighting 138; *Black Soul* 44, *45*; on "hanging on" 45; *Macpherson* 26–27, *26*, 43, 44; *MacPherson* process video *187*; oil-based paints 136, 137; on overcoming feelings of isolation 44; pace of work 43; and Petrov 128, 132, 217; on questioning her animation 217; on researching history of *MacPherson* folk song 26–27; Superlube grease 137; on working on hardest scenes first 44
*Clay* (David Ehrlich) 163
*Clayola* (David Ehrlich) 163

# Index

clay painting: characteristics of clay 4–5, 157–158, 166–167, *166*; clay compositing exercise 169–175, *170–174*; cut-out medium 176; drawing under the camera 176–177; lighting 33; pioneers 158–162; studio 164–168; table and lighting 164–165, *165*; techniques, experimental 175–178; techniques, survey of 162–164; temperature regulation 167; tools 167–168, *167*; warming up to the clay exercise 168–169, *168–169*; *see also* painting animation
close-up shots *52*, 53
Cohl, Émile 13, 195; *Fantasmagorie* 48
color adding: and animating with sand 110; hand tinting in Photoshop exercise 110–112, *110–112*; tints and filters in After Effects exercise 112–115, *112–114*
Colorfloat 136
color keying: and animating with sand 103; Color Key Effects Stack exercise 103–105, *103–105*
*Color Run* (David Ehrlich) 162
compositing with clay, clay compositing exercise 169–175, *170–174*
compositing with paint: digital approaches 144; green screen techniques 144–150, *144–150*
compositing with sand: animated masks exercise 106–110, *106–107*, *108*, *109*; blending modes 100–101, *100*, *101*, *108*; in-camera vs out-of-camera 93–95; Color Key Effects Stack exercise 103–105, *103–105*; color keying 103; Garbage Mattes exercise 98–99, *98–99*; layering 95–98, *95*, *96*, *97*; Paint Bucket effect exercise 101–102, *101–102*
computer graphics (CG) 2, 196–197, 200–201
*A Conversation with Haris* (Sheila M. Sofian) 138, *139*, 203, 204, *204*
*Conversing with Aotearoa* (C. F. Parks) 61

copyrights, and distribution 191
*Les Corbeaux* (*The Ravens*, Ernest and Gisèle Ansorge) 17, *17*, 77, *77*
*The Cow* (Alexander Petrov) 128
creativity: and limitations 20; and technical goals 20
Crockwell, Douglass, *Glenn Falls Sequence* 16
*The Crossing* (Marieka Walsh) *1*, *76*, *84*, 93, *94*, *96*
crowdsourcing 17, 25; *see also* funding
*Cumulus* (Philippe Vaucher) 86
"cushioning" 51, *51*
cuticle sticks, as tools for painting animation 138, 204
cut-out medium 176
cycles and holds 52

*Darling* (Izabela Plucinska) *157*, *164*
Darwin Staggered Mix sample footage 66
DCP (Digital Cinema Package) 185
depth of field 38–40, *39*
*Diagonal Symphony* (Viking Eggeling) 13
diffusion box *34*
diffusion paper 33
digital cameras: animating camera movements in post-production 62–63; aperture 40; Camera Controls 41; in-camera vs out-of-camera 58–59, 93–95; Digital Single Reflex Lens (DSLR) cameras 35–36, *36*, 38, 40; digital video cameras 35, 36, 49; Dragonframe camera control interface 40; exposure setting 40, *40*; frame capture 41, 81; image resolution 36–37, *37*, 62; image stabilizing feature 38; IMAX cameras 32, 129, *129*; ISO 40; lenses 37–40; and lighting 32–33; locking it down 41–42; phone cameras 35, *36*; RAW format 36–37, 91; shutter speed 40; storage and backing up 36; tilting camera *35*; webcams 35, 36, 40; and wellbeing 42; *see also* cameras; digital toolbox; under-the-camera animation

Digital Cinema Package (DCP) 185
digital output 185–186
Digital Single Reflex Lens (DSLR) cameras 35–36, *36*, 38, 40
digital technology, and animation 1–2
digital toolbox: animating camera movements in post-production 62–63; rotoscoping (or reference footage) 41, 70–71; staggered mix 64–69, *65*, *66–69*; thinking in layers 64, *64*; *see also* compositing with clay; compositing with paint; compositing with sand
digital video cameras 35, 36, 49
Disney, Walt 80
"Disney-style" character animation 49
distribution 191
*Divertimenti* (Clive Walley) 126, 181; *Divertimento 1* (*Wind of Change*) 126, 151, *152*, *153*; *Divertimento 2* (*Love Song*) 126, *127*; *Divertimento 3* (*Brushwork*) 122, *122*, 126; *Divertimento 4* (*Life Study*) 126; *Divertimento 5* (*Slap-Stick*) 126, 128, 181; *Divertimento 6* (*Dark Matter*) 128
double-framing (or animating on twos) 50, *50*
Dragonframe camera control interface 40
drawing under the camera 176–177
drawn camera moves 59, *59*
*The Dream of a Ridiculous Man* (Alexander Petrov) 128
DSLR (Digital Single Reflex Lens) cameras 35–36, *36*, 38, 40
Dunning, George, *The Flying Man* 17
dust masks 42
Dutch angle shots 53

easels 34, 133, *134*, 135, 165
Ease Out and Ease In features 63, *63*
easing 51, *51*
editing: and animated transitions 60–61; *see also* digital toolbox
EF 85mm f/1.2 lenses 39
Eggeling, Viking, *Diagonal Symphony* 13

# Index

Ehrlich, David: artist profile 217; *Clay* 163; *Clayola* 163; *Color Run* 162; *Poznanie* 163; warming up to the clay exercise 168
Electronic Press Kit (EPK) 189, 192
endings, and storyboards (Gil Alkabetz) 25
Engel, Jules, "Experimental Animation" definition 3
EPK (Electronic Press Kit) 189, 192
*Erszebet* (Robbe Vervaeke) 135
established aesthetics *see* aesthetics
evolving holds 52
exercises: additional painting animation exercises 153; animated masks 106–110, *106–107*, *108*, *109*; animating sandy morphs 82–86, *82–86*; clay compositing 169–175, *170–174*; Color Key Effects Stack 103–105, *103–105*; compositing the Roller Coaster of Luv 146–150, *146–150*; finger painting portrait with sponge transition 140–143, *140–143*; Garbage Mattes 98–99, *98–99*; hand tinting in Photoshop 110–112, *110–112*; motion painting 130–132, *130–131*; Paint Bucket effect 101–102, *101–102*; tints and filters in After Effects 112–115, *112–114*; warming up to the clay 168–169, *168–169*; *see also* Adobe After Effects
exhibition: audience reactions 193–194; audience targeting 179, 186; and digital output 185–186; distribution 191; Electronic Press Kit (EPK) 189, 192; film festivals 188–191; Making Of (process) videos 187–188; online release 191–192, *191*; other means of exhibitions 192–193
Experimental Animation, as defined by Jules Engels 3
experimental frame of mind: experimental animation 1–4; focus on sand, paint, and clay 4–5; and history of animation 11–17; purpose and contents of the book 5–8

exposure setting 40, *40*
external storage drive 36

*Fantasmagorie* (Émile Cohl) 48
*Fantasmatic* (Ernest and Gisèle Ansorge) 4
feathers, as tools for sand animation 88
festivals: Animafest Zagreb (World Festival of Animated Film Zagreb) *185*; Annecy International Animation Festival 16, *16*, 77, 185, *188*, *189*; Brookings Festival (South Dakota) 189; Cannes Film Festival 185, 209; film festivals 188–191; Hamburg Kurzfilm Festival *190*; Hiroshima International Animation Festival 163; Northwest Animation Festival *189*; Sundance Festival 185
*Fészek / Nest* (Ferenc Cakó) 79
*Fighting Pablo* (Robbe Vervaeke) 70, *70*
film, frame rates 49
film festivals 188–191
finding your voice: animation, history of 11–17; beginning the journey 17–22; image stuck in your mind 22–24; telling the story 24–27
fingers: finger painting portrait with sponge transition (exercise) 140–143, *140–143*; painting with 128, 138, *139*, 203; to spread the clay 167; *see also* hands
finishing (a project), "It's done!" flowchart 194
*Fire* (Witold Giersz) 123, 124, *124*
Fischinger, Oskar: artist profile 217; experimental nature of his work 13, 15, 16; in his Los Angeles studio *121*; motion painting 122, 130, 132; *Motion Painting No. 1* 121, *121*, 122, 126; painting animation pioneer 120–122
flat camera angle shots 53
flowchart, "It's done!" flowchart *194*
fluid frame animation 6–7; *see also* animated movement principles

*The Flying Man* (George Dunning) 17
focal lengths 38, *38*
follow-through (of an action) 57, *57*
frame-by-frame process 12, 49–51, *49*, *50*
frame capture 41; frame capture programs 81
Frame Export 41
frame rates 49, *49*
French Impressionists 123
f-stop setting 38–39, *39*
funding: crowdsourcing 17, 25; grants 16, 17, 25; patronage 17

Garbage Mattes exercise 98–99, *98–99*
Germany, experimental 1920s 15
*Gertie the Dinosaur* (Winsor McCay) *13*, 195
gestural painting 128
Giersz, Witold: artist profile 218; experimental nature of his work 16–17; *Fire* 123, 124, *124*; on French Impressionists 123; *Horse* 123, *123*, 124; on *Horse* and *Fire* 124; *Little Western* 17, *17*, 123, *123*; painting animation pioneer 123–124; on *Signum* 124; *Signum* 124, *124*; at work in his studio *123*
glass: green glass as painting surface *145*; milk (or opal) glass 34; non-reflective 31, 33; for working surface 30–31, 165; *see also* multiplanes; paint-on-glass
glasses, tinted glasses for protection 42
*Glenn Falls Sequence* (Douglass Crockwell) 16
glycerin 136, *136*, 138, 204
Google Hangouts, Q&A for online release 192, *192*
gouache 136, *136*, 138
grants 16, 17, 25; *see also* funding
Gratz, Joan: artist profile 218; clay painting and digital methods 174; clay painting pioneer 160–162; clay preparation 166; *Kubla Kahn* 160; *Lost and Found* 161, 162, 165; masonite board for working surface 31; *Mona Lisa Descending a Staircase* 48, *61*,

160, *160*, *161*; *Night Weaver* 3, *3*, *26*, *175*; on not being critical of herself 218; pace of work 43; *Pro and Con* (Joan Gratz and Joanna Priestley) *12*, *161*; *Puffer Girl* 20, *21*, *22*, *174*; on use of digital programs 20; on use of fingers to apply clay 167; working at easel 165
grease/lubricants 137
green screen techniques: basics 144–145, *144*, *145*; compositing the Roller Coaster of Luv exercise 146–150, *146–150*; creating the layers 145–146, *145–146*
Grimault, Paul *16*

Halas, John *16*
"halo effect" 95, *95*, 103, *103*, 104, 144
Hamburg Kurzfilm Festival, Corrie Parks' pass for *A Tangled Tale* *190*
hand of the artist 61–62, *61*, 94
hands: skin protectant 143; as tools for sand animation 87; see also fingers
hand tinting 94, *95*; in Photoshop exercise 110–112, *110–112*
haptic, meaning of term 1
Hayes, Ruth 205
HDCam tapes 185
health: mental health and motivation 45; and working under the camera 42; and working with sand 91
*Heart of the World* (C. F. Parks) 64, *64*, *116*, 116–117
Hemingway, Ernest: *Hemingway: A Portrait* (Erik Canuel) *190*; *The Old Man and the Sea* 128; see also *The Old Man and the Sea* (Alexander Petrov)
Hiroshima: International Animation Festival 163; Otis wall *194*
history of animation 11–17
holds and cycles 52
*Horse* (Witold Giersz) 123, *123*, 124
"hot set" 42
*Humorous Phases of Funny Faces* (J. S. Blackton) *13*

Humphries, Anna: artist profile 218; *It Might Be Real* 86, 95, *180*; on past mistakes and keeping on going 218; on sand and "going with the light" 85
*The Hunter* (Marieka Walsh) 91, 92–93, *92*, *93*, *187*

image resolution 36–37, *37*, 62
image stabilizing feature 38
image stuck in your mind 22–24
IMAX cameras 32, 129, *129*
Impressionism 123
in-camera, vs out-of-camera 58–59, 93–95
index cards, working story ideas on 24
*Inner View* (Patrick Jenkins) 122, *122*
Innocence Project 206
"in or out of an action (or of a pose)" 51
inspiration 19; image stuck in your mind 22–24
International Animated Film Association / Association Internationale du Film d'Animation (ASIFA) 16, *16*
*The Interview* (Caroline Leaf) *133*
ISO 40
isolation, overcoming feeling of 44–45
*It Might Be Real* (Anna Humphries) *86*, 95, *180*
"It's done!" flowchart *194*
Ivanov-Vano, Ivan *16*

Jenkins, Patrick: artist profile 219; on *Inner View* 122; *Inner View* 122, *122*; *Labyrinth* 3, *3*, *60*, 133; on metamorphoses and "painterly" 219; Q-tips for cleanliness 138; *Sorceress* 139, 144, *144*; top light 137; water-based paints 136; working at an easel 133, *134*; working surfaces 31, 133
*John and Michael* (Shira Avni) 165
Jones, Bryn 181
*Jovi Plastelina* 165

Kafka, Franz: *The Metamorphosis* 79; see also *The Metamorphosis of Mr. Samsa* (Caroline Leaf)

Kashkoolinia, Maryam: artist profile 219; sand animation style 85; on story and sand medium 219; *Tunnel* 53; *When I Was a Child 2*, *17*, *84*
kebab skewers: as tools for painting animation 138; as tools for sand animation 88
keeping things in perspective 42–45
Kentridge, William 178
Keylight 148
Kobiela, Dorota: *The Little Postman* 196; *Loving Vincent* (Dorota Kobiela and Hugh Welchman) 196, *197*, 201
Koch, Karl, *The Adventures of Prince Achmed* (Lotte Reiniger) *15*
Korejwo, Aleksandra: artist profile 219; *Carmen Habenaro* 80; *Carmen Torero* 7; salt animation pioneer 78, 80–81; *The Swan* 80
*Kubla Kahn* (Joan Gratz) *160*
Kuthy, Diane, phone camera stand for animation workshop (Tomlinson and Kuthy) *36*

*Labyrinth* (Patrick Jenkins) 3, *3*, *60*, 133
Lajoie, Bernard 32
Lamb, Derek 78, 158
layering: with Adobe After Effects 64, *64*, 91; and clay painting 172–173, *172–173*; and green screen techniques 145–150, *145–150*; in sand 95–98, *95*, *96*, *97*
Leaf, Caroline: on animated transitions 61; artist profile 220; under-the-camera animation as performance 19; drawn camera moves 59; hand of the artist writing credits 62; inspiration, source of 19; *The Interview* *133*; on limitations 220; on "moving things in depth as well as across" 85; on originality 7; *The Owl Who Married a Goose* 62, 76, 78–79, *78*; painting animation pioneer 120, 124–126; sand and paint-on-glass artist 175; sand animation pioneer 76, 78–79; sand beach *82*; *Sand or Peter and the Wolf* 17, 78, *78*; on sand vs painting

# Index

animation 125; on sandy morphs for workshops 82; and Sofian, meeting with 203; *The Street* 125–126, *125*, 136; *The Street* and storyboards 25; top light 137; water-based paints 136; working on *The Interview* 133
leaving trails 59–60, *60*
Leclerc, Félix, *Macpherson* folk song 26, *26*
LED lights *32*, 33, 34
lenses 37–38, *37*; depth of field 38–40, *39*; EF 85mm f/1.2 lenses 39; focal lengths 38, *38*; sweet spot 39–40; Zoom lenses 38
Lepore, Kirsten, *Bottle* 2
Li, Xin: artist profile 220; backlighting 138; oil-based paints 136; on special language of animation 220; *Spring* 66; *A Tale of Longing* 17, *120*, *144*; *The Umbrella* 32
light box 33–35, *34*, 42
Lightroom *see* Adobe Lightroom
lights: backlighting 32, *32*, 33, 34, 40, 42, 137, 138, 164; bounced light 33, *33*, 34; and clay painting 164–165, *165*; diffusion box *34*; diffusion paper 33; and digital cameras 32–33; and "hot set" 42; LED lights *32*, 33, 34; light box 33–35, *34*, 42; Motion/Control/Lighting Controls 41; and painting animation 137–138; top light 31, 32, *32*, 33, 137–138, 165
limitations: Caroline Leaf on 220; and creativity 20
lines of action 49, *56*, 57
linoleum tiles, for working surface 31, 133, 138
*The Little Boy Who Stole the Moon* (Ernest and Gisèle Ansorge) 77
*The Little Postman* (Dorota Kobiela) 196
*Little Western* (Witold Giersz) 17, *17*, 123, *123*
Live View 41
locking it down 41–42
long shots 53
*Lost and Found* (Joan Gratz) *161*, 162, 165

*Loving Vincent* (Dorota Kobiela and Hugh Welchman) case study 195–202, *197–202*
lubricants/grease 137
Luma Matte Sequence (or alpha channel) in Photoshop 109–110, *109*
Lye, Len 16

McCay, Winsor 13; *Gertie the Dinosaur* 13, 195
McCloskey, James 202, 206
McLaren, Norman 16, 64
*Macpherson* (Martine Chartrand) 26–27, *26*, 43, 44, 187
Macpherson, Frank Randolph 26–27, *26*
Maillet, Raymond *16*
Making Of (process) videos 187–188
mandalas, Tibetan Chak Pur tool for sand mandalas 88, *88*
*Mangia* (Sheila M. Sofian), Sofian, Sheila M. 203, *203*
marketing *see* exhibition
Martin, Tess, multiplane 32, *32*
masks, animated masks exercise 106–110, *106–107*, *108*, *109*
masonite boards, for working surface 31, 165
Master Null 62–63, *63*
*Méandres* (Florence Miailhe) 7
mechanical animation cameras 49
Meléndez, César Díaz: artist profile 220; on drawing with sand 221; hand of the artist *61*; multiplane light table *82*; *No Corras Tanto* 84, 91–92, *91*, *92*, 93, 220; on "pushing around" the sand 82; sand animation style 85; on storyboards 25; in studio animating with sand *4*; on working on *No Corras Tanto* 91–92, 220; *Zepo* 26, *60*; *Zepo* process video 187
Méliès, Georges 12, 195; *The Mermaid* 12; *A Trip to the Moon* 12
mental health, and motivation 45
*The Mermaid* (Alexander Petrov) 128
*The Mermaid* (Georges Méliès) 12

*The Metamorphosis of Mr. Samsa* (Caroline Leaf) 79, *79*
Miailhe, Florence: artist profile 221; *Au premier dimanche d'août* 175, *175*; *Méandres* 7
Mihanović, Zrinka Šimičić 209, 210, 211, 212, *214*
milk (or opal) glass 34
Minarik, Tanja *212*, *214*
mineral oil 166
*Miramare* (Michaela Müller) 3, 43, *181*, 209, 210, 221
*Mona Lisa Descending a Staircase* (Joan Gratz) 48, *61*, 160, *160*, *161*
Mordarski, Waldemar, *The Awakening* 78
morphs: and animated transitions 61, *61*; animating sandy morphs (exercise) 82–86, *82–86*
motion: art that moves 48; *see also* animated movement principles; motion painting
Motion Blur 63, *64*
Motion/Control/Lighting Controls 41
motion painting: concept 122; exercise 130–132, *130–131*
*Motion Painting No. 1* (Oskar Fischinger) 121, *121*, 122, 126
motivation: and balanced life 45; and social media 45
Müller, Michaela: artist profile 221; with fellow artists *214*; light box construction project 34; *Miramare* 3, 43, *181*, 209, 210, 221; performing *Up the Stairs* *212*; on preparations for shooting scenes 43; on sound design 181; tilting camera 35; *Trag/Trace/Spur* and *Up the Stairs* (Michaela Müller et al.) 209–214, *209–214*; water-based paints 136; at work *210*; work area for *Trag/Trace/Spur* performance *213*
multiplanes: concept 31–32, *32*; and depth of field 39, *39*; and layering in sand 95, *95*, 96, 97, *97*; Meléndez's multiplane light table *82*; Troshinsky's multiplane 31, *31*, *33*, 39, *39*; Walley's multiplane rig 3, 31, 126, *126*, 150–151, 227
Museum of Contemporary Art (Zagreb) 209, 210, *210*

Museum of Non-Objective Painting (now Solomon R. Guggenheim Museum), New York 16, 120
music: and painting animation 121–122; and sound design 179, 180–183; and sound mix 183–184
Muszalski, Piotr, *Toccata and Fugue in D Minor* 77, *78*
Mylar, for clay painting 164
*My Love* (Alexander Petrov) 130

Nakumura, Kazuo 122
National Film Board of Canada (NFB) 16, 64, 158; English Animation Studio 78
*Nest / Fészek* (Ferenc Cakó) *79*
Neubauer, Bärbel, on abstract films 27
New York, Museum of Non-Objective Painting (now Solomon R. Guggenheim Museum) 16, 120
*Night on Bald Mountain* (Alexander Alexeieff and Claire Parker) 15–16
*Night Weaver* (Joan Gratz) 3, *3*, *26*, *175*
Nikolić, Branko *214*
*No Corras Tanto* (César Díaz Meléndez) *84*, 91–92, *91*, *92*, *93*, 220
«noise» (digital) 40
*Norman* (Robbe Vervaeke) 52, *53*, 135, *135*, 226
Northwest Animation Festival, 2015 festival regulations *189*
NTSC video, frame rates 49

oil-based paints 136–137, 138
*The Old Man and the Sea* (Alexander Petrov) 7, 32, 44, *44*, 128–130, *129*, 137, *138*, *190*
Onion-skinning 41, *41*
online release 191–192, *191*
opal (or milk) glass 34
*The Orange Umbrella* (C. F. Parks) 22, *22*, *154*
originality 7
Orton, Mark 182; at work in his studio *182*
Otis wall (Hiroshima) *194*

out-of-camera, vs in-camera 58–59, 93–95
overlapping action 57–58, *57*
*The Owl Who Married a Goose* (Caroline Leaf) 62, *76*, 78–79, *78*

pace of work 42–45
pacing oneself 44
paint: characteristics of 4–5; different types of 136–137, 138; gouache 136, *136*, 138; oil-based 136–137, 138; tempera 136, 138, 204; water-based 136, 138; and working surfaces 31; *see also* clay painting; painting animation; paint-on-glass
Paint Bucket effect exercise 101–102, *101–102*
painting, life of a 120
painting animation: additional exercises 153; compositing the Roller Coaster of Luv exercise 146–150, *146–150*; digital approaches 144; finger painting portrait with sponge transition (exercise) 140–143, *140–143*; green screen techniques 144–150, *144–150*; "halo effect" 144; life of a painting 120; lighting 137–138; motion painting exercise 130–132, *130–131*; painting surface 132–135, 138; pioneers 120–130; studio setting 132–140; tools 138, 140, 203–204; types of paint 136–137, 138; Walley and 3D animation 150–153, *150*, *151–152*, *153*; *see also* clay painting; paint; paint-on-glass
paint-on-glass 33, 123, 126, 128–130, 132, 136, 144; *see also* clay painting; paint; painting animation
PAL video, frame rates 49
Parker, Claire, *Night on Bald Mountain* (Alexander Alexeieff and Claire Parker) 15–16
Parks, Corrie Francis: artist profile 222; *Ash Sunday* 5, *5*, *33*, 137; brushes 87; *Conversing with Aotearoa* 61; "Donald" the recorder *183*; first homebuilt

sand table and camera stand 35, *35*; Hamburg Kurzfilm Festival pass *190*; *Heart of the World* 64, *64*, *116*, 116–117; interview of H. Welchman re. *Loving Vincent* 196–202; interview of M. Müller re. *Trag/Trace/Spur* and *Up the Stairs* 209–214; interview of S. Sofian re. *Truth Has Fallen* 203–209; New Zealand roadtrip sketchbook page *18*; *The Orange Umbrella* 22, *22*, *154*; pace of work 43; *Seed* documentary, animation for *12*, 43; *Snow* 20; *A Tangled Tale* see under *A Tangled Tale* (C. F. Parks); *Three Scenarios in Which Hana Sasaki Grows a Tail* 117, *117*; *Tracks* 5, *6*, 97, *97*, *184*; on uncertainty and starting 222; *Vezo* documentary, animation for *56*, 117, 117–118, *118*; at work in studio *6*
Patel, Ishu: *Afterlife* 65, 158, *159*, 167; artist profile 222; *Bead Game* 158; on breaking cinematic rules 222; clay painting pioneer 158–159; concept sketch and finished frame for United Airlines commercial *24*; inspiration, source of 19; on staggered mix 64, 65; *Top Priority* 159, *159*; at work *158*
patronage 17; *see also* funding
paywalls 192
*Pearl's Diner* (Lynn Smith) *4*, 26, 42, 176, *176*
performance: under-the-camera animation as performance 19; live sand animation performance 80, *80*; and rehearsal 19, 43, 178
Perkins, George 34–35
*Peter and the Wolf* (Hugh Welchman) 196, 197; *see also* Sand or Peter and the Wolf (Caroline Leaf)
Petrov, Alexander: artist profile 223; backlighting 138; and Chartrand 128, 132, 217; *The Cow* 128; *The Dream of a Ridiculous Man* 128; on expressive strokes 130; glass working surface and acetate cels 31, 132; *The Mermaid* 128;

# Index

*My Love* 130; oil-based paints 136, 137; *The Old Man and the Sea* 7, 32, 44, *44*, 128–130, *129*, 137, *138*, *190*; painting animation pioneer 120, 128–130; on painting with his fingers 128; with Serguei Rechetnikoff and IMAX camera *129*; sketches and studies *48*; Superlube grease 137; on using living people for his painted characters 44; on working on hardest scenes first 44; at work in his studio *130*
Petrov, Dimitri 129, 130
phone cameras 35; phone camera stand *36*
Photoshop: alpha channel (or Luma Matte Sequence) 109–110, *109*; and exploration of medium 20; hand tinting 94, *95*; hand tinting exercise 110–112, *110–112*; and RAW format 37, 91
*Pierce, Cole* 181–182
pioneers: clay painting 158–162; painting animation 120–130; powder/sand animation 76–81
plastering tools, for sand animation 88
Plexiglas 30–31, 121, 132, *132*, 133, *133*, 138, 164, 165, 204
Plucinska, Izabela: artist profile 223; clay painting 164; *Darling* 157, *164*
polarizing filters 33
poses 53, *53*, *54*, 55
post-production: animating camera movements in 62–63; and in-camera vs out-of-camera 58–59, 93–95; *see also* digital toolbox
powder animation: concept 76; materials 86–87; pioneers 76–81; *see also* sand animation
*Poznanie* (David Ehrlich) 163
Priestley, Joanna, *Pro and Con* (Joan Gratz and Joanna Priestley) *12*, *161*
*Pro and Con* (Joan Gratz and Joanna Priestley) *12*, *161*
process (Making Of) videos 187–188
publicizing *see* exhibition

*Puffer Girl* (Joan Gratz) 20, *21*, *22*, 174
puppet animation 196, 197, 201

Q-tips, as tools for painting animation 138, 204

*The Ravens* (*Les Corbeaux,* Ernest and Gisèle Ansorge) 17, *17*, 77, *77*
RAW format 36–37, 91
Rechetnikoff, Serguei 129, *129*
recorder, "Donald" the recorder *183*
reference footage (or rotoscoping) 41, 70–71
rehearsing 19, 43, 178
Reiniger, Lotte 15; *The Adventures of Prince Achmed* 15, *15*, 16
research, and storytelling 26–27
*Rhythmus* series (Hans Richter) 13; *Rhythmus 21*, sequence from *14*
Richler, Mordecai 125
Richter, Hans: *Rhythmus* series 13; *Rhythmus 21*, sequence from *14*
rights, and distribution 191
Roller Coaster of Luv compositing exercise 146–150, *146–150*
romantic realism 129–130
rotoscoping (or reference footage) 41, 70–71
rubber stamps, for painting 138
Ruttmann, Walter: *Opus I–IV* 13; *Opus III*, frame sequence from *14*; working on L. Reiniger's *The Adventures of Prince Achmed* 15, *15*

*The Safe House* (Lee Whitmore) 26, *26*, 32, 44, *44*, *120*, 137
salt: for animation 76; and blending modes 109; salt animation pioneers 77–78, 80–81; types of salt 86–87
*The Same Moon* (Lynn Tomlinson) *163*, 175
sand animation: animated masks exercise 106–110, *106–107*, *108*, *109*; animating sandy morphs exercise 82–86, *82–86*; blending modes 100–101, *100*, *101*, *108*; characteristics of sand 4–5; color adding 110; Color Key Effects Stack exercise 103–105, *103–105*; color keying 103; combined with other animation techniques 115–118; compositing 93–95; Garbage Mattes exercise 98–99, *98–99*; "halo effect" 95, *95*, 103, *103*, 104; hand tinting in Photoshop exercise 110–112, *110–112*; Humphries on sand and "going with the light" 85; layering 95–98, *95*, *96*, *97*; Leaf on "moving things in depth as well as across" 85; Leaf's photograph of sand beach *82*; live sand animation performance 80, *80*; Meléndez on "pushing around" the sand 82; Paint Bucket effect exercise 101–102, *101–102*; planning a longer project 91–93; powder animation pioneers 76–81; processing footage *90*, 91; project ideas for exploring sand 89–90, *89*, *90*; sandy studio 81–82, *81*; tints and filters in After Effects exercise 112–115, *112–114*; tools 87–89, *88*; types of sand 86, *86*; Walsh on favorite sand 86; Walsh on sand animation and darkness 85; working surfaces 31
Sandburg, Carl, "Arithmetic" (poem) 177
*Sandburg's Arithmetic* (Lynn Smith) 177, *177*
*Sand or Peter and the Wolf* (Caroline Leaf) 17, 78, *78*
Saunders Waterford rag paper 178
Sauze, Pierre 181
Scheck, Barry 206
Schoeck, Alvaro *214*
secondary action 58, *58*
*Seed* (feature documentary), animation for (C. F. Parks) *12*, 43
Sessions, John, as Père Tanguy (in *Loving Vincent*) 199, *200*, *202*
shots, type of *52*, 53
shutter speed 40
*Siena* (Lynn Smith) 89
*Signum* (Witold Giersz) 124, *124*
sketching: A. Petrov's sketches and studies *48*; C. F. Parks' New Zealand roadtrip sketchbook

# Index

page *18*; I. Patel's concept sketch and finished frame for United Airlines commercial *24*; on paper vs with camera 23–24; thumbnail sketches 24–25, *24*

skin protectant 143

"slow in and slow out" 51

*Smile 3* (Ernest and Gisèle Ansorge) 77

Smith, Lynn: artist profile 223; black velvet under glass 134–135, *134*, 145, 146; custom camera stand 34–35; on drawn camera moves 59; on glycerin 136; pace of work 42; paper cut-outs with fluid frame techniques 3, 176; *Pearl's Diner 4*, 26, 42, 176, *176*; *Sandburg's Arithmetic* 177, *177*; *Siena* 89; *The Sound Collector* 134; *Soup of the Day* 42, *43*, 59, *139*, *184*; on testing and experimenting 223; top light 137; water-based paints 136; working surface *133*

*Snow* (C. F. Parks) 20

social media: and motivation 45; and online release 192

SoDak Animation Festival 189

Sofian, Sheila M.: artist profile 224; cat protector *42*; *A Conversation with Haris* 138, *139*, 203, 204, *204*; on embracing accidents 224; on experimenting with different brands of paint 136; her studio *204*; interviewing Bugliosi *206*; and Leaf, meeting with 203; *Mangia* 203, *203*; photograph of *203*; sponge dabbing technique 143; *Survivors* 205; top light 137; *Truth Has Fallen 5*, *42*, 138, 202–209, *202*, *205*, *206*, *208*; water-based paints 136; ways to transition out of scenes 140; working on Plexiglas *132*

softbox 33

software: Adobe Bridge 91; Adobe Lightroom 37, *90*, 91; frame capture 41; *see also* 3D animation; Adobe After Effects; Photoshop

Solomon R. Guggenheim Museum (previously Museum of Non-Objective Painting), New York 16, 120

*Sorceress* (Patrick Jenkins) *139*, 144, *144*

*The Sound Collector* (Lynn Smith) 134

sound design: and music 179, 180–183; sound mix 183–184; *see also* music

*Soup of the Day* (Lynn Smith) 42, *43*, 59, *139*, *184*

spacing and timing 49, *49*, 51; *see also* holds and cycles

sponges: finger painting portrait with sponge transition (exercise) 140–143, *140–143*; for painting 138, 203; sponge transition (*A Conversation with Haris*, S.M. Sofian) *139*

*Spring* (Xin Li) 66

squash and stretch 49, 55, *55*, *56*

staggered mix 64–66, *65*; exercise 66–69, *66–69*

staging: concept 52; how you pose subject and characters 53, *53*, *54*, 55; how you time the action 54, 55, *55*; where you place subject and characters 52, 53, *53*

Starr, Cecile 16

"state of flow" 43, 48

storage, and backing up 36

storyboards 24–25; *Ada* (Lee Whitmore) with final drawing *25*; and endings (Gil Alkabetz) 25; New Zealand roadtrip sketchbook page (C. F. Parks) *18*; *A Tangled Tale* (C. F. Parks) *23*

storytelling: animatics and storyboards 24–25; research 26–27; working abstractly 27; working out story ideas on index cards *24*; *see also* sketching; storyboards

*The Street* (Caroline Leaf) 25, 125–126, *125*, 136

stretch and squash 49, 55, *55*, *56*

*Strings* (Wendy Tilby) 139

studio space: assessment of needs 29–30; for clay painting 164–168; examples *30*, *31*; locking it down 41–42; for painting animation 132–140; for sand animation 81–82, *81*; ventilation 42, 137; working surfaces 30–31; *see also* digital cameras; lights; multiplanes

sugar, for animation 87, *87*

Sundance Festival 185

Superlube 137

*Survivors* (Sheila M. Sofian) 205

*The Swan* (Aleksandra Korejwo) 80

sweet spot (of lenses) 39–40

Szpakowicz, Piotr 154n6

*A Tale of Longing* (Xin Li) *17*, 120, 144

*A Tangled Tale* (C. F. Parks): compositing with Adobe After Effects 94–95; development phase 22–23; experimenting with dripping paint *19*; Hamburg Kurzfilm Festival pass *190*; hand tinting frames in Photoshop *95*; hand tinting in Photoshop 110–112, *110–112*; image resolution 62; instruments used in soundtrack *182*; "It's done!" flowchart *194*; layers *115*; local publicity for *186*; pace of work 43; Paint Bucket effect exercise 101–102, *101–102*; process video *187*, 188, *188*; promotional poster *180*; Q&A on Google Hangouts 192, *192*; research and learning to fly fish 27; sand animation *6*; sand animation studio *31*; scene-by-scene music and sound breakdown *182*; sound design and music 181–182; sound layering *183*; storyboard *23*; Warren Miller Performing Arts Center exhibit 193, *193*

technical goals, and creativity 20

tempera 136, 138, 204

temperature regulation, and clay painting 167

Templeton, Susie 196

Thorstensen, Gina, designs for Nicolai Troshinsky's *Astigmatismo* 21, 176, *176*

*Three Scenarios in Which Hana Sasaki Grows a Tail* (C. F. Parks) 117, *117*

thumbnail sketches 24–25, *24*

# Index

Tibetan Chak Pur tool, for sand mandalas 88, *88*
Tilby, Wendy: artist profile 224; on paint-on-glass being forgiving 224; sponge work 203; *Strings 139*
timing and spacing 49, *49*, 51; *see also* holds and cycles
timing the action 54, 55, *55*
tints and filters in After Effects exercise 112–115, *112–114*
*Toccata and Fugue in D Minor* (Piotr Muszalski) 77, *78*
Tomlinson, Lynn: artist profile 225; *The Ballad of Holland Island House 2*, 45, 70, *71*, 163–164, *163*, *164*, 167, *188*, 189; clay palette *166*; on embracing smears and smudges 225; living room studio *30*; phone camera stand for animation workshop (Tomlinson and Kuthy) *36*; rotoscoping 70, *71*; *The Same Moon* 163, *175*; on sharing her work over social media 45; tools 167–168; at work in her studio *164*
tools: for clay painting 167–168, *167*; for painting animation 138, 140, 203–204; for sand animation 87–89, *88*; *see also* digital toolbox
top light 31, 32, *32*, 33, 137–138, 165
*Top Priority* (Ishu Patel) 159, *159*
touch, and "haptic" term 1
*Toy Story* (film) 197
*Tracks* (C. F. Parks) 5, *6*, 97, *97*, 184
*Trag/Trace/Spur* and *Up the Stairs* (Michaela Müller et al.) case study 209–214, *209–214*
trailing animation 59–60, *60*
transitions: abstract transitions 89, *89*; animated transitions 60–61, *61*
trickfilm genre 12
*A Trip to the Moon* (Georges Méliès) 12
Troshinsky, Nicolai: artist profile 225; *Astigmatismo* 20, *21*, 31, *31*, 39, *39*, 54, 55, 176, *176*, 181; *Astigmatismo* process video 187; on festivals and administration work 190; inspiration, source of 19; multiplane 31, *31*; multiplane

and depth of field 39, *39*; multiplane and lighting *33*; paper cut-outs with fluid frame techniques 176; on sound design for *Astigmatismo* 181; on varying techniques 225
*Truth Has Fallen* (S.M. Sofian) 5, *42*, *138*; case study 202–209, *202*, *205*, *206*, *208*
*Tunnel* (Maryam Kashkoolinia) 53

*The Umbrella* (Xin Li) 32
under-the-camera animation: concept 1, 5; dealing with uncontrollable aspects of 45; drawing under the camera 176–178; as performance 19; and staying healthy 42; *see also* studio space
United States, experimental filmmaking grants and subsidies 16
*Up the Stairs see Trag/Trace/Spur* and *Up the Stairs* (Michaela Müller et al.) case study
Urbański, Kazimierz, salt animation 77–78

van Gogh, Vincent 196, 197, 199–200, 201; *see also Loving Vincent* (Dorota Kobiela and Hugh Welchman) case study
Van Gogh Museum 201
Vaucher, Philippe: artist profile 226; brushes 87, *88*; on compositing 94; *Cumulus* 86; on salt colored with food dye 86–87, *87*; on "tapping the glass" 226; *The Well* 49, 86, *87*, 94, *94*, *108*, 109
ventilation, in studio space 42, 137
Ventilato, Fa 181, 209, 210, 211, 212, 213, *214*
Verschuere, Brecht-Jan 135, *135*
Vervaeke, Robbe: artist profile 226; easel 34, *134*, 135; *Erszebet* 135; *Fighting Pablo* 70, *70*; green glass as painting surface *145*; on "legendary" quality of images 53; on making films vs shots 226; on musicians, collaboration with 180; *Norman* 52, 53, *53*, 135, *135*, 226; oil-based paints 136,

137; pace of work 43; on paint as an actor 135; palette *136*; on rotoscoping 70, *70*; top light 137; on work area 34
*Vezo* (documentary), animation for (C. F. Parks) 56, *117*, 117–118, *118*
video cameras (digital) 35, 36, 49
video-on-demand (VOD) platforms 192
Video Playback 41
videos: process (Making Of) videos 187–188; video frame rates 49
Vimeo 192
Vinton Studios films 160, 166
VOD (video-on-demand) platforms 192

walk cycles 52, *52*
Walley, Clive: 3D space feeling 150; artist profile 227; *Divertimenti* 126, 181; *Divertimento 1 (Wind of Change)* 126, 151, *152*, *153*; *Divertimento 2 (Love Song)* 126, *127*; *Divertimento 3 (Brushwork)* 122, *122*, 126; *Divertimento 4 (Life Study)* 126; *Divertimento 5 (Slap-Stick)* 126, 128, 181; *Divertimento 6 (Dark Matter)* 128; on gestural painting 128; multiplane rig 3, 31, 126, *126*, 150–151, 227; on music for *Divertimento 5 (Slap-Stick)* 181; *And Now You* 150, *150*, *151*; on O. Fischinger's *Motion Painting No. 1* and his rostrum camera rig 126; oil-based paints 136; on painting animation 126; painting animation pioneer 120, 126–128
Walsh, Marieka: artist profile 227; *The Crossing 1*, 76, 84, 93, *94*, *96*; on favorite sand 86; on "halo effect" 104; *The Hunter* 91, 92–93, *92*, *93*; *The Hunter* process video 187; on multiplane shots 95; on sand animation and darkness 85; sand animation style 84; on working on *The Hunter* 92, 93; working on *The Hunter* 92; on working with salt 227
warming up to the clay exercise 168–169, *168–169*

Warren Miller Performing Arts Center (Big Sky, Montana), gallery installation *192*, 193, *193*
water-based clay 166
water-based paints 136, 138
webcams, and shooting animation 35, 36, 40
Welchman, Hugh: *Loving Vincent* (Dorota Kobiela and Hugh Welchman) 196; on *Loving Vincent* (interviewed by C. F. Parks) 196–202; *Peter and the Wolf* 196, 197
*The Well* (Philippe Vaucher) *49*, 86, *87*, 94, *94*, *108*, 109
wellbeing: and working under the camera 42; and working with sand 91; *see also* mental health

*When I Was a Child* (Maryam, Kashkoolinia) *2*, *17*, 84
Whitehall, Richard 121
Whitmore, Lee: *Ada 8*, 44, 177–178, *177*, *178*, *180*; *Ada*, storyboard and final drawing from *25*; artist profile 228; on under-the-camera animation 178; paint-on-glass and drawing with pastels under camera 175–176; on research and memory 26; *The Safe House* 26, *26*, *32*, 44, *44*, *120*, *137*; on Saunders Waterford rag paper 178; three-dimensional models 44, *44*; top light 137; water-based paints 136
wooden modeling tools 167–168
working surfaces 30–31; for clay painting 164–165; for painting animation 132–135, 138
World Festival of Animated Film Zagreb (Animafest Zagreb), 2014 technical requirements *185*

Yoresh, Itzhak 162
YouTube 192

Zagreb: Animafest Zagreb 2014 technical requirements *185*; Museum of Contemporary Art 209, 210, *210*
*Zepo* (César Díaz Meléndez) *26*, *60*, 187
Zoom lenses 38

# Taylor & Francis eBooks

## Helping you to choose the right eBooks for your Library

Add Routledge titles to your library's digital collection today. Taylor and Francis ebooks contains over 50,000 titles in the Humanities, Social Sciences, Behavioural Sciences, Built Environment and Law.

Choose from a range of subject packages or create your own!

**Benefits for you**
- Free MARC records
- COUNTER-compliant usage statistics
- Flexible purchase and pricing options
- All titles DRM-free.

**Benefits for your user**
- Off-site, anytime access via Athens or referring URL
- Print or copy pages or chapters
- Full content search
- Bookmark, highlight and annotate text
- Access to thousands of pages of quality research at the click of a button.

**REQUEST YOUR FREE INSTITUTIONAL TRIAL TODAY**

**Free Trials Available**
We offer free trials to qualifying academic, corporate and government customers.

## eCollections – Choose from over 30 subject eCollections, including:

| | |
|---|---|
| Archaeology | Language Learning |
| Architecture | Law |
| Asian Studies | Literature |
| Business & Management | Media & Communication |
| Classical Studies | Middle East Studies |
| Construction | Music |
| Creative & Media Arts | Philosophy |
| Criminology & Criminal Justice | Planning |
| Economics | Politics |
| Education | Psychology & Mental Health |
| Energy | Religion |
| Engineering | Security |
| English Language & Linguistics | Social Work |
| Environment & Sustainability | Sociology |
| Geography | Sport |
| Health Studies | Theatre & Performance |
| History | Tourism, Hospitality & Events |

For more information, pricing enquiries or to order a free trial, please contact your local sales team:
**www.tandfebooks.com/page/sales**

 **Routledge** Taylor & Francis Group | The home of Routledge books | **www.tandfebooks.com**

T - #0128 - 010219 - C252 - 276/216/14 [16] - CB - 9781138190627